SWEDISH
VOCABULARY

ENGLISH-
SWEDISH

The most useful words
To expand your lexicon and sharpen
your language skills

000 words

Swedish vocabulary for English speakers - 9000 words

By Andrey Taranov

T&P Books vocabularies are intended for helping you learn, memorize and review foreign words. The dictionary is divided into themes, covering all major spheres of everyday activities, business, science, culture, etc.

The process of learning words using T&P Books' theme-based dictionaries gives you the following advantages:

- Correctly grouped source information predetermines success at subsequent stages of word memorization
- Availability of words derived from the same root allowing memorization of word units (rather than separate words)
- Small units of words facilitate the process of establishing associative links needed for consolidation of vocabulary
- Level of language knowledge can be estimated by the number of learned words

T&P Books Publishing
www.tpbooks.com

ISBN: 978-1-78071-306-9

This book is also available in E-book formats.
Please visit www.tpbooks.com or the major online bookstores.

SWEDISH VOCABULARY
for English speakers

T&P Books vocabularies are intended to help you learn, memorize, and review foreign words. The vocabulary contains over 9000 commonly used words arranged thematically.

- Vocabulary contains the most commonly used words
- Recommended as an addition to any language course
- Meets the needs of beginners and advanced learners of foreign languages
- Convenient for daily use, revision sessions, and self-testing activities
- Allows you to assess your vocabulary

Special features of the vocabulary

- Words are organized according to their meaning, not alphabetically
- Words are presented in three columns to facilitate the reviewing and self-testing processes
- Words in groups are divided into small blocks to facilitate the learning process
- The vocabulary offers a convenient and simple transcription of each foreign word

The vocabulary has 256 topics including:

Basic Concepts, Numbers, Colors, Months, Seasons, Units of Measurement, Clothing & Accessories, Food & Nutrition, Restaurant, Family Members, Relatives, Character, Feelings, Emotions, Diseases, City, Town, Sightseeing, Shopping, Money, House, Home, Office, Working in the Office, Import & Export, Marketing, Job Search, Sports, Education, Computer, Internet, Tools, Nature, Countries, Nationalities and more ...

T&P BOOKS' THEME-BASED DICTIONARIES

The Correct System for Memorizing Foreign Words

Acquiring vocabulary is one of the most important elements of learning a foreign language, because words allow us to express our thoughts, ask questions, and provide answers. An inadequate vocabulary can impede communication with a foreigner and make it difficult to understand a book or movie well.

The pace of activity in all spheres of modern life, including the learning of modern languages, has increased. Today, we need to memorize large amounts of information (grammar rules, foreign words, etc.) within a short period. However, this does not need to be difficult. All you need to do is to choose the right training materials, learn a few special techniques, and develop your individual training system.

Having a system is critical to the process of language learning. Many people fail to succeed in this regard; they cannot master a foreign language because they fail to follow a system comprised of selecting materials, organizing lessons, arranging new words to be learned, and so on. The lack of a system causes confusion and eventually, lowers self-confidence.

T&P Books' theme-based dictionaries can be included in the list of elements needed for creating an effective system for learning foreign words. These dictionaries were specially developed for learning purposes and are meant to help students effectively memorize words and expand their vocabulary.

Generally speaking, the process of learning words consists of three main elements:

- Reception (creation or acquisition) of a training material, such as a word list
- Work aimed at memorizing new words
- Work aimed at reviewing the learned words, such as self-testing

All three elements are equally important since they determine the quality of work and the final result. All three processes require certain skills and a well-thought-out approach.

New words are often encountered quite randomly when learning a foreign language and it may be difficult to include them all in a unified list. As a result, these words remain written on scraps of paper, in book margins, textbooks, and so on. In order to systematize such words, we have to create and continually update a "book of new words." A paper notebook, a netbook, or a tablet PC can be used for these purposes.

This "book of new words" will be your personal, unique list of words. However, it will only contain the words that you came across during the learning process. For example, you might have written down the words "Sunday," "Tuesday," and "Friday." However, there are additional words for days of the week, for example, "Saturday," that are missing, and your list of words would be incomplete. Using a theme dictionary, in addition to the "book of new words," is a reasonable solution to this problem.

The theme-based dictionary may serve as the basis for expanding your vocabulary.

It will be your big "book of new words" containing the most frequently used words of a foreign language already included. There are quite a few theme-based dictionaries available, and you should ensure that you make the right choice in order to get the maximum benefit from your purchase.

Therefore, we suggest using theme-based dictionaries from T&P Books Publishing as an aid to learning foreign words. Our books are specially developed for effective use in the sphere of vocabulary systematization, expansion and review.

Theme-based dictionaries are not a magical solution to learning new words. However, they can serve as your main database to aid foreign-language acquisition. Apart from theme dictionaries, you can have copybooks for writing down new words, flash cards, glossaries for various texts, as well as other resources; however, a good theme dictionary will always remain your primary collection of words.

T&P Books' theme-based dictionaries are specialty books that contain the most frequently used words in a language.

The main characteristic of such dictionaries is the division of words into themes. For example, the *City* theme contains the words "street," "crossroads," "square," "fountain," and so on. The *Talking* theme might contain words like "to talk," "to ask," "question," and "answer".

All the words in a theme are divided into smaller units, each comprising 3–5 words. Such an arrangement improves the perception of words and makes the learning process less tiresome. Each unit contains a selection of words with similar meanings or identical roots. This allows you to learn words in small groups and establish other associative links that have a positive effect on memorization.

The words on each page are placed in three columns: a word in your native language, its translation, and its transcription. Such positioning allows for the use of techniques for effective memorization. After closing the translation column, you can flip through and review foreign words, and vice versa. "This is an easy and convenient method of review – one that we recommend you do often."

Our theme-based dictionaries contain transcriptions for all the foreign words. Unfortunately, none of the existing transcriptions are able to convey the exact nuances of foreign pronunciation. That is why we recommend using the transcriptions only as a supplementary learning aid. Correct pronunciation can only be acquired with the help of sound. Therefore our collection includes audio theme-based dictionaries.

The process of learning words using T&P Books' theme-based dictionaries gives you the following advantages:

- You have correctly grouped source information, which predetermines your success at subsequent stages of word memorization
- Availability of words derived from the same root (lazy, lazily, lazybones), allowing you to memorize word units instead of separate words
- Small units of words facilitate the process of establishing associative links needed for consolidation of vocabulary
- You can estimate the number of learned words and hence your level of language knowledge
- The dictionary allows for the creation of an effective and high-quality revision process
- You can revise certain themes several times, modifying the revision methods and techniques
- Audio versions of the dictionaries help you to work out the pronunciation of words and develop your skills of auditory word perception

The T&P Books' theme-based dictionaries are offered in several variants differing in the number of words: 1.500, 3.000, 5.000, 7.000, and 9.000 words. There are also dictionaries containing 15,000 words for some language combinations. Your choice of dictionary will depend on your knowledge level and goals.

We sincerely believe that our dictionaries will become your trusty assistant in learning foreign languages and will allow you to easily acquire the necessary vocabulary.

TABLE OF CONTENTS

MISCELLANEOUS   252

MAIN 500 VERBS   259

PRONUNCIATION GUIDE

Letter	Swedish example	T&P phonetic alphabet	English example
Aa	bada	[ɑ], [ɑ:]	bath, to pass
Bb	tabell	[b]	baby, book
Cc [1]	licens	[s]	city, boss
Cc [2]	container	[k]	clock, kiss
Dd	andra	[d]	day, doctor
Ee	efter	[e]	elm, medal
Ff	flera	[f]	face, food
Gg [3]	gömma	[j]	yes, New York
Gg [4]	truga	[g]	game, gold
Hh	handla	[h]	home, have
Ii	tillhöra	[i:], [ı]	tree, big
Jj	jaga	[j]	yes, New York
Kk [5]	keramisk	[ɕ]	sheep, shop
Kk [6]	frisk	[k]	clock, kiss
Ll	tal	[l]	lace, people
Mm	medalj	[m]	magic, milk
Nn	panik	[n]	name, normal
Oo	tolv	[ɔ]	bottle, doctor
Pp	plommon	[p]	pencil, private
Qq	squash	[k]	clock, kiss
Rr	spelregler	[r]	rice, radio
Ss	spara	[s]	city, boss
Tt	tillhöra	[t]	tourist, trip
Uu	ungefär	[u], [ʉ:]	soup, menu
Vv	overall	[v]	very, river
Ww [7]	kiwi	[w]	vase, winter
Xx	sax	[ks]	box, taxi
Yy	manikyr	[y], [y:]	fuel, tuna
Zz	zoolog	[s]	city, boss
Åå	sångare	[ə]	driver, teacher
Ää	tandläkare	[æ]	chess, man
Öö	kompositör	[ø]	eternal, church

Letter	Swedish example	T&P phonetic alphabet	English example

Combinations of letters

Ss [8]	sjösjuka	[ʃ]	machine, shark
sk [9]	skicka	[ʃ]	machine, shark
s [10]	först	[ʃ]	machine, shark
J j [11]	djärv	[j]	yes, New York
Lj [12]	ljus	[j]	yes, New York
kj, tj	kjol	[ɕ]	sheep, shop
ng	omkring	[ŋ]	English, ring

Comments

[·] kj pronouns as
[··] combination **ng** transfers a nasal sound
[1] before **e, i, y**
[2] elsewhere
[3] before **e, i, ä, ö**
[4] elsewhere
[5] before **e, i, ä, ö**
[6] elsewhere
[7] in loanwords
[8] in **sj, skj, stj**
[9] before stressed **e, i, y, ä, ö**
[10] in the combination **rs**
[11] in **dj, hj, gj, kj**
[12] at the beginning of words

ABBREVIATIONS
used in the vocabulary

English abbreviations

ab.	-	about
adj	-	adjective
adv	-	adverb
anim.	-	animate
as adj	-	attributive noun used as adjective
e.g.	-	for example
etc.	-	et cetera
fam.	-	familiar
fem.	-	feminine
form.	-	formal
inanim.	-	inanimate
masc.	-	masculine
math	-	mathematics
mil.	-	military
n	-	noun
pl	-	plural
pron.	-	pronoun
sb	-	somebody
sing.	-	singular
sth	-	something
v aux	-	auxiliary verb
vi	-	intransitive verb
vi, vt	-	intransitive, transitive verb
vt	-	transitive verb

Swedish abbreviations

pl	-	plural

Swedish articles

den	-	common gender
det	-	neuter
en	-	common gender
ett	-	neuter

BASIC CONCEPTS

Basic concepts. Part 1

1. Pronouns

I, me	jag	['ja:]
you	du	[dʉ:]
he	han	['han]
she	hon	['hʊn]
it	det, den	[dɛ], [dɛn]
we	vi	['vi]
you (to a group)	ni	['ni]
they	de	[de:]

2. Greetings. Salutations. Farewells

Hello! (fam.)	Hej!	['hɛj]
Hello! (form.)	Hej! Hallå!	['hɛj], [ha'lʲo:]
Good morning!	God morgon!	[ˌgʊd 'mɔrgɔn]
Good afternoon!	God dag!	[ˌgʊd 'dag]
Good evening!	God kväll!	[ˌgʊd 'kvɛlʲ]
to say hello	att hälsa	[at 'hɛlʲsa]
Hi! (hello)	Hej!	['hɛj]
greeting (n)	hälsning (en)	['hɛlʲsnin]
to greet (vt)	att hälsa	[at 'hɛlʲsa]
How are you? (form.)	Hur står det till?	[hʉr sto: de 'tilʲ]
How are you? (fam.)	Hur är det?	[hʉr ɛr 'de:]
What's new?	Vad är nytt?	[vad æ:r 'nʏt]
Goodbye! (form.)	Adjö! Hej då!	[a'jø:], [hɛj'do:]
Bye! (fam.)	Hej då!	[hɛj'do:]
See you soon!	Vi ses!	[vi ses]
Farewell!	Adjö! Farväl!	[a'jø:], [far'vɛ:lʲ]
to say goodbye	att säga adjö	[at 'sɛ:ja a'jø:]
So long!	Hej då!	[hɛj'do:]
Thank you!	Tack!	['tak]
Thank you very much!	Tack så mycket!	['tak sɔ 'mʏkə]
You're welcome	Varsågod	['va:ʂo:gʊd]
Don't mention it!	Ingen orsak!	['iŋən 'ʊ:ʂak]

19

| It was nothing | Ingen orsak! | ['iŋən 'ʊːʂak] |

Excuse me! (fam.)	Ursäkta, ...	['ʉːˌʂɛkta ...]
Excuse me! (form.)	Ursäkta mig, ...	['ʉːˌʂɛkta mɛj ...]
to excuse (forgive)	att ursäkta	[at 'ʉːˌʂɛkta]

to apologize (vi)	att ursäkta sig	[at 'ʉːˌʂɛkta sɛj]
My apologies	Jag ber om ursäkt	[ja ber ɔm 'ʉːˌʂɛkt]
I'm sorry!	Förlåt!	[fœːˈʈoːt]
to forgive (vt)	att förlåta	[at 'fœːˌʈoːta]
It's okay! (that's all right)	Det gör inget	[dɛ jør 'iŋet]
please (adv)	snälla	['snɛla]

Don't forget!	Glöm inte!	['glʲøːm 'intə]
Certainly!	Naturligtvis!	[na'tʉrligvis]
Of course not!	Självklart inte!	['ɧɛlʲvklʲaʈ 'intə]
Okay! (I agree)	OK! Jag håller med.	[ɔ'kej] , [ja 'hoːlʲer me]
That's enough!	Det räcker!	[dɛ 'rɛkə]

3. How to address

Excuse me, ...	Ursäkta, ...	['ʉːˌʂɛkta ...]
mister, sir	herr	['hɛr]
ma'am	frun	['frʉːn]
miss	fröken	['frøːkən]
young man	unge man	['uŋə ˌman]
young man (little boy, kid)	pojke	['pojkə]
miss (little girl)	flicka	['flika]

4. Cardinal numbers. Part 1

0 zero	noll	['nɔlʲ]
1 one	ett	[ɛt]
2 two	två	['tvoː]
3 three	tre	['treː]
4 four	fyra	['fyra]

5 five	fem	['fem]
6 six	sex	['sɛks]
7 seven	sju	['ɧʉː]
8 eight	åtta	['ota]
9 nine	nio	['niːʊ]

10 ten	tio	['tiːʊ]
11 eleven	elva	['ɛlʲva]
12 twelve	tolv	['tɔlʲv]
13 thirteen	tretton	['trɛtːɔn]
14 fourteen	fjorton	['fjʊːʈɔn]

15 fifteen	**femton**	['fɛmtɔn]
16 sixteen	**sexton**	['sɛkstɔn]
17 seventeen	**sjutton**	['ɧʉːttɔn]
18 eighteen	**arton**	['aːtɔn]
19 nineteen	**nitton**	['niːttɔn]
20 twenty	**tjugo**	['ɕʉgʉ]
21 twenty-one	**tjugoett**	['ɕʉgʉˌɛt]
22 twenty-two	**tjugotvå**	['ɕʉgʉˌtvoː]
23 twenty-three	**tjugotre**	['ɕʉgʉˌtreː]
30 thirty	**trettio**	['trɛttiʉ]
31 thirty-one	**trettioett**	['trɛttiʉˌɛt]
32 thirty-two	**trettiotvå**	['trɛttiʉˌtvoː]
33 thirty-three	**trettiotre**	['trɛttiʉˌtreː]
40 forty	**fyrtio**	['fœːʈiʉ]
41 forty-one	**fyrtioett**	['fœːʈiʉˌɛt]
42 forty-two	**fyrtiotvå**	['fœːʈiʉˌtvoː]
43 forty-three	**fyrtiotre**	['fœːʈiʉˌtreː]
50 fifty	**femtio**	['fɛmtiʉ]
51 fifty-one	**femtioett**	['fɛmtiʉˌɛt]
52 fifty-two	**femtiotvå**	['fɛmtiʉˌtvoː]
53 fifty-three	**femtiotre**	['fɛmtiʉˌtreː]
60 sixty	**sextio**	['sɛkstiʉ]
61 sixty-one	**sextioett**	['sɛkstiʉˌɛt]
62 sixty-two	**sextiotvå**	['sɛkstiʉˌtvoː]
63 sixty-three	**sextiotre**	['sɛkstiʉˌtreː]
70 seventy	**sjuttio**	['ɧʉttiʉ]
71 seventy-one	**sjuttioett**	['ɧʉttiʉˌɛt]
72 seventy-two	**sjuttiotvå**	['ɧʉttiʉˌtvoː]
73 seventy-three	**sjuttiotre**	['ɧʉttiʉˌtreː]
80 eighty	**åttio**	['ottiʉ]
81 eighty-one	**åttioett**	['ottiʉ'ɛt]
82 eighty-two	**åttiotvå**	['ottiʉˌtvoː]
83 eighty-three	**åttiotre**	['ottiʉˌtreː]
90 ninety	**nittio**	['nittiʉ]
91 ninety-one	**nittioett**	['nittiʉˌɛt]
92 ninety-two	**nittiotvå**	['nittiʉˌtvoː]
93 ninety-three	**nittiotre**	['nittiʉˌtreː]

5. Cardinal numbers. Part 2

100 one hundred	**hundra (ett)**	['hundra]
200 two hundred	**tvåhundra**	['tvoːˌhundra]

300 three hundred	trehundra	['tre͵hundra]
400 four hundred	fyrahundra	['fyra͵hundra]
500 five hundred	femhundra	['fem͵hundra]

600 six hundred	sexhundra	['sɛks͵hundra]
700 seven hundred	sjuhundra	['ɧʉ:͵hundra]
800 eight hundred	åttahundra	['ota͵hundra]
900 nine hundred	niohundra	['niʊ͵hundra]

1000 one thousand	tusen (ett)	['tʉ:sən]
2000 two thousand	tvåtusen	['tvo:͵tʉ:sən]
3000 three thousand	tretusen	['tre:͵tʉ:sən]
10000 ten thousand	tiotusen	['ti:ʊ͵tʉ:sən]
one hundred thousand	hundratusen	['hundra͵tʉ:sən]
million	miljon (en)	[mi'ljʊn]
billion	miljard (en)	[mi'lja:ɖ]

6. Ordinal numbers

first (adj)	första	['fœ:ʂta]
second (adj)	andra	['andra]
third (adj)	tredje	['trɛdjə]
fourth (adj)	fjärde	['fjæ:ɖə]
fifth (adj)	femte	['fɛmtə]

sixth (adj)	sjätte	['ɧæ:tə]
seventh (adj)	sjunde	['ɧundə]
eighth (adj)	åttonde	['ottɔndə]
ninth (adj)	nionde	['ni:͵ʊndə]
tenth (adj)	tionde	['ti:͵ɔndə]

7. Numbers. Fractions

fraction	bråk (ett)	['bro:k]
one half	en halv	[en 'halʲv]
one third	en tredjedel	[en 'trɛdjə͵delʲ]
one quarter	en fjärdedel	[en 'fjæ:ɖe͵delʲ]
one eighth	en åttondedel	[en 'otɔnde͵delʲ]
one tenth	en tiondedel	[en 'ti:ɔnde͵delʲ]
two thirds	två tredjedelar	['tvo: 'trɛdjə͵delʲar]
three quarters	tre fjärdedelar	[tre: 'fjæ:ɖe͵delʲar]

8. Numbers. Basic operations

subtraction	subtraktion (en)	[subtrak'ɧʊn]
to subtract (vi, vt)	att subtrahera	[at subtra'hera]

division	division (en)	[divi'ʃʊn]
to divide (vt)	att dividera	[at divi'dera]
addition	addition (en)	[adi'ʃʊn]
to add up (vt)	att addera	[at a'deːra]
to add (vi, vt)	att addera	[at a'deːra]
multiplication	multiplikation (en)	[mʉlˈtiplika'ʃʊn]
to multiply (vt)	att multiplicera	[at mulˈtipli'sera]

9. Numbers. Miscellaneous

digit, figure	siffra (en)	['sifra]
number	tal (ett)	['talˈ]
numeral	räkneord (ett)	['rɛkneˌʊːd]
minus sign	minus (ett)	['minus]
plus sign	plus (ett)	['plʉs]
formula	formel (en)	['fɔrməlˈ]
calculation	beräkning (en)	[be'rɛkniŋ]
to count (vi, vt)	att räkna	[at 'rɛkna]
to count up	att beräkna	[at be'rɛkna]
to compare (vt)	att jämföra	[at 'jɛmˌføra]
How much?	Hur mycket?	[hʉr 'mʏkə]
How many?	Hur många?	[hʉr 'mɔŋa]
sum, total	summa (en)	['suma]
result	resultat (ett)	[resulˈ'tat]
remainder	rest (en)	['rɛst]
a few (e.g., ~ years ago)	flera	['flˈera]
few (I have ~ friends)	få, inte många	['foː], ['intə ˌmɔŋa]
a little (~ tired)	lite	['litə]
the rest	det övriga	[dɛ øv'riga]
one and a half	halvannan	[halˈ'vanan]
dozen	dussin (ett)	['dusin]
in half (adv)	i hälften	[i 'hɛlˈftən]
equally (evenly)	jämnt	['jɛmnt]
half	halva (en)	['halˈˌva]
time (three ~s)	gång (en)	['gɔŋ]

10. The most important verbs. Part 1

to advise (vt)	att råda	[at 'roːda]
to agree (say yes)	att samtycka	[at 'samˌtʏka]
to answer (vi, vt)	att svara	[at 'svara]
to apologize (vi)	att ursäkta sig	[at 'ʉːˌʂɛkta sɛj]
to arrive (vi)	att ankomma	[at 'aŋˌkɔma]

to ask (~ oneself)	**att fråga**	[at 'fro:ga]
to ask (~ sb to do sth)	**att be**	[at 'be:]
to be (vi)	**att vara**	[at 'vara]

to be afraid	**att frukta**	[at 'frʉkta]
to be hungry	**att vara hungrig**	[at 'vara 'huŋrig]
to be interested in ...	**att intressera sig**	[at intrɛ'sera sɛj]
to be needed	**att vara behövd**	[at 'vara be'hø:vd]
to be surprised	**att bli förvånad**	[at bli før'vo:nad]

to be thirsty	**att vara törstig**	[at 'vara 'tø:ʂtig]
to begin (vt)	**att begynna**	[at be'jina]
to belong to ...	**att tillhöra ...**	[at 'tilˡ͵hø:ra ...]
to boast (vi)	**att skryta**	[at 'skryta]
to break (split into pieces)	**att bryta**	[at 'bryta]

to call (~ for help)	**att tillkalla**	[at 'tilˡ͵kalˡa]
can (v aux)	**att kunna**	[at 'kuna]
to catch (vt)	**att fånga**	[at 'foŋa]
to change (vt)	**att ändra**	[at 'ɛndra]
to choose (select)	**att välja**	[at 'vɛlja]

to come down (the stairs)	**att gå ned**	[at 'go: ͵ned]
to compare (vt)	**att jämföra**	[at 'jɛm͵føra]
to complain (vi, vt)	**att klaga**	[at 'klˡaga]
to confuse (mix up)	**att förväxla**	[at før'vɛkslˡa]
to continue (vt)	**att fortsätta**	[at 'fʊt͵sæta]
to control (vt)	**att kontrollera**	[at kɔntrɔ'lˡera]

to cook (dinner)	**att laga**	[at 'lˡaga]
to cost (vt)	**att kosta**	[at 'kɔsta]
to count (add up)	**att räkna**	[at 'rɛkna]
to count on ...	**att räkna med ...**	[at 'rɛkna me ...]
to create (vt)	**att skapa**	[at 'skapa]
to cry (weep)	**att gråta**	[at 'gro:ta]

11. The most important verbs. Part 2

to deceive (vi, vt)	**att fuska**	[at 'fʉska]
to decorate (tree, street)	**att pryda**	[at 'pryda]
to defend (a country, etc.)	**att försvara**	[at fœ:'ʂvara]
to demand (request firmly)	**att kräva**	[at 'krɛ:va]
to dig (vt)	**att gräva**	[at 'grɛ:va]

to discuss (vt)	**att diskutera**	[at diskʉ'tera]
to do (vt)	**att göra**	[at 'jø:ra]
to doubt (have doubts)	**att tvivla**	[at 'tvivlˡa]
to drop (let fall)	**att tappa**	[at 'tapa]
to enter (room, house, etc.)	**att komma in**	[at 'kɔma 'in]

to excuse (forgive)	att ursäkta	[at 'ʉːˌsɛkta]
to exist (vi)	att existera	[at ɛksi'stera]
to expect (foresee)	att förutse	[at 'førʉtˌsə]
to explain (vt)	att förklara	[at før'klʲara]
to fall (vi)	att falla	[at 'falʲa]

to find (vt)	att finna	[at 'fina]
to finish (vt)	att sluta	[at 'slʉːta]
to fly (vi)	att flyga	[at 'flʲyga]
to follow ... (come after)	att följa efter ...	[at 'følja 'ɛftər ...]
to forget (vi, vt)	att glömma	[at 'glʲœma]

to forgive (vt)	att förlåta	[at 'fœːˌlʲoːta]
to give (vt)	att ge	[at jeː]
to give a hint	att ge en vink	[at jeː en 'viŋk]
to go (on foot)	att gå	[at 'goː]

to go for a swim	att bada	[at 'bada]
to go out (for dinner, etc.)	att gå ut	[at 'goː ʉt]
to guess (the answer)	att gissa	[at 'jisa]

to have (vt)	att ha	[at 'ha]
to have breakfast	att äta frukost	[at 'ɛːta 'frʉːkɔst]
to have dinner	att äta kvällsmat	[at 'ɛːta 'kvɛlʲsˌmat]
to have lunch	att äta lunch	[at 'ɛːta ˌlʉnɕ]
to hear (vt)	att höra	[at 'høːra]

to help (vt)	att hjälpa	[at 'jɛlʲpa]
to hide (vt)	att gömma	[at 'jœma]
to hope (vi, vt)	att hoppas	[at 'hɔpas]
to hunt (vi, vt)	att jaga	[at 'jaga]
to hurry (vi)	att skynda sig	[at 'ɧʏnda sɛj]

12. The most important verbs. Part 3

to inform (vt)	att informera	[at infɔr'mera]
to insist (vi, vt)	att insistera	[at insi'stera]
to insult (vt)	att förolämpa	[at 'førʊˌlʲɛmpa]
to invite (vt)	att inbjuda, att invitera	[at in'bjʉːda], [at invi'tera]
to joke (vi)	att skämta, att skoja	[at 'ɧɛmta], [at 'skɔja]

to keep (vt)	att behålla	[at be'hoːlʲa]
to keep silent	att tiga	[at 'tiga]
to kill (vt)	att döda, att mörda	[at 'døːda], [at 'møːɖa]
to know (sb)	att känna	[at 'ɕɛna]
to know (sth)	att veta	[at 'veta]
to laugh (vi)	att skratta	[at 'skrata]

| to liberate (city, etc.) | att befria | [at be'fria] |
| to like (I like ...) | att gilla | [at 'jilʲa] |

to look for ... (search)	att söka ...	[at 'sø:ka ...]
to love (sb)	att älska	[at 'ɛlʲska]
to make a mistake	att göra fel	[at 'jø:ra ˌfelʲ]

to manage, to run	att styra, att leda	[at 'styra], [at 'lʲeda]
to mean (signify)	att betyda	[at be'tyda]
to mention (talk about)	att omnämna	[at 'ɔmˌnɛmna]
to miss (school, etc.)	att missa	[at 'misa]
to notice (see)	att märka	[at 'mæ:rka]

to object (vi, vt)	att invända	[at 'inˌvɛnda]
to observe (see)	att observera	[at ɔbsɛr'vera]
to open (vt)	att öppna	[at 'øpna]
to order (meal, etc.)	att beställa	[at be'stɛlʲa]
to order (mil.)	att beordra	[at be'o:dra]
to own (possess)	att besitta, att äga	[at be'sita], [at 'ɛ:ga]

to participate (vi)	att delta	[at 'dɛlʲta]
to pay (vi, vt)	att betala	[at be'talʲa]
to permit (vt)	att tillåta	[at 'tilʲo:ta]
to plan (vt)	att planera	[at plʲa'nera]
to play (children)	att leka	[at 'lʲeka]

to pray (vi, vt)	att be	[at 'be:]
to prefer (vt)	att föredra	[at 'førədra]
to promise (vt)	att lova	[at 'lʲɔva]
to pronounce (vt)	att uttala	[at 'ʉtˌtalʲa]
to propose (vt)	att föreslå	[at 'førəˌslʲo:]
to punish (vt)	att straffa	[at 'strafa]

13. The most important verbs. Part 4

to read (vi, vt)	att läsa	[at 'lʲɛ:sa]
to recommend (vt)	att rekommendera	[at rekɔmən'dera]
to refuse (vi, vt)	att vägra	[at 'vɛgra]
to regret (be sorry)	att beklaga	[at be'klʲaga]
to rent (sth from sb)	att hyra	[at 'hyra]

to repeat (say again)	att upprepa	[at 'uprepa]
to reserve, to book	att reservera	[at resɛr'vera]
to run (vi)	att löpa, att springa	[at 'lʲø:pa], [at 'spriŋa]
to save (rescue)	att rädda	[at 'rɛda]
to say (~ thank you)	att säga	[at 'sɛ:ja]

to scold (vt)	att skälla	[at 'ʃɛlʲa]
to see (vt)	att se	[at 'se:]
to sell (vt)	att sälja	[at 'sɛlja]
to send (vt)	att skicka	[at 'ɧika]
to shoot (vi)	att skjuta	[at 'ɧʉ:ta]
to shout (vi)	att skrika	[at 'skrika]

to show (vt)	att visa	[at 'visa]
to sign (document)	att underteckna	[at 'undəˌtɛkna]
to sit down (vi)	att sätta sig	[at 'sæta sɛj]

to smile (vi)	att småle	[at 'smoːlʲe]
to speak (vi, vt)	att tala	[at 'talʲa]
to steal (money, etc.)	att stjäla	[at 'ɧɛːlʲa]
to stop (for pause, etc.)	att stanna	[at 'stana]
to stop (please ~ calling me)	att sluta	[at 'slʉːta]

to study (vt)	att studera	[at stu'dera]
to swim (vi)	att simma	[at 'sima]
to take (vt)	att ta	[at ta]
to think (vi, vt)	att tänka	[at 'tɛŋka]
to threaten (vt)	att hota	[at 'hʊta]

to touch (with hands)	att röra	[at 'røːra]
to translate (vt)	att översätta	[at 'øːvəˌsæta]
to trust (vt)	att lita på	[at 'lita pɔ]
to try (attempt)	att pröva	[at 'prøːva]
to turn (e.g., ~ left)	att svänga	[at 'svɛŋa]

to underestimate (vt)	att underskatta	[at 'undəˌskata]
to understand (vt)	att förstå	[at fœː'ʂtoː]
to unite (vt)	att förena	[at 'førena]
to wait (vt)	att vänta	[at 'vɛnta]

to want (wish, desire)	att vilja	[at 'vilja]
to warn (vt)	att varna	[at 'vaːɳa]
to work (vi)	att arbeta	[at 'arˌbeta]
to write (vt)	att skriva	[at 'skriva]
to write down	att skriva ner	[at 'skriva ner]

14. Colors

color	färg (en)	['fæːrj]
shade (tint)	nyans (en)	[ny'ans]
hue	färgton (en)	['fæːrjˌtʊn]
rainbow	regnbåge (en)	['rɛgnˌboːgə]

white (adj)	vit	['vit]
black (adj)	svart	['svaːt]
gray (adj)	grå	['groː]

green (adj)	grön	['grøːn]
yellow (adj)	gul	['gʉːlʲ]
red (adj)	röd	['røːd]
blue (adj)	blå	['blʲoː]
light blue (adj)	ljusblå	['jʉːsˌblʲoː]

pink (adj)	**rosa**	['rɔsa]
orange (adj)	**orange**	[ɔ'ranʃ]
violet (adj)	**violett**	[viʊ'lʲet]
brown (adj)	**brun**	['brɵːn]

golden (adj)	**guld-**	['gulʲd-]
silvery (adj)	**silver-**	['silʲvər-]

beige (adj)	**beige**	['bɛʃ]
cream (adj)	**cremefärgad**	['krɛːm͵fæːrjad]
turquoise (adj)	**turkos**	[tur'koːs]
cherry red (adj)	**körsbärsröd**	['ɕøːʂbæːʂ͵røːd]
lilac (adj)	**lila**	['lilʲa]
crimson (adj)	**karmosinröd**	[kar'mosin͵røːd]

light (adj)	**ljus**	['jɵːs]
dark (adj)	**mörk**	['mœːrk]
bright, vivid (adj)	**klar**	['klʲar]

colored (pencils)	**färg-**	['fæːrj-]
color (e.g., ~ film)	**färg-**	['fæːrj-]
black-and-white (adj)	**svartvit**	['svaːt͵vit]
plain (one-colored)	**enfärgad**	['ɛn͵fæːrjad]
multicolored (adj)	**mångfärgad**	['mɔŋ͵fæːrjad]

15. Questions

Who?	**Vem?**	['vem]
What?	**Vad?**	['vad]
Where? (at, in)	**Var?**	['var]
Where (to)?	**Vart?**	['vaːt]
From where?	**Varifrån?**	['varifroːn]

When?	**När?**	['næːr]
Why? (What for?)	**Varför?**	['vaːføːr]
Why? (~ are you crying?)	**Varför?**	['vaːføːr]

What for?	**För vad?**	['før vad]
How? (in what way)	**Hur?**	['hɵːr]
What? (What kind of ...?)	**Vilken?**	['vilʲkən]
Which?	**Vilken?**	['vilʲkən]

To whom?	**Till vem?**	[tilʲ 'vem]
About whom?	**Om vem?**	[ɔm 'vem]
About what?	**Om vad?**	[ɔm 'vad]
With whom?	**Med vem?**	[me 'vem]

How many?	**Hur många?**	[hɵr 'mɔŋa]
How much?	**Hur mycket?**	[hɵr 'mʏkə]
Whose?	**Vems?**	['vɛms]

16. Prepositions

with (accompanied by)	**med**	['me]
without	**utan**	['ʉtan]
to (indicating direction)	**till**	['tilʲ]
about (talking ~ ...)	**om**	['ɔm]
before (in time)	**för, inför**	['føːr], ['inføːr]
in front of ...	**framför**	['framføːr]
under (beneath, below)	**under**	['undər]
above (over)	**över**	['øːvər]
on (atop)	**på**	[pɔ]
from (off, out of)	**från**	['frɔn]
of (made from)	**av**	[av]
in (e.g., ~ ten minutes)	**om**	['ɔm]
over (across the top of)	**över**	['øːvər]

17. Function words. Adverbs. Part 1

Where? (at, in)	**Var?**	['var]
here (adv)	**här**	['hæːr]
there (adv)	**där**	['dæːr]
somewhere (to be)	**någonstans**	['noːgɔnˌstans]
nowhere (not anywhere)	**ingenstans**	['iŋənˌstans]
by (near, beside)	**vid**	['vid]
by the window	**vid fönstret**	[vid 'fœnstrət]
Where (to)?	**Vart?**	['vaːʈ]
here (e.g., come ~!)	**hit**	['hit]
there (e.g., to go ~)	**dit**	['dit]
from here (adv)	**härifrån**	['hæːriˌfroːn]
from there (adv)	**därifrån**	['dæːriˌfroːn]
close (adv)	**nära**	['næːra]
far (adv)	**långt**	['lʲɔŋt]
near (e.g., ~ Paris)	**nära**	['næːra]
nearby (adv)	**i närheten**	[i 'næːrˌhetən]
not far (adv)	**inte långt**	['intə 'lʲɔŋt]
left (adj)	**vänster**	['vɛnstər]
on the left	**till vänster**	[tilʲ 'vɛnstər]
to the left	**till vänster**	[tilʲ 'vɛnstər]
right (adj)	**höger**	['høːgər]
on the right	**till höger**	[tilʲ 'høːgər]

to the right	till höger	[tilʲ 'hø:gər]
in front (adv)	framtill	['framtilʲ]
front (as adj)	främre	['frɛmrə]
ahead (the kids ran ~)	framåt	['framo:t]

behind (adv)	bakom, baktill	['bakɔm], ['bak'tilʲ]
from behind	bakifrån	['baki‚fro:n]
back (towards the rear)	tillbaka	[tilʲ'baka]

| middle | mitt (en) | ['mit] |
| in the middle | i mitten | [i 'mitən] |

at the side	från sidan	[frɔn 'sidan]
everywhere (adv)	överallt	['ø:vər‚alʲt]
around (in all directions)	runt omkring	[runt ɔm'kriŋ]

from inside	inifrån	['ini‚fro:n]
somewhere (to go)	någonstans	['no:gɔn‚stans]
straight (directly)	rakt, rakt fram	['rakt], ['rakt fram]
back (e.g., come ~)	tillbaka	[tilʲ'baka]

| from anywhere | från var som helst | [frɔn va sɔm 'hɛlʲst] |
| from somewhere | från någonstans | [frɔn 'no:gɔn‚stans] |

firstly (adv)	för det första	['før de 'fœ:ʂta]
secondly (adv)	för det andra	['før de 'andra]
thirdly (adv)	för det tredje	['før de 'trɛdjə]

suddenly (adv)	plötsligt	['plʲøtslit]
at first (in the beginning)	i början	[i 'bœrjan]
for the first time	för första gången	['før 'fœ:ʂta 'gɔŋən]
long before …	långt innan …	['lʲɔŋt 'inan …]
anew (over again)	på nytt	[pɔ 'nʏt]
for good (adv)	för gott	[før 'gɔt]

never (adv)	aldrig	['alʲdrig]
again (adv)	igen	['ijɛn]
now (adv)	nu	['nʉ:]
often (adv)	ofta	['ɔfta]
then (adv)	då	['do:]
urgently (quickly)	brådskande	['brɔ‚skandə]
usually (adv)	vanligtvis	['van‚litvis]

by the way, …	förresten …	[fœ:'rɛstən …]
possible (that is ~)	möjligen	['mœjligən]
probably (adv)	sannolikt	[sanʉ'likt]
maybe (adv)	kanske	['kanʃə]
besides …	dessutom …	[des'ʉ:tʊm …]
that's why …	därför …	['dæ:før …]
in spite of …	i trots av …	[i 'trɔts av …]
thanks to …	tack vare …	['tak ‚varə …]
what (pron.)	vad	['vad]

that (conj.)	att	[at]
something	något	['no:gɔt]
anything (something)	något	['no:gɔt]
nothing	ingenting	['iŋəntiŋ]

who (pron.)	vem	['vem]
someone	någon	['no:gɔn]
somebody	någon	['no:gɔn]

nobody	ingen	['iŋən]
nowhere (a voyage to ~)	ingenstans	['iŋən,stans]
nobody's	ingens	['iŋəns]
somebody's	någons	['no:gɔns]

so (I'm ~ glad)	så	['so:]
also (as well)	också	['ɔkso:]
too (as well)	också	['ɔkso:]

18. Function words. Adverbs. Part 2

Why?	Varför?	['va:fø:r]
for some reason	av någon anledning	[av 'no:gɔn 'an,lʲedniŋ]
because ...	därför att ...	['dæ:før at ...]
for some purpose	av någon anledning	[av 'no:gɔn 'an,lʲedniŋ]

and	och	['ɔ]
or	eller	['ɛlʲer]
but	men	['men]
for (e.g., ~ me)	för, till	['fø:r]

too (~ many people)	för, alltför	['fø:r], ['alʲtfø:r]
only (exclusively)	bara, endast	['bara], ['ɛndast]
exactly (adv)	precis, exakt	[prɛ'sis], [ɛk'sakt]
about (more or less)	cirka	['sirka]

approximately (adv)	ungefär	['uŋə,fæ:r]
approximate (adj)	ungefärlig	['uŋə,fæ:lʲig]
almost (adv)	nästan	['nɛstan]
the rest	rest (en)	['rɛst]

the other (second)	den andra	[dɛn 'andra]
other (different)	andre	['andrə]
each (adj)	var	['var]
any (no matter which)	vilken som helst	['vilʲkən sɔm 'hɛlʲst]
many, much (a lot of)	mycken, mycket	['mʏkən], ['mʏkə]
many people	många	['mɔŋa]
all (everyone)	alla	['alʲa]

| in return for ... | i gengäld för ... | [i 'jɛŋɛld ,før ...] |
| in exchange (adv) | i utbyte | [i 'ʉt,bytə] |

| by hand (made) | för hand | [før 'hand] |
| hardly (negative opinion) | knappast | ['knapast] |

probably (adv)	sannolikt	[sanʊ'likt]
on purpose (intentionally)	med flit, avsiktligt	[me flit], ['avsiktlit]
by accident (adv)	tillfälligtvis	['tilʲfɔlitvis]

very (adv)	mycket	['mʏkə]
for example (adv)	till exempel	[tilʲ ɛk'sɛmpəl]
between	mellan	['mɛlʲan]
among	bland	['blʲand]
so much (such a lot)	så mycket	[sɔ 'mʏkə]
especially (adv)	särskilt	['sæːˌʂilʲt]

Basic concepts. Part 2

19. Weekdays

Monday	**måndag (en)**	['mɔn‚dag]
Tuesday	**tisdag (en)**	['tis‚dag]
Wednesday	**onsdag (en)**	['ʊns‚dag]
Thursday	**torsdag (en)**	['tʊːʂ‚dag]
Friday	**fredag (en)**	['fre‚dag]
Saturday	**lördag (en)**	['lʲøːdag]
Sunday	**söndag (en)**	['sœn‚dag]

today (adv)	**i dag**	[i 'dag]
tomorrow (adv)	**i morgon**	[i 'mɔrgɔn]
the day after tomorrow	**i övermorgon**	[i 'øːvə‚mɔrgɔn]
yesterday (adv)	**i går**	[i 'goːr]
the day before yesterday	**i förrgår**	[i 'fœːr‚goːr]

day	**dag (en)**	['dag]
working day	**arbetsdag (en)**	['arbets‚dag]
public holiday	**helgdag (en)**	['hɛlj‚dag]
day off	**ledig dag (en)**	['lʲedig ‚dag]
weekend	**helg, veckohelg (en)**	[hɛlj], ['vɛkɔ‚hɛlj]

all day long	**hela dagen**	['helʲa 'dagən]
the next day (adv)	**nästa dag**	['nɛsta ‚dag]
two days ago	**för två dagar sedan**	[før ‚tvoː 'dagar 'sedan]
the day before	**dagen innan**	['dagən 'inan]
daily (adj)	**daglig**	['daglig]
every day (adv)	**varje dag**	['varjə dag]

week	**vecka (en)**	['vɛka]
last week (adv)	**förra veckan**	['fœːra 'vɛkan]
next week (adv)	**i nästa vecka**	[i 'nɛsta 'vɛka]
weekly (adj)	**vecko-**	['vɛkɔ-]
every week (adv)	**varje vecka**	['varjə 'vɛka]
twice a week	**två gångar i veckan**	[tvoː 'gɔŋar i 'vɛkan]
every Tuesday	**varje tisdag**	['varjə ‚tisdag]

20. Hours. Day and night

morning	**morgon (en)**	['mɔrgɔn]
in the morning	**på morgonen**	[pɔ 'mɔrgɔnən]
noon, midday	**middag (en)**	['mid‚dag]

in the afternoon	på eftermiddagen	[pɔ 'ɛftəˌmidagən]
evening	kväll (en)	[kvɛlʲ]
in the evening	på kvällen	[pɔ 'kvɛlʲen]
night	natt (en)	['nat]
at night	om natten	[ɔm 'natən]
midnight	midnatt (en)	['midˌnat]

second	sekund (en)	[se'kund]
minute	minut (en)	[mi'nʉ:t]
hour	timme (en)	['timə]
half an hour	halvtimme (en)	['halʲvˌtimə]
a quarter-hour	kvart (en)	['kva:t]
fifteen minutes	femton minuter	['fɛmtɔn mi'nʉ:tər]
24 hours	dygn (ett)	['dʏgn]

sunrise	soluppgång (en)	['sʊlʲ ˌup'gɔŋ]
dawn	gryning (en)	['gryniŋ]
early morning	tidig morgon (en)	['tidig 'mɔrgɔn]
sunset	solnedgång (en)	['sʊlʲ 'nedˌgɔŋ]

early in the morning	tidigt på morgonen	['tidit pɔ 'mɔrgɔnən]
this morning	i morse	[i 'mɔ:ʂə]
tomorrow morning	i morgon bitti	[i 'mɔrgɔn 'biti]
this afternoon	i eftermiddag	[i 'ɛftəˌmidag]
in the afternoon	på eftermiddagen	[pɔ 'ɛftəˌmidagən]
tomorrow afternoon	i morgon eftermiddag	[i 'mɔrgɔn 'ɛftəˌmidag]
tonight (this evening)	i kväll	[i 'kvɛlʲ]
tomorrow night	i morgon kväll	[i 'mɔrgɔn 'kvɛlʲ]

at 3 o'clock sharp	precis klockan tre	[prɛ'sis 'klʲɔkan tre:]
about 4 o'clock	vid fyratiden	[vid 'fyraˌtidən]
by 12 o'clock	vid klockan tolv	[vid 'klʲɔkan 'tɔlʲv]

in 20 minutes	om tjugo minuter	[ɔm 'ɕʉgɔ mi'nʉ:tər]
in an hour	om en timme	[ɔm en 'timə]
on time (adv)	i tid	[i 'tid]

a quarter of ...	kvart i ...	['kva:ʈ i ...]
within an hour	inom en timme	['inɔm en 'timə]
every 15 minutes	varje kvart	['varjə kva:ʈ]
round the clock	dygnet runt	['dʏngnet ˌrunt]

21. Months. Seasons

January	januari	['januˌari]
February	februari	[fɛbrʉ'ari]
March	mars	['ma:ʂ]
April	april	[a'prilʲ]
May	maj	['maj]
June	juni	['ju:ni]

July	juli	['juːli]
August	augusti	[auˈgusti]
September	september	[sɛpˈtɛmbər]
October	oktober	[ɔkˈtʊbər]
November	november	[nɔˈvɛmbər]
December	december	[deˈsɛmbər]

spring	vår (en)	['voːr]
in spring	på våren	[pɔ 'voːrən]
spring (as adj)	vår-	['voːr-]

summer	sommar (en)	['sɔmar]
in summer	på sommaren	[pɔ 'sɔmarən]
summer (as adj)	sommar-	['sɔmar-]

fall	höst (en)	['høst]
in fall	på hösten	[pɔ 'høstən]
fall (as adj)	höst-	['høst-]

winter	vinter (en)	['vintər]
in winter	på vintern	[pɔ 'vintərn]
winter (as adj)	vinter-	['vintər-]

month	månad (en)	['moːnad]
this month	den här månaden	[dɛn hæːr 'moːnadən]
next month	nästa månad	['nɛsta 'moːnad]
last month	förra månaden	['fœːra 'moːnadən]

a month ago	för en månad sedan	['før en 'moːnad 'sedan]
in a month (a month later)	om en månad	[ɔm en 'moːnad]
in 2 months (2 months later)	om två månader	[ɔm tvoː 'moːnadər]
the whole month	en hel månad	[en helʲ 'moːnad]
all month long	hela månaden	['helʲa 'moːnadən]

monthly (~ magazine)	månatlig	[moˈnatlig]
monthly (adv)	månatligen	[moˈnatligən]
every month	varje månad	['varjə ˌmoːnad]
twice a month	två gånger i månaden	[tvoː 'gɔŋər i 'moːnadən]

year	år (ett)	['oːr]
this year	i år	[i 'oːr]
next year	nästa år	['nɛsta ˌoːr]
last year	i fjol, förra året	[i 'fjʊlʲ], ['fœːra 'oːret]

a year ago	för ett år sedan	['før et 'oːr 'sedan]
in a year	om ett år	[ɔm et 'oːr]
in two years	om två år	[ɔm tvoː 'oːr]

the whole year	ett helt år	[ɛt helʲt 'oːr]
all year long	hela året	['helʲa 'oːret]
every year	varje år	['varjə 'oːr]

annual (adj)	**årlig**	['o:lig]
annually (adv)	**årligen**	['o:ligən]
4 times a year	**fyra gånger om året**	['fyra 'gɔŋər ɔm 'o:ret]

date (e.g., today's ~)	**datum (ett)**	['datum]
date (e.g., ~ of birth)	**datum (ett)**	['datum]
calendar	**almanacka (en)**	['alʲmanaka]

half a year	**halvår (ett)**	['halʲv‚o:r]
six months	**halvår (ett)**	['halʲv‚o:r]
season (summer, etc.)	**årstid (en)**	['o:ʂ‚tid]
century	**sekel (ett)**	['sekəlʲ]

22. Time. Miscellaneous

time	**tid (en)**	['tid]
moment	**ögonblick (ett)**	['ø:gɔn‚blik]
instant (n)	**ögonblick (ett)**	['ø:gɔn‚blik]
instant (adj)	**ögonblicklig**	['ø:gɔn‚bliklig]
lapse (of time)	**tidsavsnitt (ett)**	['tids‚avsnit]
life	**liv (ett)**	['liv]
eternity	**evighet (en)**	['evig‚het]

epoch	**epok (en)**	[ɛ'pɔ:k]
era	**era (en)**	['era]
cycle	**cykel (en)**	['sykəlʲ]
period	**period (en)**	[peri'ʊd]
term (short-~)	**tid, period (en)**	['tid], [peri'ʊd]

the future	**framtid (en)**	['fram‚tid]
future (as adj)	**framtida**	['fram‚tida]
next time	**nästa gång**	['nɛsta ‚gɔŋ]
the past	**det förflutna**	[dɛ 'førˌflʉ:tna]
past (recent)	**förra**	['fœ:ra]
last time	**förra gången**	['fœ:ra 'gɔŋən]

later (adv)	**senare**	['senarə]
after (prep.)	**efter**	['ɛftər]
nowadays (adv)	**nuförtiden**	['nʉːˌfør'tidən]
now (adv)	**nu**	['nʉ:]
immediately (adv)	**omedelbart**	[ʊ'medəlʲˌba:t]
soon (adv)	**snart**	['sna:t]
in advance (beforehand)	**i förväg**	[i 'førˌvɛ:g]

a long time ago	**längesedan**	['lʲɛŋəˌsedan]
recently (adv)	**nyligen**	['nyligən]
destiny	**öde (ett)**	['ø:də]
memories (childhood ~)	**minnen (pl)**	['minən]
archives	**arkiv (ett)**	[ar'kiv]
during ...	**under ...**	['undər ...]

long, a long time (adv)	**länge**	['lɛŋə]
not long (adv)	**inte länge**	['intə 'lɛŋə]
early (in the morning)	**tidigt**	['tidit]
late (not early)	**sent**	['sɛnt]

forever (for good)	**för alltid**	['før 'alʲtid]
to start (begin)	**att börja**	[at 'bœrja]
to postpone (vt)	**att skjuta upp**	[at 'ɧʉːta up]

at the same time	**samtidigt**	['sam͵tidit]
permanently (adv)	**alltid, ständigt**	['alʲtid], ['stɛndit]
constant (noise, pain)	**konstant**	[kɔn'stant]
temporary (adj)	**tillfällig, temporär**	['tilʲ͵folig], [tempo'rɛr]
sometimes (adv)	**ibland**	['iblʲand]
rarely (adv)	**sällan**	['sɛlʲan]
often (adv)	**ofta**	['ɔfta]

23. Opposites

rich (adj)	**rik**	['rik]
poor (adj)	**fattig**	['fatig]

ill, sick (adj)	**sjuk**	['ɧʉːk]
well (not sick)	**frisk**	['frisk]

big (adj)	**stor**	['stʊr]
small (adj)	**liten**	['litən]

quickly (adv)	**fort, snabbt**	[fʊːt], ['snabt]
slowly (adv)	**långsamt**	['lʲɔŋ͵samt]

fast (adj)	**snabb**	['snab]
slow (adj)	**långsam**	['lʲɔŋ͵sam]

glad (adj)	**glad**	['glʲad]
sad (adj)	**sorgmodig**	['sɔrj͵mʊdig]

together (adv)	**tillsammans**	[tilʲ'samans]
separately (adv)	**separat**	[sepa'rat]

aloud (to read)	**högt**	['hœgt]
silently (to oneself)	**för sig själv**	[før ͵sɛj 'ɧɛlʲv]

tall (adj)	**hög**	['høːg]
low (adj)	**låg**	['lʲoːg]

deep (adj)	**djup**	['jʉːp]
shallow (adj)	**grund**	['grʉnd]

yes	**ja**	['ja]

no	**nej**	['nɛj]
distant (in space)	**fjärran**	['fʲæːran]
nearby (adj)	**nära**	['næːra]
far (adv)	**långt**	['lʲɔŋt]
nearby (adv)	**i närheten**	[i 'næːrˌhetən]
long (adj)	**lång**	['lʲɔŋ]
short (adj)	**kort**	['kɔːt]
good (kindhearted)	**god**	['gʊd]
evil (adj)	**ond**	['ʊnd]
married (adj)	**gift**	['jift]
single (adj)	**ogift**	[ʊ'jift]
to forbid (vt)	**att förbjuda**	[at før'bjʉːda]
to permit (vt)	**att tillåta**	[at 'tilʲoːta]
end	**slut (ett)**	['slʉːt]
beginning	**början (en)**	['bœrjan]
left (adj)	**vänster**	['vɛnstər]
right (adj)	**höger**	['høːgər]
first (adj)	**först**	[fœːʂt]
last (adj)	**sista**	['sista]
crime	**brott (ett)**	['brɔt]
punishment	**straff (ett)**	['straf]
to order (vt)	**att beordra**	[at be'oːdra]
to obey (vi, vt)	**att underordna sig**	[at 'undərˌɔːdna sɛj]
straight (adj)	**rak, rakt**	['rak], ['rakt]
curved (adj)	**krokig**	['krʊkig]
paradise	**paradis (ett)**	['paraˌdis]
hell	**helvete (ett)**	['hɛlʲvetə]
to be born	**att födas**	[at 'føːdas]
to die (vi)	**att dö**	[at 'døː]
strong (adj)	**stark**	['stark]
weak (adj)	**svag**	['svag]
old (adj)	**gammal**	['gamalʲ]
young (adj)	**ung**	['uŋ]
old (adj)	**gammal**	['gamalʲ]
new (adj)	**ny**	['ny]

| hard (adj) | hård | ['ho:d] |
| soft (adj) | mjuk | ['mjʉ:k] |

| warm (tepid) | varm | ['varm] |
| cold (adj) | kall | ['kalʲ] |

| fat (adj) | tjock | ['ɕøk] |
| thin (adj) | mager | ['magər] |

| narrow (adj) | smal | ['smalʲ] |
| wide (adj) | bred | ['bred] |

| good (adj) | bra | ['brɔ:] |
| bad (adj) | dålig | ['do:lig] |

| brave (adj) | tapper | ['tapər] |
| cowardly (adj) | feg | ['feg] |

24. Lines and shapes

square	kvadrat (en)	[kva'drat]
square (as adj)	kvadratisk	[kva'dratisk]
circle	cirkel (en)	['sirkəlʲ]
round (adj)	rund	['rund]
triangle	triangel (en)	['tri,aŋəlʲ]
triangular (adj)	triangulär	[triaŋu'lʲæ:r]

oval	oval (en)	[ʊ'valʲ]
oval (as adj)	oval	[ʊ'valʲ]
rectangle	rektangel (en)	['rɛk,taŋəlʲ]
rectangular (adj)	rätvinklig	['rɛt,viŋklig]

pyramid	pyramid (en)	[pyra'mid]
rhombus	romb (en)	['rɔmb]
trapezoid	trapets (en)	[tra'pets]
cube	kub (en)	['kʉ:b]
prism	prisma (en)	['prisma]

circumference	omkrets (en)	['ɔm,krɛts]
sphere	sfär (en)	['sfæ:r]
ball (solid sphere)	klot (ett)	['klʲot]
diameter	diameter (en)	['dia,metər]
radius	radie (en)	['radiə]
perimeter (circle's ~)	perimeter (en)	[peri'metər]
center	medelpunkt (en)	['medəlʲ,puŋkt]

horizontal (adj)	horisontal	[hʊrisɔn'talʲ]
vertical (adj)	lodrät, lod-	['lʲod,rɛt], ['lʲod-]
parallel (n)	parallell (en)	[para'lʲɛlʲ]
parallel (as adj)	parallell	[para'lʲɛlʲ]

line	linje (en)	['linjə]
stroke	linje (en)	['linjə]
straight line	rät linje (en)	[rɛːt 'linjə]
curve (curved line)	kurva (en)	['kurva]
thin (line, etc.)	tunn	['tun]
contour (outline)	kontur (en)	[kɔn'tʉːr]

intersection	skärningspunkt (en)	['ɧærniŋs͵punkt]
right angle	rät vinkel (en)	[rɛːt 'viŋkəlʲ]
segment	segment (ett)	[seg'mɛnt]
sector	sektor (en)	['sektʊr]
side (of triangle)	sida (en)	['sida]
angle	vinkel (en)	['viŋkəlʲ]

25. Units of measurement

weight	vikt (en)	['vikt]
length	längd (en)	[lʲɛŋd]
width	bredd (en)	['brɛd]
height	höjd (en)	['hœjd]
depth	djup (ett)	['jʉːp]
volume	volym (en)	[vɔ'lʲym]
area	yta, areal (en)	['yta], [are'alʲ]

gram	gram (ett)	['gram]
milligram	milligram (ett)	['mili͵gram]
kilogram	kilogram (ett)	[ɕilʲɔ'gram]
ton	ton (en)	['tʊn]
pound	skålpund (ett)	['skoːlʲ͵pund]
ounce	uns (ett)	['uns]

meter	meter (en)	['metər]
millimeter	millimeter (en)	['mili͵metər]
centimeter	centimeter (en)	[sɛnti'metər]
kilometer	kilometer (en)	[ɕilʲɔ'metər]
mile	mil (en)	['milʲ]

inch	tum (en)	['tum]
foot	fot (en)	['fʊt]
yard	yard (en)	['jaːd]

square meter	kvadratmeter (en)	[kva'drat͵metər]
hectare	hektar (ett)	[hɛk'tar]

liter	liter (en)	['litər]
degree	grad (en)	['grad]
volt	volt (en)	['vɔlʲt]
ampere	ampere (en)	[am'pɛr]
horsepower	hästkraft (en)	['hɛst͵kraft]
quantity	mängd, kvantitet (en)	['mɛŋt], [kwanti'tet]

a little bit of ...	få ..., inte många ...	['fo: ...], ['intə 'mɔŋa ...]
half	hälft (en)	['hɛlʲft]
dozen	dussin (ett)	['dusin]
piece (item)	stycke (ett)	['stʏkə]

| size | storlek (en) | ['stʊːlʲek] |
| scale (map ~) | skala (en) | ['skalʲa] |

minimal (adj)	minimal	[mini'malʲ]
the smallest (adj)	minst	['minst]
medium (adj)	medel	['medəlʲ]
maximal (adj)	maximal	[maksi'malʲ]
the largest (adj)	störst	['støːʂt]

26. Containers

canning jar (glass ~)	glasburk (en)	['glʲasˌburk]
can	burk (en)	['burk]
bucket	hink (en)	['hiŋk]
barrel	tunna (en)	['tuna]

wash basin (e.g., plastic ~)	tvättfat (ett)	['tvætˌfat]
tank (100L water ~)	tank (en)	['taŋk]
hip flask	plunta, fickflaska (en)	['plʉnta], ['fikˌflʲaska]
jerrycan	dunk (en)	['duːŋk]
tank (e.g., tank car)	tank (en)	['taŋk]

mug	mugg (en)	['mug]
cup (of coffee, etc.)	kopp (en)	['kop]
saucer	tefat (ett)	['teˌfat]
glass (tumbler)	glas (ett)	['glʲas]
wine glass	vinglas (ett)	['vinˌglʲas]
stock pot (soup pot)	kastrull, gryta (en)	[ka'strulʲ], ['gryta]

| bottle (~ of wine) | flaska (en) | ['flʲaska] |
| neck (of the bottle, etc.) | flaskhals (en) | ['flʲaskˌhalʲs] |

carafe (decanter)	karaff (en)	[ka'raf]
pitcher	kanna (en) med handtag	['kana me 'hanˌtag]
vessel (container)	behållare (en)	[be'hoːlʲarə]
pot (crock, stoneware ~)	kruka (en)	['krʉka]
vase	vas (en)	['vas]

bottle (perfume ~)	flakong (en)	[flʲa'kɔŋ]
vial, small bottle	flaska (en)	['flʲaska]
tube (of toothpaste)	tub (en)	['tʉːb]

sack (bag)	säck (en)	['sɛk]
bag (paper ~, plastic ~)	påse (en)	['poːsə]
pack (of cigarettes, etc.)	paket (ett)	[pa'ket]

box (e.g., shoebox)	**ask (en)**	['ask]
crate	**låda (en)**	['lʲoːda]
basket	**korg (en)**	['kɔrj]

27. Materials

material	**material (ett)**	[mate'rjalʲ]
wood (n)	**trä (ett)**	['trɛː]
wood-, wooden (adj)	**trä-**	['trɛː-]

| glass (n) | **glas (ett)** | ['glʲas] |
| glass (as adj) | **av glas, glas-** | [av glʲas], [glʲas-] |

| stone (n) | **sten (en)** | ['sten] |
| stone (as adj) | **sten-** | ['sten-] |

| plastic (n) | **plast (en)** | ['plʲast] |
| plastic (as adj) | **plast-** | [plʲast-] |

| rubber (n) | **gummi (ett)** | ['gumi] |
| rubber (as adj) | **gummi-** | ['gumi-] |

| cloth, fabric (n) | **tyg (ett)** | ['tyg] |
| fabric (as adj) | **tyg-** | ['tyg-] |

| paper (n) | **papper (ett)** | ['papər] |
| paper (as adj) | **papper-** | ['papər-] |

| cardboard (n) | **papp, kartong (en)** | ['pap], [ka:'tɔŋ] |
| cardboard (as adj) | **papp-, kartong-** | ['pap-], [ka:'tɔŋ-] |

polyethylene	**polyetylen (en)**	['pɔlyɛty,lʲen]
cellophane	**cellofan (en)**	[sɛlʲʊ'fan]
linoleum	**linoleum (ett)**	[li'noleum]
plywood	**kryssfaner (ett)**	['krys,fa'nɛːr]

porcelain (n)	**porslin (ett)**	[pɔ:'ʂlin]
porcelain (as adj)	**av porslin**	[av pɔ:'ʂlin]
clay (n)	**lera (en)**	['lʲera]
clay (as adj)	**ler-**	['lʲer-]
ceramic (n)	**keramik (en)**	[ɕera'mik]
ceramic (as adj)	**keramisk**	[ɕe'ramisk]

28. Metals

metal (n)	**metall (en)**	[me'talʲ]
metal (as adj)	**metall-**	[me'talʲ-]
alloy (n)	**legering (en)**	[lʲe'geːriŋ]

gold (n)	guld (ett)	['gulʲd]
gold, golden (adj)	guld-	['gulʲd-]
silver (n)	silver (ett)	['silʲvər]
silver (as adj)	silver-	['silʲvər-]

iron (n)	järn (ett)	['jæ:n]
iron-, made of iron (adj)	järn-	['jæ:n-]
steel (n)	stål (ett)	['sto:lʲ]
steel (as adj)	stål-	['sto:lʲ-]
copper (n)	koppar (en)	['kopar]
copper (as adj)	koppar-	['kopar-]

aluminum (n)	aluminium (ett)	[alʉ'mi:nium]
aluminum (as adj)	aluminium-	[alʉ'mi:nium-]
bronze (n)	brons (en)	['brɔns]
bronze (as adj)	brons-	['brɔns-]

brass	mässing (en)	['mɛsiŋ]
nickel	nickel (ett)	['nikəlʲ]
platinum	platina (en)	['plʲatina]
mercury	kvicksilver (ett)	['kvik‚silʲvər]
tin	tenn (ett)	['tɛn]
lead	bly (ett)	['blʲy]
zinc	zink (en)	['siŋk]

HUMAN BEING

Human being. The body

29. Humans. Basic concepts

human being	**människa (en)**	['mɛniɲa]
man (adult male)	**man (en)**	['man]
woman	**kvinna (en)**	['kvina]
child	**barn (ett)**	['baːɳ]
girl	**flicka (en)**	['flika]
boy	**pojke (en)**	['pɔjkə]
teenager	**tonåring (en)**	[tɔ'noːriŋ]
old man	**gammal man (en)**	['gamalⁱ ˌman]
old woman	**gumma (en)**	['guma]

30. Human anatomy

organism (body)	**organism (en)**	[ɔrga'nism]
heart	**hjärta (ett)**	['jæːʈa]
blood	**blod (ett)**	['blʲʊd]
artery	**artär (en)**	[a'ʈæːr]
vein	**ven (en)**	['veːn]
brain	**hjärna (en)**	['jæːɳa]
nerve	**nerv (en)**	['nɛrv]
nerves	**nerver** (pl)	['nɛrvər]
vertebra	**ryggkota (en)**	['rʏgˌkɔta]
spine (backbone)	**ryggrad (en)**	['rʏgˌrad]
stomach (organ)	**magsäck (en)**	['magˌsɛk]
intestines, bowels	**tarmar, inälvor** (pl)	['tarmar], [inɛlʲvʊr]
intestine (e.g., large ~)	**tarm (en)**	['tarm]
liver	**lever (en)**	['lʲevər]
kidney	**njure (en)**	['njʉːrə]
bone	**ben (ett)**	['beːn]
skeleton	**skelett (ett)**	[ske'lʲet]
rib	**revben (ett)**	['revˌbeːn]
skull	**skalle (en)**	['skalʲe]
muscle	**muskel (en)**	['muskəlʲ]
biceps	**biceps (en)**	['bisɛps]

triceps	triceps (en)	['trisɛps]
tendon	sena (en)	['seːna]
joint	led (en)	['lʲed]
lungs	lungor (pl)	['lʉŋʊr]
genitals	könsorganen (pl)	['ɕœns ɔr'ganən]
skin	hud (en)	['hʉːd]

31. Head

head	huvud (ett)	['hʉːvʉd]
face	ansikte (ett)	['ansiktə]
nose	näsa (en)	['nɛːsa]
mouth	mun (en)	['muːn]

eye	öga (ett)	['øːga]
eyes	ögon (pl)	['øːgɔn]
pupil	pupill (en)	[pʉ'pilʲ]
eyebrow	ögonbryn (ett)	['øːgɔn,bryn]
eyelash	ögonfrans (en)	['øːgɔn,frans]
eyelid	ögonlock (ett)	['øːgɔn,lʲɔk]

tongue	tunga (en)	['tuŋa]
tooth	tand (en)	['tand]
lips	läppar (pl)	['lʲɛpar]
cheekbones	kindben (pl)	['ɕind,beːn]
gum	tandkött (ett)	['tand,ɕœt]
palate	gom (en)	['gʊm]

nostrils	näsborrar (pl)	['nɛːs,bɔrar]
chin	haka (en)	['haka]
jaw	käke (en)	['ɕɛːkə]
cheek	kind (en)	['ɕind]

forehead	panna (en)	['pana]
temple	tinning (en)	['tiniŋ]
ear	öra (ett)	['øːra]
back of the head	nacke (en)	['nakə]
neck	hals (en)	['halʲs]
throat	strupe, hals (en)	['strʉpə], ['halʲs]

hair	hår (pl)	['hoːr]
hairstyle	frisyr (en)	[fri'syr]
haircut	klippning (en)	['klipniŋ]
wig	peruk (en)	[pe'rʉːk]

mustache	mustasch (en)	[mʉ'staːʃ]
beard	skägg (ett)	['ʃɛg]
to have (a beard, etc.)	att ha	[at 'ha]
braid	fläta (en)	['flʲɛːta]
sideburns	polisonger (pl)	[pɔli'sɔŋər]

red-haired (adj)	rödhårig	['rø:d‚ho:rig]
gray (hair)	grå	['gro:]
bald (adj)	skallig	['skalig]
bald patch	flint (en)	['flint]

| ponytail | hästsvans (en) | ['hɛst‚svans] |
| bangs | lugg, pannlugg (en) | [lʉg], ['pan‚lʉg] |

32. Human body

hand	hand (en)	['hand]
arm	arm (en)	['arm]
finger	finger (ett)	['fiŋər]
toe	tå (en)	['to:]
thumb	tumme (en)	['tumə]
little finger	lillfinger (ett)	['lilʲ‚fiŋər]
nail	nagel (en)	['nagəlʲ]

fist	knytnäve (en)	['knʏt‚nɛ:və]
palm	handflata (en)	['hand‚flʲata]
wrist	handled (en)	['hand‚lʲed]
forearm	underarm (en)	['undər‚arm]
elbow	armbåge (en)	['arm‚bo:gə]
shoulder	skuldra (en)	['skʉlʲdra]

leg	ben (ett)	['be:n]
foot	fot (en)	['fʊt]
knee	knä (ett)	['knɛ:]
calf (part of leg)	vad (ett)	['vad]
hip	höft (en)	['hœft]
heel	häl (en)	['hɛ:lʲ]

body	kropp (en)	['krɔp]
stomach	mage (en)	['magə]
chest	bröst (ett)	['brœst]
breast	bröst (ett)	['brœst]
flank	sida (en)	['sida]
back	rygg (en)	['rʏg]
lower back	ländrygg (en)	['lʲɛnd‚rʏg]
waist	midja (en)	['midja]

navel (belly button)	navel (en)	['navəlʲ]
buttocks	stjärtar, skinkor (pl)	['ɧæ:ʈar], ['ɧiŋkʊr]
bottom	bak (en)	['bak]

beauty mark	leverfläck (ett)	['lʲevər‚flɛk]
birthmark	födelsemärke (ett)	['fø:dəlʲsə‚mæ:rkə]
(café au lait spot)		
tattoo	tatuering (en)	[tatʉ'eriŋ]
scar	ärr (ett)	['ær]

Clothing & Accessories

33. Outerwear. Coats

clothes	kläder (pl)	['klɛːdər]
outerwear	ytterkläder	['ytəˌklɛːdər]
winter clothing	vinterkläder (pl)	['vintəˌklɛːdər]
coat (overcoat)	rock, kappa (en)	['rɔk], ['kapa]
fur coat	päls (en)	['pɛlˠs]
fur jacket	pälsjacka (en)	['pɛlˠsˌjaka]
down coat	dunjacka (en)	['dʉːnˌjaka]
jacket (e.g., leather ~)	jacka (en)	['jaka]
raincoat (trenchcoat, etc.)	regnrock (en)	['rɛgnˌrɔk]
waterproof (adj)	vattentät	['vatənˌtɛt]

34. Men's & women's clothing

shirt (button shirt)	skjorta (en)	['ɧuːʈa]
pants	byxor (pl)	['byksʊr]
jeans	jeans (en)	['jins]
suit jacket	kavaj (en)	[ka'vaj]
suit	kostym (en)	[kɔs'tym]
dress (frock)	klänning (en)	['klɛniŋ]
skirt	kjol (en)	['ɕøːlˠ]
blouse	blus (en)	['blʉːs]
knitted jacket (cardigan, etc.)	stickad tröja (en)	['stikad 'trøja]
jacket (of woman's suit)	dräktjacka, kavaj (en)	['drɛkt 'jaka], ['kavaj]
T-shirt	T-shirt (en)	['tiːʃɔːt]
shorts (short trousers)	shorts (en)	['ʃɔːʈs]
tracksuit	träningsoverall (en)	['trɛːniŋs ove'rɔːlˠ]
bathrobe	morgonrock (en)	['morgonˌrɔk]
pajamas	pyjamas (en)	[py'jamas]
sweater	sweater, tröja (en)	['svitər], ['trøja]
pullover	pullover (en)	[pu'lˠoːvər]
vest	väst (en)	['vɛst]
tailcoat	frack (en)	['frak]
tuxedo	smoking (en)	['smɔkiŋ]

uniform	uniform (en)	[uni'fɔrm]
workwear	arbetskläder (pl)	['arbetsˌklʲɛːdər]
overalls	overall (en)	['ɔveˌrɔːlʲ]
coat (e.g., doctor's smock)	rock (en)	['rɔk]

35. Clothing. Underwear

underwear	underkläder (pl)	['undəˌklʲɛːdər]
boxers, briefs	underbyxor (pl)	['undəˌbyksʊr]
panties	trosor (pl)	['trʊsʊr]
undershirt (A-shirt)	undertröja (en)	['undəˌtrøja]
socks	sockor (pl)	['sɔkʊr]

nightgown	nattlinne (ett)	['natˌlinə]
bra	behå (en)	[be'hoː]
knee highs	knästrumpor (pl)	['knɛːˌstrumpʊr]
(knee-high socks)		

pantyhose	strumpbyxor (pl)	['strumpˌbyksʊr]
stockings (thigh highs)	strumpor (pl)	['strumpʊr]
bathing suit	baddräkt (en)	['badˌdrɛkt]

36. Headwear

hat	hatt (en)	['hat]
fedora	hatt (en)	['hat]
baseball cap	baseballkeps (en)	['bejsbɔlʲ keps]
flatcap	keps (en)	['keps]

beret	basker (en)	['baskər]
hood	luva, kapuschong (en)	['lʉːva], [kapʉ'ʃɔːŋ]
panama hat	panamahatt (en)	['panamaˌhat]
knit cap (knitted hat)	luva (en)	['lʉːva]

headscarf	sjalett (en)	[ʃa'lʲet]
women's hat	hatt (en)	['hat]
hard hat	hjälm (en)	['jɛlʲm]
garrison cap	båtmössa (en)	['bɔtˌmœsa]
helmet	hjälm (en)	['jɛlʲm]

| derby | plommonstop (ett) | ['plʲʊmɔnˌstʊp] |
| top hat | hög hatt, cylinder (en) | ['høːg ˌhat], [sy'lindər] |

37. Footwear

| footwear | skodon (pl) | ['skʊdʊn] |
| shoes (men's shoes) | skor (pl) | ['skʊr] |

shoes (women's shoes)	damskor (pl)	['dam͜skʊr]
boots (e.g., cowboy ~)	stövlar (pl)	['støvlʲar]
slippers	tofflor (pl)	['tɔflʲʊr]

tennis shoes (e.g., Nike ~)	tennisskor (pl)	['tɛnis͜skʊr]
sneakers (e.g., Converse ~)	canvas skor (pl)	['kanvas ͜skʊr]
sandals	sandaler (pl)	[san'dalʲer]

cobbler (shoe repairer)	skomakare (en)	['skʊ͜makarə]
heel	klack (en)	['klʲak]
pair (of shoes)	par (ett)	['par]

shoestring	skosnöre (ett)	['skʊ͜snø:rə]
to lace (vt)	att snöra	[at 'snø:ra]
shoehorn	skohorn (ett)	['skʊ͜hu:ŋ]
shoe polish	skokräm (en)	['skʊ͜krɛm]

38. Textile. Fabrics

cotton (n)	bomull (en)	['bʊ͜mulʲ]
cotton (as adj)	bomull-	['bʊ͜mulʲ-]
flax (n)	lin (ett)	['lin]
flax (as adj)	lin	['lin]

silk (n)	siden (ett)	['sidən]
silk (as adj)	siden-	['sidən-]
wool (n)	ull (en)	['ulʲ]
wool (as adj)	ull-	['ulʲ-]

velvet	sammet (en)	['samet]
suede	mocka (en)	['mɔka]
corduroy	manchester (en)	['man͜ɕestər]

nylon (n)	nylon (ett)	[ny'lʲɔn]
nylon (as adj)	nylon-	[ny'lʲɔn-]
polyester (n)	polyester (en)	[pɔlʲy'ɛstər]
polyester (as adj)	polyester-	[pɔlʲy'ɛstər-]

leather (n)	läder, skinn (ett)	['lʲɛ:dər], ['ɧin]
leather (as adj)	läder-, av läder	['lʲɛ:dər-], [av 'lʲɛ:dər]
fur (n)	päls (en)	['pɛlʲs]
fur (e.g., ~ coat)	päls-	['pɛlʲs-]

39. Personal accessories

| gloves | handskar (pl) | ['hanskar] |
| mittens | vantar (pl) | ['vantar] |

scarf (muffler)	halsduk (en)	['halˡsˌdʉːk]
glasses (eyeglasses)	glasögon (pl)	['glˡasˌøːgɔn]
frame (eyeglass ~)	båge (en)	['bɔːgə]
umbrella	paraply (ett)	[paraˈplˡy]
walking stick	käpp (en)	['ɕɛp]
hairbrush	hårborste (en)	['hoːrˌbɔːʂtə]
fan	solfjäder (en)	['sʉlˡˌfjɛːdər]

tie (necktie)	slips (en)	['slips]
bow tie	fluga (en)	['flʉːga]
suspenders	hängslen (pl)	['hɛŋslˡən]
handkerchief	näsduk (en)	['nɛsˌdʉk]

comb	kam (en)	['kam]
barrette	hårklämma (ett)	['hoːrˌklˡɛma]
hairpin	hårnål (en)	['hoːˌŋoːlˡ]
buckle	spänne (ett)	['spɛnə]

| belt | bälte (ett) | ['bɛlˡtə] |
| shoulder strap | rem (en) | ['rem] |

bag (handbag)	väska (en)	['vɛska]
purse	damväska (en)	['damˌvɛska]
backpack	ryggsäck (en)	['rygˌsɛk]

40. Clothing. Miscellaneous

fashion	mode (ett)	['mʊdə]
in vogue (adj)	modern	[mʊˈdɛːŋ]
fashion designer	modedesigner (en)	['mʊdə deˈsajnər]

collar	krage (en)	['kragə]
pocket	ficka (en)	['fika]
pocket (as adj)	fick-	['fik-]
sleeve	ärm (en)	['æːrm]
hanging loop	hängband (ett)	['hɛŋ band]
fly (on trousers)	gylf (en)	['gylˡf]

zipper (fastener)	blixtlås (ett)	['blikstˌlˡoːs]
fastener	knäppning (en)	['knɛpniŋ]
button	knapp (en)	['knap]
buttonhole	knapphål (ett)	['knapˌhoːlˡ]
to come off (ab. button)	att lossna	[at 'lˡɔsna]

to sew (vi, vt)	att sy	[at sy]
to embroider (vi, vt)	att brodera	[at brʊˈdera]
embroidery	broderi (ett)	[brʊdeˈriː]
sewing needle	synål (en)	['syˌnoːlˡ]
thread	tråd (en)	['troːd]
seam	söm (en)	['søːm]

to get dirty (vi)	att smutsa ned sig	[at 'smutsa ned sɛj]
stain (mark, spot)	fläck (en)	['flˡɛk]
to crease, crumple (vi)	att bli skrynklig	[at bli 'skrʏŋklig]
to tear, to rip (vt)	att riva	[at 'riva]
clothes moth	mal (en)	['malˡ]

41. Personal care. Cosmetics

toothpaste	tandkräm (en)	['tandˌkrɛm]
toothbrush	tandborste (en)	['tandˌbɔːʂtə]
to brush one's teeth	att borsta tänderna	[at 'bɔːʂta 'tɛndɛːŋa]

razor	hyvel (en)	['hyvəlˡ]
shaving cream	rakkräm (en)	['rakˌkrɛm]
to shave (vi)	att raka sig	[at 'raka sɛj]

| soap | tvål (en) | ['tvoːlˡ] |
| shampoo | schampo (ett) | ['ɧamˌpʊ] |

scissors	sax (en)	['saks]
nail file	nagelfil (en)	['nagəlˡˌfilˡ]
nail clippers	nageltång (en)	['nagəlˡˌtɔŋ]
tweezers	pincett (en)	[pin'sɛt]

cosmetics	kosmetika (en)	[kɔs'mɛtika]
face mask	ansiktsmask (en)	[an'siktsˌmask]
manicure	manikyr (en)	[mani'kyr]
to have a manicure	att få manikyr	[at foː mani'kyr]
pedicure	pedikyr (en)	[pedi'kyr]

make-up bag	kosmetikväska (en)	[kɔsmɛ'tikˌvɛska]
face powder	puder (ett)	['pʉːdər]
powder compact	puderdosa (en)	['pʉːdɛˌdoːsa]
blusher	rouge (ett)	['ruːʃ]

perfume (bottled)	parfym (en)	[par'fym]
toilet water (lotion)	eau de toilette (en)	['ɔːdetuaˌlˡet]
lotion	rakvatten (ett)	['rakˌvatən]
cologne	eau de cologne (en)	['ɔːdekɔˌlˡɔŋˡ]

eyeshadow	ögonskugga (en)	['øːgɔnˌskuga]
eyeliner	ögonpenna (en)	['øːgɔnˌpɛna]
mascara	mascara (en)	[ma'skara]

lipstick	läppstift (ett)	['lˡɛpˌstift]
nail polish, enamel	nagellack (ett)	['nagəlˡˌlˡak]
hair spray	hårspray (en)	['hoːrˌsprɛj]
deodorant	deodorant (en)	[deʊdʊ'rant]
cream	kräm (en)	['krɛm]
face cream	ansiktskräm (en)	[an'siktsˌkrɛm]

hand cream	handkräm (en)	['hand‚krɛm]
anti-wrinkle cream	anti-rynkor kräm (en)	['anti‚rʏŋkʊr 'krɛm]
day cream	dagkräm (en)	['dag‚krɛm]
night cream	nattkräm (en)	['nat‚krɛm]
day (as adj)	dag-	['dag-]
night (as adj)	natt-	['nat-]

tampon	tampong (en)	[tam'pɔŋ]
toilet paper (toilet roll)	toalettpapper (ett)	[tʊa'lʲet‚papər]
hair dryer	hårtork (en)	['hoː‚tʊrk]

42. Jewelry

jewelry	smycken (pl)	['smʏkən]
precious (e.g., ~ stone)	ädel-	['ɛ:dəl-]
hallmark stamp	stämpel (en)	['stɛmpəlʲ]

ring	ring (en)	['riŋ]
wedding ring	vigselring (en)	['vigsəlʲ‚riŋ]
bracelet	armband (ett)	['arm‚band]

earrings	örhängen (pl)	['øːr‚hɛŋən]
necklace (~ of pearls)	halsband (ett)	['halʲs‚band]
crown	krona (en)	['krʊna]
bead necklace	halsband (ett)	['halʲs‚band]

diamond	diamant (en)	[dia'mant]
emerald	smaragd (en)	[sma'ragd]
ruby	rubin (en)	[rʉ'biːn]
sapphire	safir (en)	[sa'fir]
pearl	pärlor (pl)	['pæː[ʲʊːr]
amber	rav, bärnsten (en)	['rav], ['bæːnʃtən]

43. Watches. Clocks

watch (wristwatch)	armbandsur (ett)	['armbands‚ʉːr]
dial	urtavla (en)	['ʉː‚tavlʲa]
hand (of clock, watch)	visare (en)	['visarə]
metal watch band	armband (ett)	['arm‚band]
watch strap	armband (ett)	['arm‚band]

battery	batteri (ett)	[batɛ'riː]
to be dead (battery)	att bli urladdad	[at bli 'ʉː‚lʲadad]
to change a battery	att byta batteri	[at 'byta batɛ'riː]
to run fast	att gå för fort	[at 'goː før 'foːt]
to run slow	att gå för långsamt	[at 'goː før 'lʲɔŋ‚samt]
wall clock	väggklocka (en)	['vɛg‚klʲɔka]
hourglass	sandklocka (en)	['sand‚klʲɔka]

sundial	solklocka (en)	['sʊlʲˌklʲɔka]
alarm clock	väckarklocka (en)	['vɛkarˌklʲɔka]
watchmaker	urmakare (en)	['ʉrˌmakarə]
to repair (vt)	att reparera	[at repa'rera]

Food. Nutricion

44. Food

meat	kött (ett)	['ɕœt]
chicken	höna (en)	['høːna]
Rock Cornish hen (poussin)	kyckling (en)	['ɕyklɪŋ]
duck	anka (en)	['aŋka]
goose	gås (en)	['goːs]
game	vilt (ett)	['vilʲt]
turkey	kalkon (en)	[kalʲˈkʊn]
pork	fläsk (ett)	['flʲɛsk]
veal	kalvkött (en)	['kalʲvˌɕœt]
lamb	lammkött (ett)	['lʲamˌɕœt]
beef	oxkött, nötkött (ett)	['ʊksˌɕœt], ['nøːtˌɕœt]
rabbit	kanin (en)	[ka'nin]
sausage (bologna, pepperoni, etc.)	korv (en)	['kɔrv]
vienna sausage (frankfurter)	wienerkorv (en)	['viŋɛrˌkɔrv]
bacon	bacon (ett)	['bɛjkɔn]
ham	skinka (en)	['ɧiŋka]
gammon	skinka (en)	['ɧiŋka]
pâté	paté (en)	[pa'te]
liver	lever (en)	['lʲevər]
hamburger (ground beef)	köttfärs (en)	['ɕœtˌfæːʂ]
tongue	tunga (en)	['tuŋa]
egg	ägg (ett)	['ɛg]
eggs	ägg (pl)	['ɛg]
egg white	äggvita (en)	['ɛgˌviːta]
egg yolk	äggula (en)	['ɛgˌʉːlʲa]
fish	fisk (en)	['fisk]
seafood	fisk och skaldjur	['fisk ɔ 'skalʲjʉːr]
crustaceans	kräftdjur (pl)	['krɛftˌjuːr]
caviar	kaviar (en)	['kavˌjar]
crab	krabba (en)	['kraba]
shrimp	räka (en)	['rɛːka]
oyster	ostron (ett)	['ʊstrʊn]
spiny lobster	languster (en)	[lʲaŋ'gustər]

| octopus | bläckfisk (en) | ['blɛkˌfisk] |
| squid | bläckfisk (en) | ['blʲɛkˌfisk] |

sturgeon	stör (en)	['stø:r]
salmon	lax (en)	['lʲaks]
halibut	hälleflundra (en)	['hɛlʲeˌflʉndra]

cod	torsk (en)	['tɔ:ʂk]
mackerel	makrill (en)	['makrilʲ]
tuna	tonfisk (en)	['tʊnˌfisk]
eel	ål (en)	['o:lʲ]
trout	öring (en)	['ø:riŋ]
sardine	sardin (en)	[sa:'dʲi:n]
pike	gädda (en)	['jɛda]
herring	sill (en)	['silʲ]

bread	bröd (ett)	['brø:d]
cheese	ost (en)	['ʊst]
sugar	socker (ett)	['sɔkər]
salt	salt (ett)	['salʲt]

rice	ris (ett)	['ris]
pasta (macaroni)	pasta (en), makaroner (pl)	['pasta], [maka'rʊnər]
noodles	nudlar (pl)	['nʉ:dlʲar]

butter	smör (ett)	['smœ:r]
vegetable oil	vegetabilisk olja (en)	[vegeta'bilisk 'ɔlja]
sunflower oil	solrosolja (en)	['sʊlʲrʊsˌɔlja]
margarine	margarin (ett)	[marga'rin]

| olives | oliver (pl) · | [ʊ:'livər] |
| olive oil | olivolja (en) | [ʊ'livˌɔlja] |

milk	mjölk (en)	['mjœlʲk]
condensed milk	kondenserad mjölk (en)	[kɔndɛn'serad ˌmjœlʲk]
yogurt	yoghurt (en)	['jo:gʉ:t]
sour cream	gräddfil, syrad grädden (en)	['grɛdfilʲ], [syrad 'gredən]
cream (of milk)	grädde (en)	['grɛdə]

| mayonnaise | majonnäs (en) | [majo'nɛs] |
| buttercream | kräm (en) | ['krɛm] |

cereal grains (wheat, etc.)	gryn (en)	['gryn]
flour	mjöl (ett)	['mjø:lʲ]
canned food	konserv (en)	[kɔn'sɛrv]

cornflakes	cornflakes (pl)	['kɔ:ɳˌflɛjks]
honey	honung (en)	['hɔnʉŋ]
jam	sylt, marmelad (en)	['sylʲt], [marme'lʲad]
chewing gum	tuggummi (ett)	['tugˌgumi]

55

45. Drinks

water	vatten (ett)	['vatən]
drinking water	dricksvatten (ett)	['driks,vatən]
mineral water	mineralvatten (ett)	[mine'ralʲˌvatən]
still (adj)	icke kolsyrat	['ikə 'kɔlʲˌsyrat]
carbonated (adj)	kolsyrat	['kɔlʲˌsyrat]
sparkling (adj)	kolsyrat	['kɔlʲˌsyrat]
ice	is (en)	['is]
with ice	med is	[me 'is]
non-alcoholic (adj)	alkoholfri	[alʲkʊ'holʲˌfri:]
soft drink	alkoholfri dryck (en)	[alʲkʊ'holʲfri 'drʏk]
refreshing drink	läskedryck (en)	['lɛskəˌdrik]
lemonade	lemonad (en)	[lʲemɔ'nad]
liquors	alkoholhaltiga drycker (pl)	[alʲkʊ'holʲˌhalʲtiga 'drʏkər]
wine	vin (ett)	['vin]
white wine	vitvin (ett)	['vitˌvin]
red wine	rödvin (ett)	['rø:dˌvin]
liqueur	likör (en)	[li'kø:r]
champagne	champagne (en)	[ɧam'panʲ]
vermouth	vermouth (en)	['vɛrmut]
whiskey	whisky (en)	['viski]
vodka	vodka (en)	['vodka]
gin	gin (ett)	['dʒin]
cognac	konjak (en)	['kɔnʲak]
rum	rom (en)	['rɔm]
coffee	kaffe (ett)	['kafə]
black coffee	svart kaffe (ett)	['sva:ʈ 'kafə]
coffee with milk	kaffe med mjölk (ett)	['kafə me mjœlʲk]
cappuccino	cappuccino (en)	['kaputʃinʊ]
instant coffee	snabbkaffe (ett)	['snabˌkafə]
milk	mjölk (en)	['mjœlʲk]
cocktail	cocktail (en)	['kɔktɛjlʲ]
milkshake	milkshake (en)	['milʲkʃɛjk]
juice	juice (en)	['ju:s]
tomato juice	tomatjuice (en)	[tʊ'matju:s]
orange juice	apelsinjuice (en)	[apɛlʲ'sinju:s]
freshly squeezed juice	nypressad juice (en)	['nʏˌprɛsad 'ju:s]
beer	öl (ett)	['ø:lʲ]
light beer	ljust öl (ett)	['jʉ:stˌø:lʲ]
dark beer	mörkt öl (ett)	['mœ:rkt ˌø:lʲ]

tea	te (ett)	['te:]
black tea	svart te (ett)	['svaːʈ ˌteː]
green tea	grönt te (ett)	['grœnt teː]

46. Vegetables

vegetables	grönsaker (pl)	['grøːnˌsakər]
greens	grönsaker (pl)	['grøːnˌsakər]

tomato	tomat (en)	[tʊ'mat]
cucumber	gurka (en)	['gurka]
carrot	morot (en)	['mʊˌrʊt]
potato	potatis (en)	[pʊ'tatis]
onion	lök (en)	['lʲøːk]
garlic	vitlök (en)	['vitˌlʲøːk]

cabbage	kål (en)	['koːlʲ]
cauliflower	blomkål (en)	['blʲumˌkoːlʲ]
Brussels sprouts	brysselkål (en)	['brʏsɛlʲˌkoːlʲ]
broccoli	broccoli (en)	['brɔkɔli]

beetroot	rödbeta (en)	['røːdˌbeta]
eggplant	aubergine (en)	[ɔbɛr'ʒin]
zucchini	squash, zucchini (en)	['skvɔːɕ], [su'kini]
pumpkin	pumpa (en)	['pumpa]
turnip	rova (en)	['rʊva]

parsley	persilja (en)	[pɛ'ʂilja]
dill	dill (en)	['dilʲ]
lettuce	sallad (en)	['salʲad]
celery	selleri (en)	['sɛlʲeri]
asparagus	sparris (en)	['sparis]
spinach	spenat (en)	[spe'nat]

pea	ärter (pl)	['æːʈər]
beans	bönor (pl)	['bønʊr]
corn (maize)	majs (en)	['majs]
kidney bean	böna (en)	['bøna]

bell pepper	peppar (en)	['pɛpar]
radish	rädisa (en)	['rɛːdisa]
artichoke	kronärtskocka (en)	['krʊnæːʈˌskɔka]

47. Fruits. Nuts

fruit	frukt (en)	['frukt]
apple	äpple (ett)	['ɛplʲe]
pear	päron (ett)	['pæːrɔn]

lemon	**citron (en)**	[si'trʊn]
orange	**apelsin (en)**	[apɛlˈ'sin]
strawberry (garden ~)	**jordgubbe (en)**	['jʊːdˌgʊbə]
mandarin	**mandarin (en)**	[manda'rin]
plum	**plommon (ett)**	['plʲʊmɔn]
peach	**persika (en)**	['pɛʂika]
apricot	**aprikos (en)**	[apri'kʊs]
raspberry	**hallon (ett)**	['halʲɔn]
pineapple	**ananas (en)**	['ananas]
banana	**banan (en)**	['banan]
watermelon	**vattenmelon (en)**	['vatənˌme'lʲʊn]
grape	**druva (en)**	['drʉːva]
sour cherry	**körsbär (ett)**	['ɕøːʂˌbæːr]
sweet cherry	**fågelbär (ett)**	['foːgəlʲˌbæːr]
melon	**melon (en)**	[me'lʲʊn]
grapefruit	**grapefrukt (en)**	['grɛjpˌfrʉkt]
avocado	**avokado (en)**	[avɔ'kadʊ]
papaya	**papaya (en)**	[pa'paja]
mango	**mango (en)**	['maŋgʊ]
pomegranate	**granatäpple (en)**	[gra'natˌɛplʲe]
redcurrant	**röda vinbär (ett)**	['røːda 'vinbæːr]
blackcurrant	**svarta vinbär (ett)**	['svaːʈa 'vinbæːr]
gooseberry	**krusbär (ett)**	['krʉːsˌbæːr]
bilberry	**blåbär (ett)**	['blʲoːˌbæːr]
blackberry	**björnbär (ett)**	['bjøːɳˌbæːr]
raisin	**russin (ett)**	['rusin]
fig	**fikon (ett)**	['fikɔn]
date	**dadel (en)**	['dadəlʲ]
peanut	**jordnöt (en)**	['jʊːdˌnøːt]
almond	**mandel (en)**	['mandəlʲ]
walnut	**valnöt (en)**	['valʲˌnøːt]
hazelnut	**hasselnöt (en)**	['hasəlʲˌnøːt]
coconut	**kokosnöt (en)**	['kʊkʊsˌnøːt]
pistachios	**pistaschnötter** (pl)	['pistaʃˌnœtər]

48. Bread. Candy

bakers' confectionery (pastry)	**konditorivaror** (pl)	[kɔnditʊ'riːˌvarʊr]
bread	**bröd (ett)**	['brøːd]
cookies	**småkakor** (pl)	['smoːkakʊr]
chocolate (n)	**choklad (en)**	[ʃɔk'lʲad]
chocolate (as adj)	**choklad-**	[ʃɔk'lʲad-]

candy (wrapped)	konfekt, karamell (en)	[kɔnˈfɛkt], [karaˈmɛlʲ]
cake (e.g., cupcake)	kaka, bakelse (en)	[ˈkaka], [ˈbakəlʲsə]
cake (e.g., birthday ~)	tårta (en)	[ˈtoːʈa]

| pie (e.g., apple ~) | paj (en) | [ˈpaj] |
| filling (for cake, pie) | fyllning (en) | [ˈfylʲniŋ] |

jam (whole fruit jam)	sylt (en)	[ˈsylʲt]
marmalade	marmelad (en)	[marmeˈlʲad]
waffles	våffle (en)	[ˈvɔflʲe]
ice-cream	glass (en)	[ˈɡlʲas]
pudding	pudding (en)	[ˈpudiŋ]

49. Cooked dishes

course, dish	rätt (en)	[ˈræt]
cuisine	kök (ett)	[ˈɕøːk]
recipe	recept (ett)	[reˈsɛpt]
portion	portion (en)	[pɔːˈtʃʊn]

| salad | sallad (en) | [ˈsalʲad] |
| soup | soppa (en) | [ˈsɔpa] |

clear soup (broth)	buljong (en)	[buˈljɔŋ]
sandwich (bread)	smörgås (en)	[ˈsmœrˌɡoːs]
fried eggs	stekt ägg (en)	[ˈstɛkt ˌɛɡ]

| hamburger (beefburger) | hamburgare (en) | [ˈhamburɡarə] |
| beefsteak | biffstek (en) | [ˈbifˌstɛk] |

side dish	tillbehör (ett)	[ˈtilʲbeˌhør]
spaghetti	spagetti	[spaˈɡɛti]
mashed potatoes	potatismos (ett)	[pʊˈtatisˌmʊs]
pizza	pizza (en)	[ˈpitsa]
porridge (oatmeal, etc.)	gröt (en)	[ˈɡrøːt]
omelet	omelett (en)	[ɔməˈlʲet]

boiled (e.g., ~ beef)	kokt	[ˈkʊkt]
smoked (adj)	rökt	[ˈrœkt]
fried (adj)	stekt	[ˈstɛkt]
dried (adj)	torkad	[ˈtɔrkad]
frozen (adj)	fryst	[ˈfrʏst]
pickled (adj)	sylt-	[ˈsylʲt-]

sweet (sugary)	söt	[ˈsøːt]
salty (adj)	salt	[ˈsalʲt]
cold (adj)	kall	[ˈkalʲ]
hot (adj)	het, varm	[ˈhet], [ˈvarm]
bitter (adj)	bitter	[ˈbitər]
tasty (adj)	läcker	[ˈlʲɛkər]

to cook in boiling water	**att koka**	[at 'kʊka]
to cook (dinner)	**att laga**	[at 'lʲaga]
to fry (vt)	**att steka**	[at 'steka]
to heat up (food)	**att värma upp**	[at 'væːrma up]

to salt (vt)	**att salta**	[at 'salʲta]
to pepper (vt)	**att peppra**	[at 'pepra]
to grate (vt)	**att riva**	[at 'riva]
peel (n)	**skal (ett)**	['skalʲ]
to peel (vt)	**att skala**	[at 'skalʲa]

50. Spices

salt	**salt (ett)**	['salʲt]
salty (adj)	**salt**	['salʲt]
to salt (vt)	**att salta**	[at 'salʲta]

black pepper	**svartpeppar (en)**	['svaːʈˌpɛpar]
red pepper (milled ~)	**rödpeppar (en)**	['røːdˌpɛpar]
mustard	**senap (en)**	['seːnap]
horseradish	**pepparrot (en)**	['pɛpaˌrʊt]

condiment	**krydda (en)**	['krʏda]
spice	**krydda (en)**	['krʏda]
sauce	**sås (en)**	['soːs]
vinegar	**ättika (en)**	['ætika]

anise	**anis (en)**	['anis]
basil	**basilika (en)**	[ba'silika]
cloves	**nejlika (en)**	['nɛjlika]

ginger	**ingefära (en)**	['iŋəˌfæːra]
coriander	**koriander (en)**	[kɔri'andər]
cinnamon	**kanel (en)**	[ka'nelʲ]

sesame	**sesam (en)**	['sesam]
bay leaf	**lagerblad (ett)**	['lʲagərˌblʲad]
paprika	**paprika (en)**	['paprika]
caraway	**kummin (en)**	['kumin]
saffron	**saffran (en)**	['safran]

51. Meals

| food | **mat (en)** | ['mat] |
| to eat (vi, vt) | **att äta** | [at 'ɛːta] |

| breakfast | **frukost (en)** | ['frʉːkɔst] |
| to have breakfast | **att äta frukost** | [at 'ɛːta 'frʉːkɔst] |

lunch	lunch (en)	['lʉnɕ]
to have lunch	att äta lunch	[at 'ɛːta ˌlʉnɕ]
dinner	kvällsmat (en)	['kvɛlʲsˌmat]
to have dinner	att äta kvällsmat	[at 'ɛːta 'kvɛlʲsˌmat]

appetite	aptit (en)	['aptit]
Enjoy your meal!	Smaklig måltid!	['smaklig 'moːlʲtid]

to open (~ a bottle)	att öppna	[at 'øpna]
to spill (liquid)	att spilla	[at 'spilʲa]
to spill out (vi)	att spillas ut	[at 'spilʲas ʉt]

to boil (vi)	att koka	[at 'kʊka]
to boil (vt)	att koka	[at 'kʊka]
boiled (~ water)	kokt	['kʊkt]

to chill, cool down (vt)	att avkyla	[at 'avˌɕylʲa]
to chill (vi)	att avkylas	[at 'avˌɕylʲas]

taste, flavor	smak (en)	['smak]
aftertaste	bismak (en)	['bismak]

to slim down (lose weight)	att vara på diet	[at 'vara pɔ diˈet]
diet	diet (en)	[diˈet]
vitamin	vitamin (ett)	[vitaˈmin]
calorie	kalori (en)	[kalʲoˈriː]

vegetarian (n)	vegetarian (en)	[vegetiriˈan]
vegetarian (adj)	vegetarisk	[vegeˈtarisk]

fats (nutrient)	fett (ett)	['fɛt]
proteins	proteiner (pl)	[prɔteˈiːnər]
carbohydrates	kolhydrater (pl)	['kɔlʲhyˌdratər]
slice (of lemon, ham)	skiva (en)	['ɧiva]
piece (of cake, pie)	bit (en)	['bit]
crumb	smula (en)	['smʉlʲa]
(of bread, cake, etc.)		

52. Table setting

spoon	sked (en)	['ɧed]
knife	kniv (en)	['kniv]
fork	gaffel (en)	['gafəlʲ]

cup (e.g., coffee ~)	kopp (en)	['kop]
plate (dinner ~)	tallrik (en)	['talʲrik]

saucer	tefat (ett)	['teˌfat]
napkin (on table)	servett (en)	[sɛr'vɛt]
toothpick	tandpetare (en)	['tandˌpetarə]

53. Restaurant

restaurant	**restaurang (en)**	[rɛstʊ'raŋ]
coffee house	**kafé (ett)**	[ka'fe:]
pub, bar	**bar (en)**	['bar]
tearoom	**tehus (ett)**	['te:ˌhʉs]
waiter	**servitör (en)**	[sɛrvi'tø:r]
waitress	**servitris (en)**	[sɛrvi'tris]
bartender	**bartender (en)**	['ba:ˌtɛndər]
menu	**meny (en)**	[me'ny]
wine list	**vinlista (en)**	['vinˌlista]
to book a table	**att reservera bord**	[at resɛr'vera bʊ:d]
course, dish	**rätt (en)**	['ræt]
to order (meal)	**att beställa**	[at be'stɛlʲa]
to make an order	**att beställa**	[at be'stɛlʲa]
aperitif	**aperitif (en)**	[aperi'tif]
appetizer	**förrätt (en)**	['fœ:ræt]
dessert	**dessert (en)**	[dɛ'sɛ:r]
check	**nota (en)**	['nʊta]
to pay the check	**att betala notan**	[at be'talʲa 'nʊtan]
to give change	**att ge tillbaka växel**	[at je: tilʲ'baka 'vɛksəlʲ]
tip	**dricks (en)**	['driks]

Family, relatives and friends

54. Personal information. Forms

name (first name)	**namn (ett)**	['namn]
surname (last name)	**efternamn (ett)**	['ɛftəˌnamn]
date of birth	**födelsedatum (ett)**	['føːdəlˈsəˌdatum]
place of birth	**födelseort (en)**	['føːdəlˈsəˌɔːt]
nationality	**nationalitet (en)**	[natɧunaliˈtet]
place of residence	**bostadsort (en)**	['bostadsˌɔːt]
country	**land (ett)**	['lˈand]
profession (occupation)	**yrke (ett),**	['yrkə],
	profession (en)	[prɔfeˈɧun]
gender, sex	**kön (ett)**	['ɕøːn]
height	**höjd (en)**	['hœjd]
weight	**vikt (en)**	['vikt]

55. Family members. Relatives

mother	**mor (en)**	['mur]
father	**far (en)**	['far]
son	**son (en)**	['son]
daughter	**dotter (en)**	['dotər]
younger daughter	**yngsta dotter (en)**	['yŋsta 'dotər]
younger son	**yngste son (en)**	['yŋstə son]
eldest daughter	**äldsta dotter (en)**	['ɛlˈsta 'dotər]
eldest son	**äldste son (en)**	['ɛlˈstə 'son]
brother	**bror (en)**	['brur]
elder brother	**storebror (en)**	['sturəˌbrur]
younger brother	**lillebror (en)**	['lilˈeˌbrur]
sister	**syster (en)**	['sʏstər]
elder sister	**storasyster (en)**	['sturaˌsʏstər]
younger sister	**lillasyster (en)**	['lilˈaˌsʏstər]
cousin (masc.)	**kusin (en)**	[kʉˈsiːn]
cousin (fem.)	**kusin (en)**	[kʉˈsiːn]
mom, mommy	**mamma (en)**	['mama]
dad, daddy	**pappa (en)**	['papa]
parents	**föräldrar (pl)**	[førˈɛlˈdrar]
child	**barn (ett)**	['baːɳ]

children	barn (pl)	['bɑːŋ]
grandmother	mormor, farmor (en)	['mʊrmʊr], ['farmʊr]
grandfather	morfar, farfar (en)	['mʊrfar], ['farfar]
grandson	barnbarn (ett)	['bɑːŋˌbɑːŋ]
granddaughter	barnbarn (ett)	['bɑːŋˌbɑːŋ]
grandchildren	barnbarn (pl)	['bɑːŋˌbɑːŋ]

uncle	farbror, morbror (en)	['farˌbrʊr], ['mʊrˌbrʊr]
aunt	faster, moster (en)	['fastər], ['mʊstər]
nephew	brorson, systerson (en)	['brʊrˌsɔn], ['sʏstəˌsɔn]
niece	brorsdotter, systerdotter (en)	['brʊːsˌdɔtər], ['sʏstəˌdɔtər]

mother-in-law (wife's mother)	svärmor (en)	['svæːrˌmʊr]
father-in-law (husband's father)	svärfar (en)	['svæːrˌfar]
son-in-law (daughter's husband)	svärson (en)	['svæːˌsɔn]

stepmother	styvmor (en)	['stʏvˌmʊr]
stepfather	styvfar (en)	['stʏvˌfar]

infant	spädbarn (ett)	['spɛːdˌbɑːŋ]
baby (infant)	spädbarn (ett)	['spɛːdˌbɑːŋ]
little boy, kid	baby, bäbis (en)	['bɛːbi], ['bɛːbis]

wife	hustru (en)	['hʉstrʉ]
husband	man (en)	['man]

spouse (husband)	make, äkta make (en)	['makə], ['ɛkta ˌmakə]
spouse (wife)	hustru (en)	['hʉstrʉ]

married (masc.)	gift	['jift]
married (fem.)	gift	['jift]
single (unmarried)	ogift	[ʊˈjift]
bachelor	ungkarl (en)	['ʊŋˌkar]
divorced (masc.)	frånskild	['froːnˌɧilʲd]

widow	änka (en)	['ɛŋka]
widower	änkling (en)	['ɛŋkliŋ]

relative	släkting (en)	['slʲɛktiŋ]
close relative	nära släkting (en)	['næːra 'slʲɛktiŋ]

distant relative	fjärran släkting (en)	['fjæːran 'slʲɛktiŋ]
relatives	släktingar (pl)	['slʲɛktiŋar]

orphan (boy or girl)	föräldralöst barn (ett)	[førˈɛlʲdralʲœst 'bɑːŋ]
guardian (of a minor)	förmyndare (en)	['førˌmʏndarə]
to adopt (a boy)	att adoptera	[at adɔp'tera]
to adopt (a girl)	att adoptera	[at adɔp'tera]

56. Friends. Coworkers

friend (masc.)	**vän (en)**	['vɛːn]
friend (fem.)	**väninna (en)**	[vɛːˈnina]
friendship	**vänskap (en)**	['vɛnˌskap]
to be friends	**att vara vänner**	[at 'vara 'vɛnər]
buddy (masc.)	**vän (en)**	['vɛːn]
buddy (fem.)	**väninna (en)**	[vɛːˈnina]
partner	**partner (en)**	['paːtnər]
chief (boss)	**chef (en)**	['ʃef]
superior (n)	**överordnad (en)**	['øːvərˌɔːdnat]
owner, proprietor	**ägare (en)**	['ɛːgarə]
subordinate (n)	**underordnad (en)**	['undərˌɔːdnat]
colleague	**kollega (en)**	[kɔˈlʲeːga]
acquaintance (person)	**bekant (en)**	[beˈkant]
fellow traveler	**resekamrat (en)**	['resəˌkamˈrat]
classmate	**klasskamrat (en)**	['klʲasˌkamˈrat]
neighbor (masc.)	**granne (en)**	['granə]
neighbor (fem.)	**granne (en)**	['granə]
neighbors	**grannar (pl)**	['granar]

57. Man. Woman

woman	**kvinna (en)**	['kvina]
girl (young woman)	**tjej, flicka (en)**	[ɕej], ['flika]
bride	**brud (en)**	['bruːd]
beautiful (adj)	**vacker**	['vakər]
tall (adj)	**lång**	['lʲɔŋ]
slender (adj)	**slank**	['slʲaŋk]
short (adj)	**kort**	['kɔːt]
blonde (n)	**blondin (en)**	[blʲɔnˈdin]
brunette (n)	**brunett (en)**	[bruˈnɛt]
ladies' (adj)	**dam-**	['dam-]
virgin (girl)	**jungfru (en)**	['jʉŋfruː]
pregnant (adj)	**gravid**	[graˈvid]
man (adult male)	**man (en)**	['man]
blond (n)	**blond man (en)**	['blʲɔnd man]
brunet (n)	**brunhårig (en)**	['brʉnˌhoːrig]
tall (adj)	**lång**	['lʲɔŋ]
short (adj)	**kort**	['kɔːt]
rude (rough)	**ohövlig**	[ʉːˈhøvlig]

stocky (adj)	**undersätsig**	['undə͵sœtsig]
robust (adj)	**robust**	[rʊ'bust]
strong (adj)	**stark**	['stark]
strength	**styrka (en)**	['styrka]

stout, fat (adj)	**tjock**	['çøk]
swarthy (adj)	**mörkhyad**	['mœːrk͵hyad]
slender (well-built)	**slank**	['slʲaŋk]
elegant (adj)	**elegant**	[ɛlʲe'gant]

58. Age

age	**ålder (en)**	['ɔlʲdər]
youth (young age)	**ungdom (en)**	['uŋ͵dʊm]
young (adj)	**ung**	['uŋ]

younger (adj)	**yngre**	['yŋrə]
older (adj)	**äldre**	['ɛlʲdrə]

young man	**yngling (en)**	['yŋliŋ]
teenager	**tonåring (en)**	[tɔ'noːriŋ]
guy, fellow	**grabb (en)**	['grab]

old man	**gammal man (en)**	['gamalʲ ͵man]
old woman	**gumma (en)**	['guma]

adult (adj)	**vuxen**	['vuksən]
middle-aged (adj)	**medelålders**	['medəlʲ͵ɔldɛş]
elderly (adj)	**äldre**	['ɛlʲdrə]
old (adj)	**gammal**	['gamalʲ]

retirement	**pension (en)**	[pan'ɧʊn]
to retire (from job)	**att gå i pension**	[at 'goː i pan'ɧʊn]
retiree	**pensionär (en)**	[panɧʊ'næːr]

59. Children

child	**barn (ett)**	['baːɳ]
children	**barn (pl)**	['baːɳ]
twins	**tvillingar (pl)**	['tviliɳar]

cradle	**vagga (en)**	['vaga]
rattle	**skallra (en)**	['skalʲra]
diaper	**blöja (en)**	['blʲœja]

pacifier	**napp (en)**	['nap]
baby carriage	**barnvagn (en)**	['baːɳ͵vagn]
kindergarten	**dagis (ett), förskola (en)**	['dagis], ['fœː͵şkʊlʲa]

babysitter	barnflicka (en)	['baːɳˌflika]
childhood	barndom (en)	['baːɳˌdʊm]
doll	docka (en)	['dɔka]
toy	leksak (en)	['lʲekˌsak]
construction set (toy)	byggleksak (en)	['bʏglʲekˌsak]

well-bred (adj)	väluppfostrad	['vɛlʲˌup'fʊstrad]
ill-bred (adj)	ouppfostrad	['oʊpˌfostrad]
spoiled (adj)	bortskämd	['bɔːtʃɛːmd]

to be naughty	att vara stygg	[at 'vara stʏg]
mischievous (adj)	okynnig	[ʊː'ɕʏnig]
mischievousness	okynnighet (en)	[ʊː'ɕʏnigˌhet]
mischievous child	okynnig barn (en)	[ʊː'ɕʏnig 'baːɳ]

obedient (adj)	lydig	['lʲydig]
disobedient (adj)	olydig	[ʊː'lʲydig]

docile (adj)	foglig	['foglʲig]
clever (smart)	klok	['klʲʊk]
child prodigy	underbarn (ett)	['undəˌbaːɳ]

60. Married couples. Family life

to kiss (vt)	att kyssa	[at 'ɕysa]
to kiss (vi)	att kyssas	[at 'ɕysas]
family (n)	familj (en)	[fa'milj]
family (as adj)	familje-	[fa'miljə-]
couple	par (ett)	['par]
marriage (state)	äktenskap (ett)	['ɛktənˌskap]
hearth (home)	hemmets härd (en)	['hɛmǝts hæːd]
dynasty	dynasti (en)	[dynas'ti]

date	date, träff (en)	['dɛjt], ['trɛf]
kiss	kyss (en)	['ɕys]

love (for sb)	kärlek (en)	['ɕæːˌlʲek]
to love (sb)	att älska	[at 'ɛlʲska]
beloved	älskling	['ɛlʲsklin]

tenderness	ömhet (en)	['ømˌhet]
tender (affectionate)	öm	['øːm]
faithfulness	trohet (en)	['trʊˌhet]
faithful (adj)	trogen	['trʊgən]
care (attention)	omsorg (en)	['ɔmˌsorj]
caring (~ father)	omtänksam	['ɔmˌtɛŋksam]
newlyweds	de nygifta	[de 'nyˌjifta]
honeymoon	smekmånad (en)	['smekˌmɔːnad]
to get married (ab. woman)	att gifta sig	[at 'jifta sɛj]

to get married (ab. man)	**att gifta sig**	[at 'jifta sɛj]
wedding	**bröllop (ett)**	['brœlˡɔp]
golden wedding	**guldbröllop (ett)**	['gulˡdˌbrœlˡɔp]
anniversary	**årsdag (en)**	['oːʂˌdag]
lover (masc.)	**älskare (en)**	['ɛlˡskarə]
mistress (lover)	**älskarinna (en)**	[ɛlˡska'rina]
adultery	**otrohet (en)**	[uː'truhet]
to cheat on …	**att vara otrogen**	[at 'vara uː'trugən]
(commit adultery)		
jealous (adj)	**svartsjuk**	['svaːʈˌɧʉːk]
to be jealous	**att vara svartsjuk**	[at 'vara 'svaːʈˌɧʉːk]
divorce	**skilsmässa (en)**	['ɧilˡsˌmɛsa]
to divorce (vi)	**att skilja sig**	[at 'ɧilja sɛj]
to quarrel (vi)	**att gräla**	[at 'grɛːlˡa]
to be reconciled	**att försona sig**	[at fœ:'ʂuna sɛj]
(after an argument)		
together (adv)	**tillsammans**	[tilˡ'samans]
sex	**sex (ett)**	['sɛks]
happiness	**lycka (en)**	['lˡyka]
happy (adj)	**lycklig**	['lˡyklig]
misfortune (accident)	**olycka (en)**	[uː'lˡyka]
unhappy (adj)	**olycklig**	[uː'lˡyklig]

Character. Feelings. Emotions

61. Feelings. Emotions

feeling (emotion)	känsla (en)	['ɕɛnsⁱa]
feelings	känslor (pl)	['ɕɛnslⁱʊr]
to feel (vt)	att känna	[at 'ɕɛna]
hunger	hunger (en)	['huŋər]
to be hungry	att vara hungrig	[at 'vara 'huŋrig]
thirst	törst (en)	['tø:ʂt]
to be thirsty	att vara törstig	[at 'vara 'tø:ʂtig]
sleepiness	sömnighet (en)	['sœmnigˌhet]
to feel sleepy	att vara sömnig	[at 'vara 'sœmnig]
tiredness	trötthet (en)	['trœtˌhet]
tired (adj)	trött	['trœt]
to get tired	att bli trött	[at bli 'trœt]
mood (humor)	humör (ett)	[hʉ'mœ:r]
boredom	leda (en)	['lⁱeda]
to be bored	att ha tråkigt	[at ha 'tro:kit]
seclusion	avstängdhet (en)	['avstɛŋdˌhet]
to seclude oneself	att isolera sig	[at isʊ'lⁱera sɛj]
to worry (make anxious)	att bekymra, att oroa	[at be'ɕymra], [at 'ʊ:rʊa]
to be worried	att bekymra sig	[at be'ɕymra sɛj]
worrying (n)	bekymmer (pl)	[be'ɕymər]
anxiety	oro (en)	['ʊrʊ]
preoccupied (adj)	bekymrad	[be'ɕymrad]
to be nervous	att vara nervös	[at 'vara nɛr'vø:s]
to panic (vi)	att råka i panik	[at 'ro:ka i pa'nik]
hope	hopp (ett)	['hɔp]
to hope (vi, vt)	att hoppas	[at 'hɔpas]
certainty	säkerhet (en)	['sɛ:kərˌhet]
certain, sure (adj)	säker	['sɛ:kər]
uncertainty	osäkerhet (en)	[ʊ'sɛ:kərhet]
uncertain (adj)	osäker	[ʊ'sɛ:kər]
drunk (adj)	full	['fulⁱ]
sober (adj)	nykter	['nyktər]
weak (adj)	svag	['svag]
happy (adj)	lyckad	['lⁱykad]
to scare (vt)	att skrämma	[at 'skrɛma]

| fury (madness) | raseri (ett) | [rase'riː] |
| rage (fury) | raseri (ett) | [rase'riː] |

depression	depression (en)	[deprɛ'ʃʊn]
discomfort (unease)	obehag (ett)	['ʊbeˌhag]
comfort	komfort (en)	[kɔm'fɔːt]
to regret (be sorry)	att beklaga	[at be'klʲaga]
regret	beklagande (ett)	[be'klʲagandə]
bad luck	otur (en)	[ʊ'tʉr]
sadness	sorg (en)	['sɔrj]

shame (remorse)	skam (en)	['skam]
gladness	glädje (en)	['glʲɛdjə]
enthusiasm, zeal	entusiasm (en)	[æntusi'asm]
enthusiast	entusiast (en)	[æntusi'ast]
to show enthusiasm	att visa entusiasm	[at 'visa æntusi'asm]

62. Character. Personality

character	karaktär (en)	[karak'tæːr]
character flaw	karaktärsbrist (en)	[karak'tæːʂˌbrist]
mind	sinne (ett)	['sinə]
reason	förstånd (ett)	[fœː'ʂtɔnd]

conscience	samvete (ett)	['samvetə]
habit (custom)	vana (en)	['vana]
ability (talent)	förmåga (en)	[før'moːga]
can (e.g., ~ swim)	att kunna	[at 'kuna]

patient (adj)	tålmodig	[tɔːlʲ'mʊdig]
impatient (adj)	otålig	[ʊ'toːlig]
curious (inquisitive)	nyfiken	['nyˌfikən]
curiosity	nyfikenhet (en)	['nyˌfikənhet]

modesty	blygsamhet (en)	['blʲygsamˌhet]
modest (adj)	blygsam	['blʲygsam]
immodest (adj)	oblyg	[ʊ'blʲyg]

laziness	lättja (en)	['lʲætja]
lazy (adj)	lat	['lʲat]
lazy person (masc.)	latmask (en)	['lʲatˌmask]

cunning (n)	list (en)	['list]
cunning (as adj)	listig	['listig]
distrust	misstro (en)	['misˌtrʊ]
distrustful (adj)	misstrogen	['misˌtrʊgən]

generosity	generositet (en)	[ɧenerɔsi'tet]
generous (adj)	generös	[ɧene'røːs]
talented (adj)	talangfull	[ta'lʲaŋˌfulʲ]

talent	talang (en)	[ta'lʲaŋ]
courageous (adj)	modig	['mʊdig]
courage	mod (ett)	['mʊd]
honest (adj)	ärlig	['æːlʲig]
honesty	ärlighet (en)	['æːlʲigˌhet]
careful (cautious)	försiktig	[fœ:'ʂiktig]
brave (courageous)	modig	['mʊdig]
serious (adj)	allvarlig	[alʲ'vaːlʲig]
strict (severe, stern)	sträng	['strɛŋ]
decisive (adj)	beslutsam	[be'slʉːtsam]
indecisive (adj)	obeslutsam	['ʊbeˌslʉːtsam]
shy, timid (adj)	blyg	['blʲyg]
shyness, timidity	blyghet (en)	['blʲygˌhet]
confidence (trust)	tillit (en)	['tilʲit]
to believe (trust)	att tro	[at 'trʊ]
trusting (credulous)	tillitsfull	['tilʲitsˌfulʲ]
sincerely (adv)	uppriktigt	['upˌriktit]
sincere (adj)	uppriktig	['upˌriktig]
sincerity	uppriktighet (en)	['upˌriktighet]
open (person)	öppen	['øpən]
calm (adj)	stilla	['stilʲa]
frank (sincere)	uppriktig	['upˌriktig]
naïve (adj)	naiv	[na'iːv]
absent-minded (adj)	förströdd	[fœ:'ʂtrœd]
funny (odd)	rolig	['rʊlig]
greed	girighet (en)	['jiriˌhet]
greedy (adj)	girig	['jirig]
stingy (adj)	snål	['snoːlʲ]
evil (adj)	ond	['ʊnd]
stubborn (adj)	hårdnackad	['hoːdˌnakad]
unpleasant (adj)	obehaglig	['ʊbeˌhaglig]
selfish person (masc.)	egoist (en)	[ɛgʊ'ist]
selfish (adj)	egoistisk	[ɛgʊ'istisk]
coward	ynkrygg (en)	['yŋkrᵥg]
cowardly (adj)	feg	['feg]

63. Sleep. Dreams

to sleep (vi)	att sova	[at 'sɔva]
sleep, sleeping	sömn (en)	['sœmn]
dream	dröm (en)	['drøːm]
to dream (in sleep)	att drömma	[at 'drœma]
sleepy (adj)	sömnig	['sœmnig]

bed	säng (en)	['sɛŋ]
mattress	madrass (en)	[mad'ras]
blanket (comforter)	täcke (ett)	['tɛkə]
pillow	kudde (en)	['kudə]
sheet	lakan (ett)	['lʲakan]

insomnia	sömnlöshet (en)	['sœmnlʲøsˌhet]
sleepless (adj)	sömnlös	['sœmnˌlʲøːs]
sleeping pill	sömnpille (ett)	['sœmnˌpilʲe]
to take a sleeping pill	att ta ett sömnpille	[at ta ɛt 'sœmnˌpilʲe]

to feel sleepy	att vara sömnig	[at 'vara 'sœmnig]
to yawn (vi)	att gäspa	[at 'jɛspa]
to go to bed	att gå till sängs	[at 'goː tilʲ 'sɛŋs]
to make up the bed	att bädda	[at 'bɛda]
to fall asleep	att falla i sömn	[at 'falʲa i 'sœmn]

nightmare	mardröm (en)	['maːdˌrøm]
snore, snoring	snarkning (en)	['snarkniŋ]
to snore (vi)	att snarka	[at 'snarka]

alarm clock	väckarklocka (en)	['vɛkarˌklʲɔka]
to wake (vt)	att väcka	[at 'vɛka]
to wake up	att vakna	[at 'vakna]
to get up (vi)	att gå upp	[at 'goː 'up]
to wash up (wash face)	att tvätta sig	[at 'tvæta sɛj]

64. Humour. Laughter. Gladness

humor (wit, fun)	humor (en)	['hʉːmʊr]
sense of humor	sinne (ett) för humor	['sinə før 'hʉːmʊr]
to enjoy oneself	att ha roligt	[at ha 'rʊlit]
cheerful (merry)	glad, munter	['glʲad], ['muntər]
merriment (gaiety)	uppsluppenhet (en)	['upˌslupənhet]

smile	leende (ett)	['lʲeəndə]
to smile (vi)	att småle	[at 'smoːlʲe]
to start laughing	att börja skratta	[at 'bœrja 'skrata]
to laugh (vi)	att skratta	[at 'skrata]
laugh, laughter	skratt (ett)	['skrat]

anecdote	anekdot (en)	[anɛk'dɔt]
funny (anecdote, etc.)	rolig	['rʊlig]
funny (odd)	lustig, löjlig	['lʉːstig], ['lʲœjlig]

to joke (vi)	att skämta, att skoja	[at 'ɧɛmta], [at 'skɔja]
joke (verbal)	skämt, skoj (ett)	['ɧɛmt], ['skɔj]
joy (emotion)	glädje (en)	['glʲɛdjə]
to rejoice (vi)	att glädja sig	[at 'glʲɛdja sɛj]
joyful (adj)	glad	['glʲad]

65. Discussion, conversation. Part 1

communication	kommunikation (en)	[kɔmɵnika'ʃɵn]
to communicate	att kommunicera	[at kɔmɵni'sera]
conversation	samtal (ett)	['samtalʲ]
dialog	dialog (en)	[dia'lʲɔg]
discussion (discourse)	diskussion (en)	[diskɵ'ʃɵn]
dispute (debate)	debatt (en)	[de'bat]
to dispute	att diskutera	[at diskɵ'tera]
interlocutor	samtalspartner (en)	['samtalʲs 'pa:tnər]
topic (theme)	ämne (ett)	['ɛmnə]
point of view	synpunkt (en)	['syn͵puŋkt]
opinion (point of view)	mening (en)	['meniŋ]
speech (talk)	tal (ett)	['talʲ]
discussion (of report, etc.)	diskussion (en)	[diskɵ'ʃɵn]
to discuss (vt)	att dryfta, att diskutera	[at 'dryfta], [at diskɵ'tera]
talk (conversation)	samtal (ett)	['samtalʲ]
to talk (to chat)	att samtala	[at 'samtalʲa]
meeting	möte (ett)	['mø:tə]
to meet (vi, vt)	att mötas	[at 'mø:tas]
proverb	ordspråk (ett)	['ʊ:d͵spro:k]
saying	ordstäv (ett)	['ʊ:d͵stɛ:v]
riddle (poser)	gåta (en)	['go:ta]
to pose a riddle	att utgöra en gåta	[at 'ɵt͵jø:ra en 'go:ta]
password	lösenord (ett)	['lʲø:sən͵ʊ:d]
secret	hemlighet (en)	['hɛmlig͵het]
oath (vow)	ed (en)	['ɛd]
to swear (an oath)	att svära	[at 'svæ:ra]
promise	löfte (ett)	['lʲœftə]
to promise (vt)	att lova	[at 'lʲɔva]
advice (counsel)	råd (ett)	['ro:d]
to advise (vt)	att råda	[at 'ro:da]
to follow one's advice	att följa råd	[at 'følja rad]
to listen to ... (obey)	att hörsamma	[at 'hø:r͵sama]
news	nyhet (en)	['nyhet]
sensation (news)	sensation (en)	[sɛnsa'ʃɵn]
information (data)	upplysningar (pl)	['up͵lysniŋar]
conclusion (decision)	slutsats (en)	['slɵ:tsats]
voice	röst, stämma (en)	['rœst], ['stɛma]
compliment	komplimang (en)	[kɔmpli'maŋ]
kind (nice)	älskvärd	['ɛlʲsk͵væ:d]
word	ord (ett)	['ʊ:d]
phrase	fras (en)	['fras]

answer	svar (ett)	['svar]
truth	sanning (en)	['saniŋ]
lie	lögn (en)	['lˢœgn]

thought	tanke (en)	['taŋkə]
idea (inspiration)	idé (en)	[i'de:]
fantasy	fantasi (en)	[fanta'si:]

66. Discussion, conversation. Part 2

respected (adj)	respekterad	[rɛspɛk'terad]
to respect (vt)	att respektera	[at rɛspɛk'tera]
respect	respekt (en)	[rɛ'spɛkt]
Dear ... (letter)	Ärade ...	['æ:radə ...]

to introduce (sb to sb)	att introducera	[at intrɔdu'sera]
to make acquaintance	att göra bekantskap med	[at 'jø:ra be'kantˌskap me]
intention	avsikt (en)	['avsikt]
to intend (have in mind)	att ha för avsikt	[at 'ha før 'avsikt]
wish	önskan (en)	['ønskan]
to wish (~ good luck)	att önska	[at 'ønska]

surprise (astonishment)	överraskning (en)	['ø:vəˌrɔskniŋ]
to surprise (amaze)	att förvåna	[at før'vo:na]
to be surprised	att bli förvånad	[at bli før'vo:nad]

to give (vt)	att ge	[at je:]
to take (get hold of)	att ta	[at ta]
to give back	att ge tillbaka	[at je: tilˢ'baka]
to return (give back)	att returnera	[at retur'nera]

to apologize (vi)	att ursäkta sig	[at 'u:ˌsɛkta sɛj]
apology	ursäkt (en)	['u:ˌsɛkt]
to forgive (vt)	att förlåta	[at 'fœ:ˌlˢo:ta]

to talk (speak)	att tala	[at 'talˢa]
to listen (vi)	att lyssna	[at 'lˢysna]
to hear out	att höra på	[at 'hø:ra pɔ]
to understand (vt)	att förstå	[at fœ:'ʂto:]

to show (to display)	att visa	[at 'visa]
to look at ...	att titta	[at 'tita]
to call (yell for sb)	att kalla	[at 'kalˢa]
to distract (disturb)	att distrahera	[at distra'hera]
to disturb (vt)	att störa	[at 'stø:ra]
to pass (to hand sth)	att överlämna	[at 'ø:vəˌlˢɛmna]

demand (request)	begäran (en)	[be'jæ:ran]
to request (ask)	att begära	[at 'bejæ:ra]
demand (firm request)	krav (ett)	['krav]

to demand (request firmly)	**att kräva**	[at 'krɛ:va]
to tease (call names)	**att reta**	[at 'reta]
to mock (make fun of)	**att håna**	[at 'ho:na]
mockery, derision	**hån (ett)**	['ho:n]
nickname	**öknamn (ett)**	['ø:kˌnamn]

insinuation	**insinuation (en)**	[insinʉa'ʃʉn]
to insinuate (imply)	**att insinuera**	[at insinʉ'era]
to mean (vt)	**att betyda**	[at be'tyda]

description	**beskrivning (en)**	[bɛ'skrivniŋ]
to describe (vt)	**att beskriva**	[at be'skriva]
praise (compliments)	**beröm (ett)**	[be'rø:m]
to praise (vt)	**att berömma**	[at be'rœma]

disappointment	**besvikelse (en)**	[bɛ'svikəlˈsə]
to disappoint (vt)	**att göra besviken**	[at 'jø:ra bɛ'sviken]
to be disappointed	**att bli besviken**	[at bli bɛ'sviken]

supposition	**antagande (ett)**	[aŋ'tagandə]
to suppose (assume)	**att anta, att förmoda**	[at 'anta], [at før'mʊda]
warning (caution)	**varning (en)**	['va:ɳiŋ]
to warn (vt)	**att varna**	[at 'va:ɳa]

67. Discussion, conversation. Part 3

to talk into (convince)	**att övertala**	[at 'ø:vəˌtalˈa]
to calm down (vt)	**att lugna**	[at 'lʉgna]

silence (~ is golden)	**tystnad (en)**	['tʏstnad]
to be silent (not speaking)	**att tiga**	[at 'tiga]
to whisper (vi, vt)	**att viska**	[at 'viska]
whisper	**viskning (en)**	['viskniŋ]

frankly, sincerely (adv)	**uppriktigt**	['upˌriktit]
in my opinion ...	**enligt min mening ...**	['ɛnlit min 'meniŋ ...]

detail (of the story)	**detalj (en)**	[de'talj]
detailed (adj)	**detaljerad**	[deta'ljɛrad]
in detail (adv)	**i detalj**	[i de'talj]

hint, clue	**vink (en)**	['viŋk]
to give a hint	**att ge en vink**	[at je: en 'viŋk]

look (glance)	**blick (en)**	['blik]
to have a look	**att kasta en blick**	[at 'kasta en 'blik]
fixed (look)	**stel**	['stɛlˈ]
to blink (vi)	**att blinka**	[at 'bliŋka]
to wink (vi)	**att blinka**	[at 'bliŋka]
to nod (in assent)	**att nicka**	[at 'nika]

sigh	suck (en)	['suk]
to sigh (vi)	att sucka	[at 'suka]
to shudder (vi)	att rysa	[at 'rysa]
gesture	gest (en)	['ɧɛst]
to touch (one's arm, etc.)	att röra	[at 'røːra]
to seize	att greppa	[at 'grɛpa]
(e.g., ~ by the arm)		
to tap (on the shoulder)	att klappa	[at 'klʲapa]

Look out!	Se upp!	['se up]
Really?	Verkligen?	['vɛrkligən]
Are you sure?	Är du säker?	[ær dʉ 'sɛːkər]
Good luck!	Lycka till!	['lʲyka tilʲ]
I see!	Det är klart!	[dɛ æːr 'klʲaːt]
What a pity!	Det är synd!	[dɛ æːr 'sʏnd]

68. Agreement. Refusal

consent	samtycke (ett)	['sam‚tʏkə]
to consent (vi)	att samtycka	[at 'sam‚tʏka]
approval	godkännande (ett)	['gʊd‚ɕɛnandə]
to approve (vt)	att godkänna	[at 'gʊd‚ɕɛna]
refusal	avslag (ett)	['av‚slʲag]
to refuse (vi, vt)	att vägra	[at 'vɛgra]

Great!	Utmärkt!	['ʉt‚mæːrkt]
All right!	Okej!	[ɔ'kej]
Okay! (I agree)	OK! Jag håller med.	[ɔ'kej] , [ja 'hoːlʲer me]

forbidden (adj)	förbjuden	[før'bjʉːdən]
it's forbidden	det är förbjudet	[dɛ æːr før'bjʉːdət]
it's impossible	det är omöjligt	[dɛ æːr ʊ'mœjlit]
incorrect (adj)	felaktig, oriktig	['felʲ‚aktig], ['ʊ‚riktig]

to reject (~ a demand)	att avslå	[at 'av‚slʲoː]
to support (cause, idea)	att stödja	[at 'stœdja]
to accept (~ an apology)	att acceptera	[at aksɛp'tera]

to confirm (vt)	att bekräfta	[at be'krɛfta]
confirmation	bekräftelse (en)	[be'krɛftəlʲsə]
permission	tillåtelse (en)	['til‚lʲoːtəlʲsə]
to permit (vt)	att tillåta	[at 'tilʲoːta]
decision	beslut (ett)	[be'slʉːt]
to say nothing	att tiga	[at 'tiga]
(hold one's tongue)		

condition (term)	betingelse (en)	[be'tiŋəlʲsə]
excuse (pretext)	förevändning (en)	[førə‚vɛndniŋ]
praise (compliments)	beröm (ett)	[be'røːm]
to praise (vt)	att berömma	[at be'rœma]

69. Success. Good luck. Failure

success	framgång (en)	['framgɔŋ]
successfully (adv)	med framgång	[me 'framgɔŋ]
successful (adj)	framgångsrik, lyckad	['fram‚gɔŋsrik], ['lʲykad]

luck (good luck)	tur, lycka (en)	[tʉ:r], ['lʲyka]
Good luck!	Lycka till!	['lʲyka tilʲ]
lucky (e.g., ~ day)	tursam, lyckad	['tʉ:ʂam], ['lʲykad]
lucky (fortunate)	tursam	['tʉ:ʂam]

failure	misslyckande, fiasko (ett)	['mis‚lʲykandə], [fi'askʉ]
misfortune	otur (en)	[ʉ:'tʉr]
bad luck	otur (en)	[ʉ:'tʉr]
unsuccessful (adj)	misslyckad	['mis‚lʲykad]
catastrophe	katastrof (en)	[kata'strɔf]

pride	stolthet (en)	['stɔlʲt‚het]
proud (adj)	stolt	['stɔlʲt]
to be proud	att vara stolt	[at 'vara 'stɔlʲt]

winner	segrare (en)	['sɛg‚rarə]
to win (vi)	att vinna	[at 'vina]
to lose (not win)	att förlora	[at fœ:'lʲʉra]
try	försök (ett)	['fœ:‚ʂø:k]
to try (vi)	att pröva, att försöka	[at 'prø:va], [at fœ:'ʂø:ka]
chance (opportunity)	chans (en)	['ʃans]

70. Quarrels. Negative emotions

shout (scream)	skrik (ett)	['skrik]
to shout (vi)	att skrika	[at 'skrika]
to start to cry out	att börja skrika	[at 'bœrja 'skrika]

quarrel	gräl (ett)	['grɛ:lʲ]
to quarrel (vi)	att gräla	[at 'grɛ:lʲa]
fight (squabble)	skandal (en)	[skan'dalʲ]
to make a scene	att göra skandal	[at 'jø:ra skan'dalʲ]
conflict	konflikt (en)	[kɔn'flikt]
misunderstanding	missförstånd (ett)	['misfœ:‚ʂtɔnd]

insult	förolämpning (en)	[førʉ'lʲɛmpniŋ]
to insult (vt)	att förolämpa	[at 'førʉ‚lʲɛmpa]
insulted (adj)	förolämpad	[førʉ'lʲɛmpad]
resentment	förnärmelse (en)	[fœ:'ɳæ:rməlʲsə]
to offend (vt)	att förnärma	[at fœ:'ɳæ:rma]
to take offense	att bli förnärmad	[at bli fœ:'ɳæ:rmad]
indignation	indignation (en)	[indigna'ɧʉn]

to be indignant	**att bli indignerad**	[at bli indi'nⁱerad]
complaint	**klagomål (ett)**	['klⁱagʊˌmoːlⁱ]
to complain (vi, vt)	**att klaga**	[at 'klⁱaga]

apology	**ursäkt (en)**	['ʉːˌsɛkt]
to apologize (vi)	**att ursäkta sig**	[at 'ʉːˌsɛkta sɛj]
to beg pardon	**att be om förlåtelse**	[at 'be ɔm fœːˈlɔtəlⁱsə]

criticism	**kritik (en)**	[kri'tik]
to criticize (vt)	**att kritisera**	[at kriti'sera]
accusation	**anklagelse (en)**	['aŋˌklⁱagəlⁱsə]
to accuse (vt)	**att anklaga**	[at 'aŋˌklⁱaga]

revenge	**hämnd (en)**	['hɛmnd]
to avenge (get revenge)	**att hämnas**	[at 'hɛmnas]
to pay back	**att hämnas**	[at 'hɛmnas]

disdain	**förakt (ett)**	[fø'rakt]
to despise (vt)	**att förakta**	[at fø'rakta]
hatred, hate	**hat (ett)**	['hat]
to hate (vt)	**att hata**	[at 'hata]

nervous (adj)	**nervös**	[nɛr'vøːs]
to be nervous	**att vara nervös**	[at 'vara nɛr'vøːs]
angry (mad)	**arg, vred**	[arj], ['vred]
to make angry	**att göra arg**	[at 'jøːra arj]

humiliation	**förödmjukelse (en)**	['førœdˌmjʉːkəlⁱsə]
to humiliate (vt)	**att förödmjuka**	[at 'førœdˌmjʉːka]
to humiliate oneself	**att förödmjuka sig**	[at 'førœdˌmjʉːka sɛj]

shock	**chock (en)**	['ʃɔk]
to shock (vt)	**att chocka**	[at 'ʃɔka]

trouble (e.g., serious ~)	**knipa (en)**	['knipa]
unpleasant (adj)	**obehaglig**	['ʊbeˌhaglig]

fear (dread)	**rädsla (en)**	['rɛdslⁱa]
terrible (storm, heat)	**fruktansvärd**	['frʉktansˌvæːd]
scary (e.g., ~ story)	**skrämmande**	['skrɛmandə]
horror	**fasa, skräck (en)**	['fasa], ['skrɛk]
awful (crime, news)	**förfärlig**	[før'fæːlⁱig]

to begin to tremble	**att begynna att rysa**	[at be'jina at 'rysa]
to cry (weep)	**att gråta**	[at 'groːta]
to start crying	**att börja gråta**	[at 'bœrja 'groːta]
tear	**tår (en)**	['toːr]

fault	**skuld (en)**	['skʉlⁱd]
guilt (feeling)	**skuldkänsla (en)**	['skʉlⁱdˌɕɛnslⁱa]
dishonor (disgrace)	**skam, vanära (en)**	[skam], ['va'næːra]
protest	**protest (en)**	[prʊ'tɛst]

stress	**stress (en)**	['strɛs]
to disturb (vt)	**att störa**	[at 'stø:ra]
to be furious	**att vara arg**	[at 'vara arj]
mad, angry (adj)	**arg, vred**	[arj], ['vred]
to end (~ a relationship)	**att avbryta**	[at 'av͵bryta]
to swear (at sb)	**att svära**	[at 'svæ:ra]
to scare (become afraid)	**att bli skrämd**	[at bli 'skrɛmd]
to hit (strike with hand)	**att slå**	[at 'slʲo:]
to fight (street fight, etc.)	**att slåss**	[at 'slʲɔs]
to settle (a conflict)	**att lösa**	[at 'lʲø:sa]
discontented (adj)	**missnöjd**	['mis͵nœjd]
furious (adj)	**rasande**	['rasandə]
It's not good!	**Det är inte bra!**	[dɛ æ:r 'intə bra]
It's bad!	**Det är dåligt!**	[dɛ æ:r 'do:lit]

Medicine

71. Diseases

sickness	sjukdom (en)	['ɧʉ:kˌdʊm]
to be sick	att vara sjuk	[at 'vara 'ɧʉ:k]
health	hälsa, sundhet (en)	['hɛlʲsa], ['sundˌhet]

runny nose (coryza)	snuva (en)	['snʉ:va]
tonsillitis	halsfluss, angina (en)	['halʲsˌflʉs], [aŋ'gina]
cold (illness)	förkylning (en)	[førˈçylʲniŋ]
to catch a cold	att bli förkyld	[at bli førˈçylʲd]

bronchitis	bronkit (en)	[brɔŋ'kit]
pneumonia	lunginflammation (en)	['lʉŋˌinflʲama'ɧʊn]
flu, influenza	influensa (en)	[inflʉ'ɛnsa]

nearsighted (adj)	närsynt	['næ:ˌsʏnt]
farsighted (adj)	långsynt	['lʲɔŋˌsʏnt]
strabismus (crossed eyes)	skelögdhet (en)	['ɧelʲøgdˌhet]
cross-eyed (adj)	skelögd	['ɧelʲˌøgd]
cataract	grå starr (en)	['gro: 'star]
glaucoma	grön starr (en)	['grø:n 'star]

stroke	stroke (en), hjärnslag (ett)	['stro:k], ['jæ:nˌɧlʲag]
heart attack	infarkt (en)	[in'farkt]
myocardial infarction	hjärtinfarkt (en)	['jæ:ʈ in'farkt]
paralysis	förlamning (en)	[fœ:'lʲamniŋ]
to paralyze (vt)	att förlama	[at fœ:'lʲama]

allergy	allergi (en)	[alʲer'gi]
asthma	astma (en)	['astma]
diabetes	diabetes (en)	[dia'betəs]

toothache	tandvärk (en)	['tandˌvæ:rk]
caries	karies (en)	['karies]

diarrhea	diarré (en)	[dia're:]
constipation	förstoppning (en)	[fœ:'ʂtɔpniŋ]
stomach upset	magbesvär (ett)	['magˌbe'svɛ:r]
food poisoning	matförgiftning (en)	['matˌfør'jiftniŋ]
to get food poisoning	att få matförgiftning	[at fo: 'matˌfør'jiftniŋ]

arthritis	artrit (en)	[a'ʈrit]
rickets	rakitis (en)	[ra'kitis]

rheumatism	reumatism (en)	[revma'tism]
atherosclerosis	åderförkalkning (en)	['o:dɛrførˌkalʲkniŋ]

gastritis	gastrit (en)	[ga'strit]
appendicitis	appendicit (en)	[apɛndi'sit]
cholecystitis	cholecystit (en)	[holəsys'tit]
ulcer	magsår (ett)	['magˌso:r]

measles	mässling (en)	['mɛsˌliŋ]
rubella (German measles)	röda hund (en)	['rø:da 'hund]
jaundice	gulsot (en)	['gɐ:lʲˌsʊt]
hepatitis	hepatit (en)	[hepa'tit]

schizophrenia	schizofreni (en)	[skitsɔfre'ni:]
rabies (hydrophobia)	rabies (en)	['rabies]
neurosis	neuros (en)	[nev'rɔs]
concussion	hjärnskakning (en)	['jæ:nˌʂkakniŋ]

cancer	cancer (en)	['kansər]
sclerosis	skleros (en)	[sklʲe'rɔs]
multiple sclerosis	multipel skleros (en)	[mɐlʲ'tipəlʲ sklʲe'rɔs]

alcoholism	alkoholism (en)	[alʲkʊhɔ'lizm]
alcoholic (n)	alkoholist (en)	[alʲkʊhɔ'list]
syphilis	syfilis (en)	['syfilis]
AIDS	AIDS	['ɛjds]

tumor	tumör (en)	[tɐ'mø:r]
malignant (adj)	elakartad	['ɛlʲakˌa:ʈad]
benign (adj)	godartad	['gʊdˌa:ʈad]

fever	feber (en)	['febər]
malaria	malaria (en)	[ma'lʲaria]
gangrene	kallbrand (en)	['kalʲˌbrand]
seasickness	sjösjuka (en)	['ɧø:ˌɧɐ:ka]
epilepsy	epilepsi (en)	[epilʲep'si:]

epidemic	epidemi (en)	[ɛpide'mi:]
typhus	tyfus (en)	['tyfɐs]
tuberculosis	tuberkulos (en)	[tɐbɛrkɐ'lʲɔs]
cholera	kolera (en)	['kʊlʲera]
plague (bubonic ~)	pest (en)	['pɛst]

72. Symptoms. Treatments. Part 1

symptom	symptom (ett)	[sʏmp'tɔm]
temperature	temperatur (en)	[tɛmpəra'tɐ:r]
high temperature (fever)	hög temperatur (en)	['hø:g tɛmpəra'tɐ:r]
pulse	puls (en)	['pulʲs]
dizziness (vertigo)	yrsel, svindel (en)	['y:ʂəlʲ], ['svindəlʲ]

hot (adj)	**varm**	['varm]
shivering	**rysning (en)**	['rʏsniŋ]
pale (e.g., ~ face)	**blek**	['blʲek]

cough	**hosta (en)**	['hʊsta]
to cough (vi)	**att hosta**	[at 'hʊsta]
to sneeze (vi)	**att nysa**	[at 'nysa]
faint	**svimning (en)**	['svimniŋ]
to faint (vi)	**att svimma**	[at 'svima]

bruise (hématome)	**blåmärke (ett)**	['blʲoːˌmæːrkə]
bump (lump)	**bula (en)**	['bʉːlʲa]
to bang (bump)	**att slå sig**	[at 'slʲoː sɛj]
contusion (bruise)	**blåmärke (ett)**	['blʲoːˌmæːrkə]
to get a bruise	**att slå sig**	[at 'slʲoː sɛj]

to limp (vi)	**att halta**	[at 'halʲta]
dislocation	**vrickning (en)**	['vrikniŋ]
to dislocate (vt)	**att förvrida**	[at førˈvrida]
fracture	**brott (ett), fraktur (en)**	['brɔt], [frakˈtʉːr]
to have a fracture	**att få en fraktur**	[at foː en frakˈtʉːr]

cut (e.g., paper ~)	**skärsår (ett)**	['ɧæːˌsoːr]
to cut oneself	**att skära sig**	[at 'ɧæːra sɛj]
bleeding	**blödning (en)**	['blʲœdniŋ]

burn (injury)	**brännsår (ett)**	['brɛnˌsoːr]
to get burned	**att bränna sig**	[at 'brɛna sɛj]

to prick (vt)	**att sticka**	[at 'stika]
to prick oneself	**att sticka sig**	[at 'stika sɛj]
to injure (vt)	**att skada**	[at 'skada]
injury	**skada (en)**	['skada]
wound	**sår (ett)**	['soːr]
trauma	**trauma (en)**	['travma]

to be delirious	**att tala i feberyra**	[at 'talʲa i 'febəryra]
to stutter (vi)	**att stamma**	[at 'stama]
sunstroke	**solsting (ett)**	['sʊlʲˌstiŋ]

73. Symptoms. Treatments. Part 2

pain, ache	**värk, smärta (en)**	['væːrk], ['smɛʈa]
splinter (in foot, etc.)	**sticka (en)**	['stika]

sweat (perspiration)	**svett (en)**	['svɛt]
to sweat (perspire)	**att svettas**	[at 'svɛtas]
vomiting	**kräkning (en)**	['krɛkniŋ]
convulsions	**kramper (pl)**	['krampər]
pregnant (adj)	**gravid**	[gra'vid]

to be born	att födas	[at 'fø:das]
delivery, labor	förlossning (en)	[fœ:'l'ɔsniŋ]
to deliver (~ a baby)	att föda	[at 'fø:da]
abortion	abort (en)	[a'bɔːt]

breathing, respiration	andning (en)	['andniŋ]
in-breath (inhalation)	inandning (en)	['in,andniŋ]
out-breath (exhalation)	utandning (en)	['ʉt,andniŋ]
to exhale (breathe out)	att andas ut	[at 'andas ʉt]
to inhale (vi)	att andas in	[at 'andas in]

disabled person	handikappad person (en)	['handi,kapad pɛ'ʂʊn]
cripple	krympling (en)	['krʏmpliŋ]
drug addict	narkoman (en)	[narkʊ'man]

deaf (adj)	döv	['dø:v]
mute (adj)	stum	['stu:m]
deaf mute (adj)	dövstum	['dø:v,stu:m]

mad, insane (adj)	mentalsjuk, galen	['mental'ɧʉ:k], ['gal'en]
madman (demented person)	dåre, galning (en)	['do:rə], ['gal'niŋ]
madwoman	dåre, galning (en)	['do:rə], ['gal'niŋ]
to go insane	att bli sinnessjuk	[at bli 'sinɛs,ɧʉ:k]

gene	gen (en)	['jen]
immunity	immunitet (en)	[imʉni'te:t]
hereditary (adj)	ärftlig	['æ:rftlig]
congenital (adj)	medfödd	['med,fœd]

virus	virus (ett)	['vi:rʉs]
microbe	mikrob (en)	[mi'krɔb]
bacterium	bakterie (en)	[bak'teriə]
infection	infektion (en)	[infɛk'ɧʊn]

74. Symptoms. Treatments. Part 3

| hospital | sjukhus (ett) | ['ɧʉ:k,hʉs] |
| patient | patient (en) | [pasi'ent] |

diagnosis	diagnos (en)	[dia'gnɔs]
cure	kur (en)	['kʉ:r]
medical treatment	behandling (en)	[be'handliŋ]
to get treatment	att bli behandlad	[at bli be'handl'ad]
to treat (~ a patient)	att behandla	[at be'handl'a]
to nurse (look after)	att sköta	[at 'ɧø:ta]
care (nursing ~)	vård (en)	['vo:d]

| operation, surgery | operation (en) | [ɔpera'ɧʊn] |
| to bandage (head, limb) | att förbinda | [at før'binda] |

bandaging	förbindning (en)	[før'bindniŋ]
vaccination	vaccination (en)	[vaksina'ʃʉn]
to vaccinate (vt)	att vaksinera	[at vaksi'nera]
injection, shot	injektion (en)	[injɛk'ʃʉn]
to give an injection	att ge en spruta	[at je: en 'sprʉta]
attack	anfall (ett), attack (en)	['anfalʲ], [a'tak]
amputation	amputation (en)	[ampʉta'ʃʉn]
to amputate (vt)	att amputera	[at ampʉ'tera]
coma	koma (ett)	['kɔma]
to be in a coma	att ligga i koma	[at 'liga i 'kɔma]
intensive care	intensivavdelning (en)	[intɛn'siv‚av'dɛlʲniŋ]
to recover (~ from flu)	att återhämta sig	[at 'oːter‚hɛmta sɛj]
condition (patient's ~)	tillstånd (ett)	['tilʲ‚stɔnd]
consciousness	medvetande (ett)	['med‚vetandə]
memory (faculty)	minne (ett)	['minə]
to pull out (tooth)	att dra ut	[at 'dra ʉt]
filling	plomb (en)	['plʲɔmb]
to fill (a tooth)	att plombera	[at plʲɔm'bera]
hypnosis	hypnos (en)	[hʏp'nɔs]
to hypnotize (vt)	att hypnotisera	[at 'hʏpnoti‚sera]

75. Doctors

doctor	läkare (en)	['lʲɛːkarə]
nurse	sjuksköterska (en)	['ʃʉːk‚ʃøːtɛʂka]
personal doctor	personlig läkare (en)	[pɛ'ʂʉnlig 'lʲɛːkarə]
dentist	tandläkare (en)	['tand‚lʲɛːkarə]
eye doctor	ögonläkare (en)	['øːgɔn‚lʲɛːkarə]
internist	terapeut (en)	[tera'peft]
surgeon	kirurg (en)	[ɕi'rʉrg]
psychiatrist	psykiater (en)	[syki'atər]
pediatrician	barnläkare (en)	['baːɳ‚lʲɛːkarə]
psychologist	psykolog (en)	[sykʉ'lʲɔg]
gynecologist	gynekolog (en)	[ginekʉ'lʲɔg]
cardiologist	kardiolog (en)	[kaːdiʉ'lʲɔg]

76. Medicine. Drugs. Accessories

medicine, drug	medicin (en)	[medi'sin]
remedy	medel (ett)	['medəlʲ]
to prescribe (vt)	att ordinera	[at oːdi'nera]
prescription	recept (ett)	[re'sɛpt]

tablet, pill	tablett (en)	[tab'lʲet]
ointment	salva (en)	['salʲva]
ampule	ampull (en)	[am'pulʲ]
mixture	mixtur (en)	[miks'tʉːr]
syrup	sirap (en)	['sirap]
pill	piller (ett)	['pilʲer]
powder	pulver (ett)	['pulʲvər]

gauze bandage	gasbinda (en)	['gas͵binda]
cotton wool	vadd (en)	['vad]
iodine	jod (en)	['jʊd]

Band-Aid	plåster (ett)	['plʲɔstər]
eyedropper	pipett (en)	[pi'pɛt]
thermometer	termometer (en)	[tɛrmʊ'metər]
syringe	spruta (en)	['sprʉta]

| wheelchair | rullstol (en) | ['rʉlʲ͵stʊlʲ] |
| crutches | kryckor (pl) | ['krʏkʊr] |

painkiller	smärtstillande medel (ett)	['smæːt͵stilʲande 'medəlʲ]
laxative	laxermedel (ett)	['lʲaksər 'medəlʲ]
spirits (ethanol)	sprit (en)	['sprit]
medicinal herbs	läkeväxter (pl)	['lʲɛkə͵vɛkstər]
herbal (~ tea)	ört-	['øːt-]

77. Smoking. Tobacco products

tobacco	tobak (en)	['tʊbak]
cigarette	cigarett (en)	[siga'rɛt]
cigar	cigarr (en)	[si'gar]
pipe	pipa (en)	['pipa]
pack (of cigarettes)	paket (ett)	[pa'ket]

matches	tändstickor (pl)	['tɛnd͵stikʊr]
matchbox	tändsticksask (en)	['tɛndstiks͵ask]
lighter	tändare (en)	['tɛndarə]
ashtray	askkopp (en), askfat (ett)	['askop], ['askfat]
cigarette case	cigarettui (ett)	[siga'rɛt etʉ'iː]
cigarette holder	munstycke (ett)	['mun͵stʏkə]
filter (cigarette tip)	filter (ett)	['filʲtər]

to smoke (vi, vt)	att röka	[at 'røːka]
to light a cigarette	att tända en cigarett	[at 'tɛnda en siga'rɛt]
smoking	rökning (en)	['rœkniŋ]
smoker	rökare (en)	['røːkarə]
stub, butt (of cigarette)	stump, fimp (en)	['stump], [fimp]
smoke, fumes	rök (en)	['røːk]
ash	aska (en)	['aska]

HUMAN HABITAT

City

78. City. Life in the city

city, town	**stad (en)**	['stad]
capital city	**huvudstad (en)**	['hʉːvʉdˌstad]
village	**by (en)**	['by]
city map	**stadskarta (en)**	['stadsˌkaːʈa]
downtown	**centrum (ett)**	['sɛntrum]
suburb	**förort (en)**	['førˌʊːʈ]
suburban (adj)	**förorts-**	['førˌʊːʈs-]
outskirts	**utkant (en)**	['ʉtˌkant]
environs (suburbs)	**omgivningar (pl)**	['ɔmˌjiːvniŋar]
city block	**kvarter (ett)**	[kvaˈʈər]
residential block (area)	**bostadskvarter (ett)**	['bʊstadsˌkvaːˈʈər]
traffic	**trafik (en)**	[traˈfik]
traffic lights	**trafikljus (ett)**	[traˈfikˌjʉːs]
public transportation	**offentlig transport (en)**	[ɔˈfɛntli transˈpɔːʈ]
intersection	**korsning (en)**	['kɔːʂniŋ]
crosswalk	**övergångsställe (ett)**	['øːvərgɔŋsˌstɛlʲe]
pedestrian underpass	**gångtunnel (en)**	['gɔŋˌtunəlʲ]
to cross (~ the street)	**att gå över**	[at 'goː 'øːvər]
pedestrian	**fotgängare (en)**	['fʊtˌjenarə]
sidewalk	**trottoar (en)**	[trotʊˈar]
bridge	**bro (en)**	['brʊ]
embankment (river walk)	**kaj (en)**	['kaj]
fountain	**fontän (en)**	[fɔnˈtɛn]
allée (garden walkway)	**allé (en)**	[aˈlʲeː]
park	**park (en)**	['park]
boulevard	**boulevard (en)**	[bʊlʲeˈvaːd]
square	**torg (ett)**	['tɔrj]
avenue (wide street)	**aveny (en)**	[aveˈny]
street	**gata (en)**	['gata]
side street	**sidogata (en)**	['sidʊˌgata]
dead end	**återvändsgränd (en)**	['oːtərvɛnsˌgrɛnd]
house	**hus (ett)**	['hʉs]
building	**byggnad (en)**	['bygnad]

skyscraper	skyskrapa (en)	['ɧyˌskrapa]
facade	fasad (en)	[fa'sad]
roof	tak (ett)	['tak]
window	fönster (ett)	['fœnstər]
arch	båge (en)	['boːgə]
column	kolonn (en)	[kʊ'lɔn]
corner	knut (en)	['knʉt]

store window	skyltfönster (ett)	['ɧylˡtˌfœnstər]
signboard (store sign, etc.)	skylt (en)	['ɧylˡt]
poster	affisch (en)	[a'fiːʃ]
advertising poster	reklamplakat (ett)	[rɛ'klˡamˌplˡa'kat]
billboard	reklamskylt (en)	[rɛ'klˡamˌɧylˡt]

garbage, trash	sopor, avfall (ett)	['sʊpʊr], ['avfalˡ]
trashcan (public ~)	soptunna (en)	['sʊpˌtuna]
to litter (vi)	att skräpa ner	[at 'skrɛːpa ner]
garbage dump	soptipp (en)	['sʊpˌtip]

phone booth	telefonkiosk (en)	[telˡe'fɔnˌɕøsk]
lamppost	lyktstolpe (en)	['lˡykˌstɔlˡpə]
bench (park ~)	bänk (ett)	['bɛŋk]

police officer	polis (en)	[pʊ'lis]
police	polis (en)	[pʊ'lis]
beggar	tiggare (en)	['tigarə]
homeless (n)	hemlös (ett)	['hɛmlˡøːs]

79. Urban institutions

store	affär, butik (en)	[a'fæːr], [bu'tik]
drugstore, pharmacy	apotek (ett)	[apʊ'tek]
eyeglass store	optiker (en)	['ɔptikər]
shopping mall	köpcenter (ett)	['ɕøːpˌsɛntɛr]
supermarket	snabbköp (ett)	['snabˌɕøːp]

bakery	bageri (ett)	[bage'riː]
baker	bagare (en)	['bagarə]
pastry shop	konditori (ett)	[kɔnditʊ'riː]
grocery store	speceriaffär (en)	[spese'ri a'fæːr]
butcher shop	slaktare butik (en)	['slˡaktarə bu'tik]

produce store	grönsakshandel (en)	['grøːnsaksˌhandəlˡ]
market	marknad (en)	['marknad]

coffee house	kafé (ett)	[ka'feː]
restaurant	restaurang (en)	[rɛstɔ'raŋ]
pub, bar	pub (en)	['pub]
pizzeria	pizzeria (en)	[pitse'ria]
hair salon	frisersalong (en)	['frisər ʂaˌlˡɔŋ]

post office	post (en)	['pɔst]
dry cleaners	kemtvätt (en)	['ɕemtvæt]
photo studio	fotoateljé (en)	['fʊtʊ ɑtə͵lje:]

shoe store	skoaffär (en)	['skʊːa͵fæ:r]
bookstore	bokhandel (en)	['bʊk͵handəlʲ]
sporting goods store	sportaffär (en)	['spɔːt a'fæ:r]

clothes repair shop	klädreparationer (en)	['klʲɛd 'repara͵ɧʊnər]
formal wear rental	kläduthyrning (en)	['klʲɛd ʉ'ty:nɪŋ]
video rental store	filmuthyrning (en)	['filʲm ʉ'ty:nɪŋ]

circus	cirkus (en)	['sirkʉs]
zoo	zoo (ett)	['sʊ:]
movie theater	biograf (en)	[biʊ'graf]
museum	museum (ett)	[mʉ'seʊm]
library	bibliotek (ett)	[bibliʊ'tek]

| theater | teater (en) | [te'atər] |
| opera (opera house) | opera (en) | ['ʊpera] |

| nightclub | nattklubb (en) | ['nat͵klʉb] |
| casino | kasino (ett) | [ka'sinʊ] |

mosque	moské (en)	[mʊs'ke:]
synagogue	synagoga (en)	['syna͵gɔga]
cathedral	katedral (en)	[katɛ'dralʲ]

| temple | tempel (ett) | ['tɛmpəlʲ] |
| church | kyrka (en) | ['ɕyrka] |

college	institut (ett)	[insti'tʉt]
university	universitet (ett)	[univɛsi'tet]
school	skola (en)	['skʊlʲa]

| prefecture | prefektur (en) | [prefɛk'tʉ:r] |
| city hall | rådhus (en) | ['rɔd͵hʉs] |

| hotel | hotell (ett) | [hʊ'tɛlʲ] |
| bank | bank (en) | ['baŋk] |

| embassy | ambassad (en) | [amba'sad] |
| travel agency | resebyrå (en) | ['reseby͵rɔ:] |

| information office | informationsbyrå (en) | [infɔrma'ɧʊns by͵rɔ:] |
| currency exchange | växelkontor (ett) | ['vɛksəlʲ kɔn'tʊr] |

| subway | tunnelbana (en) | ['tunəlʲ͵bana] |
| hospital | sjukhus (ett) | ['ɧʉ:k͵hʉs] |

| gas station | bensinstation (en) | [bɛn'sin͵sta'ɧʊn] |
| parking lot | parkeringsplats (en) | [par'keriŋs͵plʲats] |

80. Signs

signboard (store sign, etc.)	skylt (en)	['ʃylʲt]
notice (door sign, etc.)	inskrift (en)	['in‚skrift]
poster	poster, löpsedel (en)	['pɔstər], ['løp‚sedəlʲ]
direction sign	vägvisare (en)	['vɛːg‚visarə]
arrow (sign)	pil (en)	['pilʲ]
caution	varning (en)	['vaːɳiŋ]
warning sign	varningsskylt (en)	['vaːɳiŋs ‚ʃylʲt]
to warn (vt)	att varna	[at 'vaːɳa]
rest day (weekly ~)	fridag (en)	['friˌdag]
timetable (schedule)	tidtabell (en)	['tid ta'bɛlʲ]
opening hours	öppettider (pl)	['øpet‚tiːdər]
WELCOME!	VÄLKOMMEN!	['vɛlʲ‚kɔmən]
ENTRANCE	INGÅNG	['in‚gɔŋ]
EXIT	UTGÅNG	['ʉt‚gɔŋ]
PUSH	TRYCK	['trʏk]
PULL	DRAG	['drag]
OPEN	ÖPPET	['øpet]
CLOSED	STÄNGT	['stɛŋt]
WOMEN	DAMER	['damər]
MEN	HERRAR	['hɛ'rar]
DISCOUNTS	RABATT	[ra'bat]
SALE	REA	['rea]
NEW!	NYHET!	['nyhet]
FREE	GRATIS	['gratis]
ATTENTION!	OBS!	['ɔbs]
NO VACANCIES	FUIIBOKAT	['fulʲ‚bʉkat]
RESERVED	RESERVERAT	[resɛr'verat]
ADMINISTRATION	ADMINISTRATION	[administra'ʃʊn]
STAFF ONLY	ENDAST PERSONAL	['ɛndast pɛʂʊ'nalʲ]
BEWARE OF THE DOG!	VARNING FÖR HUNDEN	['vaːɳiŋ før 'hundən]
NO SMOKING	RÖKNING FÖRBJUDEN	['rœkniŋ før'bjʉ:dən]
DO NOT TOUCH!	FÅR EJ VIDRÖRAS!	['foːr ej 'vidrø:ras]
DANGEROUS	FARLIG	['faːʎig]
DANGER	FARA	['fara]
HIGH VOLTAGE	HÖGSPÄNNING	['høːg‚spɛniŋ]
NO SWIMMING!	BADNING FÖRBJUDEN	['badniŋ før'bjʉ:dən]
OUT OF ORDER	UR FUNKTION	['ʉr funk'ʃʊn]
FLAMMABLE	BRANDFARLIG	['brand‚faːʎig]
FORBIDDEN	FÖRBJUD	[før'bjʉ:d]

| NO TRESPASSING! | TIllTRÄDE FÖRBJUDET | ['tilᵊtrɛ:də før'bjɯ:dət] |
| WET PAINT | NYMÅLAT | ['ny‚mo:lᵊat] |

81. Urban transportation

bus	buss (en)	['bus]
streetcar	spårvagn (en)	['spo:r‚vagn]
trolley bus	trådbuss (en)	['tro:d‚bus]
route (of bus, etc.)	rutt (en)	['rut]
number (e.g., bus ~)	nummer (ett)	['numər]

to go by ...	att åka med ...	[at 'o:ka me ...]
to get on (~ the bus)	att stiga på ...	[at 'stiga pɔ ...]
to get off ...	att stiga av ...	[at 'stiga 'av ...]

stop (e.g., bus ~)	hållplats (en)	['ho:lᵊ‚plats]
next stop	nästa hållplats (en)	['nɛsta 'ho:lᵊ‚plats]
terminus	slutstation (en)	['slɯt‚sta'ʃʊn]
schedule	tidtabell (en)	['tid ta'bɛlᵊ]
to wait (vt)	att vänta	[at 'vɛnta]

ticket	biljett (en)	[bi'lᵊet]
fare	biljettpris (ett)	[bi'lᵊet‚pris]
cashier (ticket seller)	kassör (en)	[ka'sø:r]
ticket inspection	biljettkontroll (en)	[bi'lᵊet kɔn'trolᵊ]
ticket inspector	kontrollant (en)	[kɔntrɔ'lᵊant]

to be late (for ...)	att komma för sent	[at 'kɔma før 'sɛnt]
to miss (~ the train, etc.)	att komma för sent till ...	[at 'kɔma før 'sɛnt tilᵊ ...]
to be in a hurry	att skynda sig	[at 'ʃynda sɛj]

taxi, cab	taxi (en)	['taksi]
taxi driver	taxichaufför (en)	['taksi ʃɔ'fø:r]
by taxi	med taxi	[me 'taksi]
taxi stand	taxihållplats (en)	['taksi 'ho:lᵊ‚plᵊats]
to call a taxi	att ringa efter taxi	[at 'riŋa ‚ɛftə 'taksi]
to take a taxi	att ta en taxi	[at ta en 'taksi]

traffic	trafik (en)	[tra'fik]
traffic jam	trafikstopp (ett)	[tra'fik‚stɔp]
rush hour	rusningstid (en)	['rusniŋs‚tid]
to park (vi)	att parkera	[at par'kera]
to park (vt)	att parkera	[at par'kera]
parking lot	parkeringsplats (en)	[par'keriŋs‚plᵊats]

subway	tunnelbana (en)	['tunəlᵊ‚bana]
station	station (en)	[sta'ʃʊn]
to take the subway	att ta tunnelbanan	[at ta 'tunəlᵊ‚banan]
train	tåg (ett)	['to:g]
train station	tågstation (en)	['to:g‚sta'ʃʊn]

82. Sightseeing

monument	monument (ett)	[mɔnu'mɛnt]
fortress	fästning (en)	['fɛstniŋ]
palace	palats (ett)	[pa'lʲats]
castle	borg (en)	['bɔrj]
tower	torn (ett)	['tʊːn]
mausoleum	mausoleum (ett)	[maʊsʊ'lʲeum]
architecture	arkitektur (en)	[arkitɛk'tʉːr]
medieval (adj)	medeltida	['medəlʲˌtida]
ancient (adj)	gammal	['gamalʲ]
national (adj)	nationell	[natɧʊ'nɛlʲ]
famous (monument, etc.)	berömd	[be'rœmd]
tourist	turist (en)	[tu'rist]
guide (person)	guide (en)	['gajd]
excursion, sightseeing tour	utflykt (en)	['ʉtˌflʲykt]
to show (vt)	att visa	[at 'visa]
to tell (vt)	att berätta	[at be'ræta]
to find (vt)	att hitta	[at 'hita]
to get lost (lose one's way)	att gå vilse	[at 'gɔː 'vilʲsə]
map (e.g., subway ~)	karta (en)	['kaːʈa]
map (e.g., city ~)	karta (en)	['kaːʈa]
souvenir, gift	souvenir (en)	[sʊvɛ'niːr]
gift shop	souvenirbutik (en)	[sʊvɛ'niːr bu'tik]
to take pictures	att fotografera	[at fʊtʊgra'fera]
to have one's picture taken	att bli fotograferad	[at bli fʊtʊgra'ferad]

83. Shopping

to buy (purchase)	att köpa	[at 'ɕøːpa]
purchase	inköp (ett)	['inˌɕøːp]
to go shopping	att shoppa	[at 'ʃɔpa]
shopping	shopping (en)	['ʃɔpiŋ]
to be open (ab. store)	att vara öppen	[at 'vara 'øpən]
to be closed	att vara stängd	[at 'vara stɛŋd]
footwear, shoes	skodon (pl)	['skʊdʊn]
clothes, clothing	kläder (pl)	['klʲɛːdər]
cosmetics	kosmetika (en)	[kɔs'mɛtika]
food products	matvaror (pl)	['matˌvarʊr]
gift, present	gåva, present (en)	['goːva], [pre'sɛnt]
salesman	försäljare (en)	[fœ:'ʂɛljarə]
saleswoman	försäljare (en)	[fœ:'ʂɛljarə]

check out, cash desk	kassa (en)	['kasa]
mirror	spegel (en)	['spegəlʲ]
counter (store ~)	disk (en)	['disk]
fitting room	provrum (ett)	['prʊvˌru:m]

to try on	att prova	[at 'prʊva]
to fit (ab. dress, etc.)	att passa	[at 'pasa]
to like (I like …)	att gilla	[at 'jilʲa]

price	pris (ett)	['pris]
price tag	prislapp (en)	['pris‚lʲap]
to cost (vt)	att kosta	[at 'kɔsta]
How much?	Hur mycket?	[hʉr 'mʏkə]
discount	rabatt (en)	[ra'bat]

inexpensive (adj)	billig	['bilig]
cheap (adj)	billig	['bilig]
expensive (adj)	dyr	['dyr]
It's expensive	Det är dyrt	[dɛ æ:r 'dy:t]

rental (n)	uthyrning (en)	['ʉt‚hyŋiŋ]
to rent (~ a tuxedo)	att hyra	[at 'hyra]
credit (trade credit)	kredit (en)	[kre'dit]
on credit (adv)	på kredit	[pɔ kre'dit]

84. Money

money	pengar (pl)	['pɛŋar]
currency exchange	växling (en)	['vɛksliŋ]
exchange rate	kurs (en)	['ku:ʂ]
ATM	bankomat (en)	[baŋkʊ'mat]
coin	mynt (ett)	['mʏnt]

| dollar | dollar (en) | ['dɔlʲar] |
| euro | euro (en) | ['ɛvrɔ] |

lira	lire (en)	['lirə]
Deutschmark	mark (en)	['mark]
franc	franc (en)	['fran]
pound sterling	pund sterling (ett)	['puŋ stɛr'liŋ]
yen	yen (en)	['jɛn]

debt	skuld (en)	['skʉlʲd]
debtor	gäldenär (en)	[jɛlʲdɛ'næ:r]
to lend (money)	att låna ut	[at 'lʲo:na ʉt]
to borrow (vi, vt)	att låna	[at 'lʲo:na]

bank	bank (en)	['baŋk]
account	konto (ett)	['kɔntʊ]
to deposit (vt)	att sätta in	[at 'sæta in]

to deposit into the account	att sätta in på kontot	[at 'sæta in pɔ 'kɔntʊt]
to withdraw (vt)	att ta ut från kontot	[at ta ʉt frɔn 'kɔntʊt]
credit card	kreditkort (ett)	[kre'dit͵kɔːt]
cash	kontanter (pl)	[kɔn'tantər]
check	check (en)	['ɕɛk]
to write a check	att skriva en check	[at 'skriva en 'ɕɛk]
checkbook	checkbok (en)	['ɕɛk͵bʊk]
wallet	plånbok (en)	['plʲoːn͵bʊk]
change purse	börs (en)	['bø:ʂ]
safe	säkerhetsskåp (ett)	['sɛːkərhets͵skoːp]
heir	arvinge (en)	['arviŋə]
inheritance	arv (ett)	['arv]
fortune (wealth)	förmögenhet (en)	[før'møgən͵het]
lease	hyra (en)	['hyra]
rent (money)	hyra (en)	['hyra]
to rent (sth from sb)	att hyra	[at 'hyra]
price	pris (ett)	['pris]
cost	kostnad (en)	['kɔstnad]
sum	summa (en)	['suma]
to spend (vt)	att lägga ut	[at 'lʲɛga ʉt]
expenses	utgifter (pl)	['ʉt͵jiftər]
to economize (vi, vt)	att spara	[at 'spara]
economical	sparsam	['spa:ʂam]
to pay (vi, vt)	att betala	[at be'talʲa]
payment	betalning (en)	[be'talʲniŋ]
change (give the ~)	växel (en)	['vɛksəlʲ]
tax	skatt (en)	['skat]
fine	bot (en)	['bʊt]
to fine (vt)	att bötfälla	[at 'bøt͵fɛlʲa]

85. Post. Postal service

post office	post (en)	['pɔst]
mail (letters, etc.)	post (en)	['pɔst]
mailman	brevbärare (en)	['brev͵bæ:rarə]
opening hours	öppettider (pl)	['øpet͵ti:dər]
letter	brev (ett)	['brev]
registered letter	rekommenderat brev (ett)	[rekɔmən'derat brev]
postcard	postkort (ett)	['pɔst͵kɔːt]
telegram	telegram (ett)	[telʲe'gram]

package (parcel)	**postpaket (ett)**	['pɔst paˌket]
money transfer	**pengaöverföring (en)**	['pɛŋaˌøvə'fø:riŋ]
to receive (vt)	**att ta emot**	[at ta ɛmo:t]
to send (vt)	**att skicka**	[at 'ɧika]
sending	**avsändning (en)**	['avˌsɛndniŋ]
address	**adress (en)**	[a'drɛs]
ZIP code	**postnummer (ett)**	['pɔstˌnumər]
sender	**avsändare (en)**	['avˌsɛndarə]
receiver	**mottagare (en)**	['mɔtˌtagarə]
name (first name)	**förnamn (ett)**	['fœ:ˌŋamn]
surname (last name)	**efternamn (ett)**	['ɛftəˌŋamn]
postage rate	**tariff (en)**	[ta'rif]
standard (adj)	**vanlig**	['vanlig]
economical (adj)	**ekonomisk**	[ɛkʊ'nɔmisk]
weight	**vikt (en)**	['vikt]
to weigh (~ letters)	**att väga**	[at 'vɛ:ga]
envelope	**kuvert (ett)**	[kɵ:'vær]
postage stamp	**frimärke (ett)**	['friˌmærkə]
to stamp an envelope	**att sätta på frimärke**	[at 'sæta pɔ 'friˌmærkə]

Dwelling. House. Home

86. House. Dwelling

house	hus (ett)	['hʉs]
at home (adv)	hemma	['hɛma]
yard	gård (en)	['goːd]
fence (iron ~)	stängsel (en)	['stɛŋsəlʲ]
brick (n)	tegel, mursten (en)	['tegəlʲ], ['mʉːˌsten]
brick (as adj)	tegel-	['tegəlʲ-]
stone (n)	sten (en)	['sten]
stone (as adj)	sten-	['sten-]
concrete (n)	betong (en)	[be'tɔŋ]
concrete (as adj)	betong-	[be'tɔŋ-]
new (new-built)	ny	['ny]
old (adj)	gammal	['gamalʲ]
decrepit (house)	fallfärdig	['falʲˌfæːdɪg]
modern (adj)	modern	[mʊ'dɛːn]
multistory (adj)	flervånings-	['flʲerˌvoːniŋs-]
tall (~ building)	hög	['høːg]
floor, story	våning (en)	['voːniŋ]
single-story (adj)	envånings-	['ɛnˌvoːniŋs-]
1st floor	bottenvåning (en)	['bɔtenˌvoːniŋ]
top floor	övre våning (en)	['øvrə 'voːniŋ]
roof	tak (ett)	['tak]
chimney	skorsten (en)	['skɔːˌsten]
roof tiles	taktegel (ett)	['takˌtegəlʲ]
tiled (adj)	tegel-	['tegəlʲ-]
attic (storage place)	vind, vindsvåning (en)	['vind], ['vindsˌvoːniŋ]
window	fönster (ett)	['fœnstər]
glass	glas (ett)	['glʲas]
window ledge	fönsterbleck (ett)	['fœnstərˌblʲek]
shutters	fönsterluckor (pl)	['fœnstəˌlʲʉ'kʊr]
wall	mur, vägg (en)	['mʉːr], [vɛg]
balcony	balkong (en)	[balʲ'kɔŋ]
downspout	stuprör (ett)	['stʉpˌrøːr]
upstairs (to be ~)	uppe	['upə]
to go upstairs	att gå upp	[at 'goː 'up]
to come down (the stairs)	att gå ned	[at 'goː ˌned]
to move (to new premises)	att flytta	[at 'flʲyta]

87. House. Entrance. Lift

entrance	ingång (en)	['inˌgɔn]
stairs (stairway)	trappa (en)	['trapa]
steps	steg (pl)	['steg]
banister	räcke (ett)	['rɛkə]
lobby (hotel ~)	lobby (en)	['lˠɔbi]

mailbox	brevlåda (en)	['brev.lˠo:da]
garbage can	soptunna (en)	['sʊpˌtuna]
trash chute	sopnedkast (ett)	['sʊpnedˌkast]

elevator	hiss (en)	['his]
freight elevator	lasthiss (en)	['lˠastˌhis]
elevator cage	hisskorg (en)	['hisˌkɔrj]
to take the elevator	att ta hissen	[at ta 'hisən]

apartment	lägenhet (en)	['lˠe:gənˌhet]
residents (~ of a building)	invånare (pl)	[in'vo:narə]
neighbor (masc.)	granne (en)	['granə]
neighbor (fem.)	granne (en)	['granə]
neighbors	grannar (pl)	['granar]

88. House. Electricity

electricity	elektricitet (en)	[ɛlˠektrisi'tet]
light bulb	glödlampa (en)	['glˠø:dˌlˠampa]
switch	strömbrytare (en)	['strø:mˌbrytarə]
fuse (plug fuse)	propp (en)	['prɔp]

cable, wire (electric ~)	ledning (en)	['lˠedniŋ]
wiring	ledningsnät (ett)	['lˠedniŋsˌnɛ:t]
electricity meter	elmätare (en)	['ɛlˠˌmɛ:tarə]
readings	avläsningar (pl)	['avˌlˠɛsniŋar]

89. House. Doors. Locks

door	dörr (en)	['dœr]
gate (vehicle ~)	port (en)	['pɔ:t]
handle, doorknob	dörrhandtag (ett)	['dœrˌhantag]
to unlock (unbolt)	att låsa upp	[at 'lˠo:sa up]
to open (vt)	att öppna	[at 'øpna]
to close (vt)	att stänga	[at 'stɛŋa]

key	nyckel (en)	['nʏkəlˠ]
bunch (of keys)	knippa (en)	['knipa]
to creak (door, etc.)	att gnissla	[at 'gnislˠa]

creak	knarr (ett)	['knar]
hinge (door ~)	gångjärn (ett)	['gɔŋˌjæːn]
doormat	dörrmatta (en)	['dœrˌmata]

door lock	dörrlås (ett)	['dœrˌlʲoːs]
keyhole	nyckelhål (ett)	['nʏkəlʲˌhoːlʲ]
crossbar (sliding bar)	regel (en)	['regəlʲ]
door latch	skjutregel (en)	['ɧʉːtˌregəlʲ]
padlock	hänglås (ett)	['hɛŋˌlʲoːs]

to ring (~ the door bell)	att ringa	[at 'riŋa]
ringing (sound)	ringning (en)	['riŋniŋ]
doorbell	ringklocka (en)	['riŋˌklʲɔka]
doorbell button	knapp (en)	['knap]
knock (at the door)	knackning (en)	['knakniŋ]
to knock (vi)	att knacka	[at 'knaka]

code	kod (en)	['kɔd]
combination lock	kodlås (ett)	['kɔdˌlʲoːs]
intercom	dörrtelefon (en)	['dœrˌtelʲeˈfɔn]
number (on the door)	nummer (ett)	['numər]
doorplate	dörrskylt (en)	['dœrˌɧylʲt]
peephole	kikhål, titthål (ett)	['kikˌhoːlʲ], ['titˌhoːlʲ]

90. Country house

village	by (en)	['by]
vegetable garden	koksträdgård (en)	['kʉksˌtrɛˈgoːɖ]
fence	stängsel (ett)	['stɛŋsəlʲ]

| picket fence | staket (ett) | [staˈket] |
| wicket gate | grind (en) | ['grind] |

| granary | spannmålsbod (en) | ['spanmoːlʲsˌbʉd] |
| root cellar | jordkällare (en) | ['jʉˌɕɛlʲarə] |

| shed (garden ~) | bod (en), skjul (ett) | ['bʉd], [ɧʉːl] |
| well (water) | brunn (en) | ['brun] |

| stove (wood-fired ~) | ugn (en) | ['ugn] |
| to stoke the stove | att elda | [at 'ɛlʲda] |

| firewood | ved (en) | ['ved] |
| log (firewood) | vedträ (ett) | ['vedˌtrɛː] |

| veranda | veranda (en) | [veˈranda] |
| deck (terrace) | terrass (en) | [tɛˈras] |

| stoop (front steps) | yttertrappa (en) | ['ytəˌtrapa] |
| swing (hanging seat) | gunga (en) | ['guŋa] |

91. Villa. Mansion

country house	fritidshus (ett)	['fritids,hʉs]
villa (seaside ~)	villa (en)	['vilʲa]
wing (~ of a building)	vinge (en)	['viŋə]

garden	trädgård (en)	['trɛ:go:d]
park	park (en)	['park]
tropical greenhouse	växthus (ett)	['vɛkst,hʉs]
to look after (garden, etc.)	att ta hand	[at ta 'hand]

swimming pool	simbassäng (en)	['simba,sɛŋ]
gym (home gym)	gym (ett)	['dʒym]
tennis court	tennisbana (en)	['tɛnis,bana]
home theater (room)	hemmabio (en)	['hɛma,bi:ʊ]
garage	garage (ett)	[ga'raʃ]

private property	privategendom (en)	[pri'vat 'ɛgən,dʊm]
private land	privat tomt (en)	[pri'vat tɔmt]

warning (caution)	varning (en)	['va:ɳiŋ]
warning sign	varningsskylt (en)	['va:ŋiŋs ,ʃylʲt]

security	säkerhet (en)	['sɛ:kər,het]
security guard	säkerhetsvakt (en)	['sɛ:kərhets,vakt]
burglar alarm	tjuvlarm (ett)	['ɕʉvlʲarm]

92. Castle. Palace

castle	borg (en)	['bɔrj]
palace	palats (ett)	[pa'lʲats]
fortress	fästning (en)	['fɛstniŋ]

wall (round castle)	mur (en)	['mʉ:r]
tower	torn (ett)	['tʊ:ɳ]
keep, donjon	huvudtorn (ett)	['hʉ:vʉd,tʊ:ɳ]

portcullis	fällgaller (pl)	['fɛlʲ,galʲər]
underground passage	underjordisk gång (en)	['undəjʉ:disk 'gɔŋ]
moat	vallgrav (en)	['valʲ,grav]

chain	kedja (en)	['ɕedja]
arrow loop	skottglugg (en)	['skɔt,glʉg]

magnificent (adj)	praktfull	['prakt,fulʲ]
majestic (adj)	majestätisk	[majɛ'stɛtisk]

impregnable (adj)	ointaglig	['ojn,taglig]
medieval (adj)	medeltida	['medəlʲ,tida]

93. Apartment

apartment	**lägenhet (en)**	['lɛːgənˌhet]
room	**rum (ett)**	['ruːm]
bedroom	**sovrum (ett)**	['sɔvˌrum]
dining room	**matsal (en)**	['matsalʲ]
living room	**vardagsrum (ett)**	['vaːɖasˌrum]
study (home office)	**arbetsrum (ett)**	['arbetsˌrum]
entry room	**entréhall (en)**	[ɛntreːhalʲ]
bathroom (room with a bath or shower)	**badrum (ett)**	['badˌruːm]
half bath	**toalett (en)**	[tʊa'lʲet]
ceiling	**tak (ett)**	['tak]
floor	**golv (ett)**	['gɔlʲv]
corner	**hörn (ett)**	['høːɳ]

94. Apartment. Cleaning

to clean (vi, vt)	**att städa**	[at 'stɛda]
to put away (to stow)	**att lägga undan**	[at 'lʲɛga 'undan]
dust	**damm (ett)**	['dam]
dusty (adj)	**dammig**	['damig]
to dust (vt)	**att damma**	[at 'dama]
vacuum cleaner	**dammsugare (en)**	['damˌsʉgarə]
to vacuum (vt)	**att dammsuga**	[at 'damˌsʉga]
to sweep (vi, vt)	**att sopa, att feja**	[at 'sʊpa], [att 'fɛja]
sweepings	**skräp, dam (ett)**	['skrɛp], ['dam]
order	**ordning (en)**	['ɔːɖniŋ]
disorder, mess	**oreda (en)**	[ʊ'reda]
mop	**mopp (en)**	['mɔp]
dust cloth	**trasa (en)**	['trasa]
short broom	**sopkvast (en)**	['sʊpˌkvast]
dustpan	**sopskyffel (en)**	['sʊpˌɕʏfəlʲ]

95. Furniture. Interior

furniture	**möbel (en)**	['møːbəlʲ]
table	**bord (ett)**	['bʉːɖ]
chair	**stol (en)**	['stʉlʲ]
bed	**säng (en)**	['sɛŋ]
couch, sofa	**soffa (en)**	['sɔfa]
armchair	**fåtölj, länstol (en)**	[fo'tœlj], ['lɛnˌstʉlʲ]
bookcase	**bokhylla (en)**	['bʊkˌhylʲa]

shelf	**hylla (en)**	['hylʲa]
wardrobe	**garderob (en)**	[ga:də'rɔ:b]
coat rack (wall-mounted ~)	**knagg (en)**	['knag]
coat stand	**klädhängare (en)**	['klʲɛd,hɛŋarə]

bureau, dresser	**byrå (en)**	['byro:]
coffee table	**soffbord (ett)**	['sɔf,bʊ:d]

mirror	**spegel (en)**	['spegəlʲ]
carpet	**matta (en)**	['mata]
rug, small carpet	**liten matta (en)**	['litən 'mata]

fireplace	**kamin (en), eldstad (ett)**	[ka'min], ['ɛlʲd,stad]
candle	**ljus (ett)**	['jʉ:s]
candlestick	**ljusstake (en)**	['jʉ:s,stakə]

drapes	**gardiner** (pl)	[ga:'dʲinər]
wallpaper	**tapet (en)**	[ta'pet]
blinds (jalousie)	**persienn (en)**	[pɛ'sjen]

table lamp	**bordslampa (en)**	['bʊ:ds,lʲampa]
wall lamp (sconce)	**vägglampa (en)**	['vɛg,lʲampa]
floor lamp	**golvlampa (en)**	['gɔlʲv,lʲampa]
chandelier	**ljuskrona (en)**	['jʉ:s,krʊna]

leg (of chair, table)	**ben (ett)**	['be:n]
armrest	**armstöd (ett)**	['arm,stø:d]
back (backrest)	**rygg (en)**	['rʲyg]
drawer	**låda (en)**	['lʲo:da]

96. Bedding

bedclothes	**sängkläder** (pl)	['sɛŋ,klʲɛ:dər]
pillow	**kudde (en)**	['kudə]
pillowcase	**örngott (ett)**	['ø:n̪,gɔt]
duvet, comforter	**duntäcke (ett)**	['dʉ:n,tɛkə]
sheet	**lakan (ett)**	['lʲakan]
bedspread	**överkast (ett)**	['ø:və,kast]

97. Kitchen

kitchen	**kök (ett)**	['çø:k]
gas	**gas (en)**	['gas]
gas stove (range)	**gasspis (en)**	['gas,spis]
electric stove	**elektrisk spis (en)**	[ɛ'lʲektrisk ,spis]
oven	**bakugn (en)**	['bak,ugn]
microwave oven	**mikrovågsugn (en)**	['mikrʊvɔgs,ugn]
refrigerator	**kylskåp (ett)**	['çylʲ,sko:p]

freezer	**frys (en)**	['frys]
dishwasher	**diskmaskin (en)**	['disk,ma'ɧi:n]
meat grinder	**köttkvarn (en)**	['ɕœt,kvaːŋ]
juicer	**juicepress (en)**	['juːs,prɛs]
toaster	**brödrost (en)**	['brøːd,rɔst]
mixer	**mixer (en)**	['miksər]
coffee machine	**kaffebryggare (en)**	['kafə,brʏgarə]
coffee pot	**kaffekanna (en)**	['kafə,kana]
coffee grinder	**kaffekvarn (en)**	['kafə,kvaːŋ]
kettle	**tekittel (en)**	['te,ɕitəlʲ]
teapot	**tekanna (en)**	['te,kana]
lid	**lock (ett)**	['lʲɔk]
tea strainer	**tesil (en)**	['te,silʲ]
spoon	**sked (en)**	['ɧed]
teaspoon	**tesked (en)**	['te,ɧed]
soup spoon	**matsked (en)**	['mat,ɧed]
fork	**gaffel (en)**	['gafəlʲ]
knife	**kniv (en)**	['kniv]
tableware (dishes)	**servis (en)**	[sɛr'vis]
plate (dinner ~)	**tallrik (en)**	['talʲrik]
saucer	**tefat (ett)**	['te,fat]
shot glass	**shotglas (ett)**	['ʃot,glʲas]
glass (tumbler)	**glas (ett)**	['glʲas]
cup	**kopp (en)**	['kop]
sugar bowl	**sockerskål (en)**	['sɔkə:, skoːlʲ]
salt shaker	**saltskål (en)**	['salʲt,skoːlʲ]
pepper shaker	**pepparskål (en)**	['pɛpa,skoːlʲ]
butter dish	**smörfat (en)**	['smœr,fat]
stock pot (soup pot)	**kastrull, gryta (en)**	[ka'strulʲ], ['gryta]
frying pan (skillet)	**stekpanna (en)**	['stek,pana]
ladle	**slev (en)**	['slʲev]
colander	**durkslag (ett)**	['durk,slʲag]
tray (serving ~)	**bricka (en)**	['brika]
bottle	**flaska (en)**	['flʲaska]
jar (glass)	**glasburk (en)**	['glʲas,burk]
can	**burk (en)**	['burk]
bottle opener	**flasköppnare (en)**	['flʲask,øpnarə]
can opener	**burköppnare (en)**	['burk,øpnarə]
corkscrew	**korkskruv (en)**	['kɔrk,skruːv]
filter	**filter (ett)**	['filʲtər]
to filter (vt)	**att filtrera**	[at filʲ'trera]
trash, garbage (food waste, etc.)	**sopor, avfall (ett)**	['supʊr], ['avfalʲ]
trash can (kitchen ~)	**sophink (en)**	['sup,hiŋk]

98. Bathroom

bathroom	**badrum (ett)**	['bad,ruːm]
water	**vatten (ett)**	['vatən]
faucet	**kran (en)**	['kran]
hot water	**varmvatten (ett)**	['varm,vatən]
cold water	**kallvatten (ett)**	['kalʲ,vatən]
toothpaste	**tandkräm (en)**	['tand,krɛm]
to brush one's teeth	**att borsta tänderna**	[at 'bɔːʂta 'tɛndɛːɳa]
toothbrush	**tandborste (en)**	['tand,bɔːʂtə]
to shave (vi)	**att raka sig**	[at 'raka sɛj]
shaving foam	**raklödder (ett)**	['rak,lʲødər]
razor	**hyvel (en)**	['hyvəlʲ]
to wash (one's hands, etc.)	**att tvätta**	[at 'tvæta]
to take a bath	**att tvätta sig**	[at 'tvæta sɛj]
shower	**dusch (en)**	['duʃ]
to take a shower	**att duscha**	[at 'duʃa]
bathtub	**badkar (ett)**	['bad,kar]
toilet (toilet bowl)	**toalettstol (en)**	[tʊa'lʲet,stʊlʲ]
sink (washbasin)	**handfat (ett)**	['hand,fat]
soap	**tvål (en)**	['tvoːlʲ]
soap dish	**tvålskål (en)**	['tvoːlʲ,skoːlʲ]
sponge	**svamp (en)**	['svamp]
shampoo	**schampo (ett)**	['ʃam,pʊ]
towel	**handduk (en)**	['hand,dɵːk]
bathrobe	**morgonrock (en)**	['mɔrgɔn,rɔk]
laundry (process)	**tvätt (en)**	['tvæt]
washing machine	**tvättmaskin (en)**	['tvæt,ma'ɧiːn] .
to do the laundry	**att tvätta kläder**	[at 'tvæta 'klʲɛːdər]
laundry detergent	**tvättmedel (ett)**	['tvæt,medəlʲ]

99. Household appliances

TV set	**teve (en)**	['teve]
tape recorder	**bandspelare (en)**	['band,spelʲarə]
VCR (video recorder)	**video (en)**	['videʊ]
radio	**radio (en)**	['radiʊ]
player (CD, MP3, etc.)	**spelare (en)**	['spelʲarə]
video projector	**videoprojektor (en)**	['videʊ prʊ'jɛktʊr]
home movie theater	**hemmabio (en)**	['hɛma,biːʊ]
DVD player	**DVD spelare (en)**	[deve'deː ,spelʲarə]

| amplifier | förstärkare (en) | [fœː'stæːkarə] |
| video game console | spelkonsol (en) | ['spelʲ kɔn'sɔlʲ] |

video camera	videokamera (en)	['videʊˌkamera]
camera (photo)	kamera (en)	['kamera]
digital camera	digitalkamera (en)	[digi'talʲ ˌkamera]

vacuum cleaner	dammsugare (en)	['damˌsʉgarə]
iron (e.g., steam ~)	strykjärn (ett)	['strykˌjæːn]
ironing board	strykbräda (en)	['strykˌbrɛːda]

telephone	telefon (en)	[telʲe'fɔn]
cell phone	mobiltelefon (en)	[mɔ'bilʲ telʲe'fɔn]
typewriter	skrivmaskin (en)	['skrivˌma'ɧiːn]
sewing machine	symaskin (en)	['syˌma'ɧiːn]

microphone	mikrofon (en)	[mikrʊ'fɔn]
headphones	hörlurar (pl)	['hœːˌlʲʉːrar]
remote control (TV)	fjärrkontroll (en)	['fjæːrˌkɔn'trolʲ]

CD, compact disc	cd-skiva (en)	['sede ˌɧiva]
cassette, tape	kassett (en)	[ka'sɛt]
vinyl record	skiva (en)	['ɧiva]

100. Repairs. Renovation

renovations	renovering (en)	[renʊ'veriŋ]
to renovate (vt)	att renovera	[at renʊ'vera]
to repair, to fix (vt)	att reparera	[at repa'rera]
to put in order	att bringa ordning	[at 'briŋa 'ɔːɖniŋ]
to redo (do again)	att göra om	[at 'jøːra ɔm]

paint	färg (en)	['fæːrj]
to paint (~ a wall)	att måla	[at 'mɔːlʲa]
house painter	målare (en)	['mɔːlʲarə]
paintbrush	pensel (en)	['pɛnsəlʲ]
whitewash	kalkfärg (en)	['kalʲkˌfæːrj]
to whitewash (vt)	att vitlimma	[at 'vitˌlima]

wallpaper	tapet (en)	[ta'pet]
to wallpaper (vt)	att tapetsera	[at tapet'sera]
varnish	fernissa (en)	[fɛ'nisa]
to varnish (vt)	att lackera	[at lʲa'kera]

101. Plumbing

| water | vatten (ett) | ['vatən] |
| hot water | varmvatten (ett) | ['varmˌvatən] |

| cold water | kallvatten (ett) | ['kalʲˌvatən] |
| faucet | kran (en) | ['kran] |

drop (of water)	droppe (en)	['drɔpə]
to drip (vi)	att droppa	[at 'drɔpa]
to leak (ab. pipe)	att läcka	[at 'lɛka]
leak (pipe ~)	läcka (en)	['lʲɛka]
puddle	pöl, puss (en)	['pøːlʲ], ['pus]

pipe	rör (ett)	['røːr]
valve (e.g., ball ~)	ventil (en)	[vɛn'tilʲ]
to be clogged up	att bli igensatt	[at bli 'ijɛnsat]

tools	verktyg (pl)	['vɛrkˌtyg]
adjustable wrench	skiftnyckel (en)	['ɧiftˌnʏkəlʲ]
to unscrew (lid, filter, etc.)	att skruva ur	[at 'skrʉːva ʉːr]
to screw (tighten)	att skruva fast	[at 'skrʉːva fast]

to unclog (vt)	att rensa	[at 'rɛnsa]
plumber	rörmokare (en)	['røːrˌmɔkarə]
basement	källare (en)	['ɕɛlʲarə]
sewerage (system)	avlopp (ett)	['avˌlʲɔp]

102. Fire. Conflagration

fire (accident)	eld (en)	['ɛlʲd]
flame	flamma (en)	['flʲama]
spark	gnista (en)	['gnista]
smoke (from fire)	rök (en)	['røːk]
torch (flaming stick)	fackla (en)	['faklʲa]
campfire	bål (ett)	['boːlʲ]

gas, gasoline	bensin (en)	[bɛn'sin]
kerosene (type of fuel)	fotogen (en)	[futʊ'ɧen]
flammable (adj)	brännbar	['brɛnˌbar]
explosive (adj)	explosiv	[ɛksplʲɔ'siv]
NO SMOKING	RÖKNING FÖRBJUDEN	['rœkniŋ førˈbjʉːdən]

safety	säkerhet (en)	['sɛːkərˌhet]
danger	fara (en)	['fara]
dangerous (adj)	farlig	['faːlʲig]

to catch fire	att fatta eld	[at 'fata ˌɛlʲd]
explosion	explosion (en)	[ɛksplʲɔ'fʲʊn]
to set fire	att sätta eld	[at 'sæta ˌɛlʲd]
arsonist	mordbrännare (en)	['mʊːdˌbrɛnarə]
arson	mordbrand (en)	['mʊːdˌbrand]

| to blaze (vi) | att flamma | [at 'flʲama] |
| to burn (be on fire) | att brinna | [at 'brina] |

to burn down	att brinna ned	[at 'brina ned]
to call the fire department	att ringa brandkår	[at 'riŋa 'brand͵koːr]
firefighter, fireman	brandman (en)	['brand͵man]
fire truck	brandbil (en)	['brand͵bilʲ]
fire department	brandkår (en)	['brand͵koːr]
fire truck ladder	brandbilstege (en)	['brandbilʲ͵stegə]

fire hose	slang (en)	['slʲaŋ]
fire extinguisher	brandsläckare (en)	['brand͵slʲɛkarə]
helmet	hjälm (en)	['jɛlʲm]
siren	siren (en)	[si'ren]

to cry (for help)	att skrika	[at 'skrika]
to call for help	att ropa på hjälp	[at 'rʊpa pɔ jɛlʲp]
rescuer	räddare (en)	['rɛdarə]
to rescue (vt)	att rädda	[at 'rɛda]

to arrive (vi)	att ankomma	[at 'aŋ͵kɔma]
to extinguish (vt)	att släcka	[at 'slʲɛka]
water	vatten (ett)	['vatən]
sand	sand (en)	['sand]

ruins (destruction)	ruiner (pl)	[rʉ'iːnər]
to collapse (building, etc.)	att falla ihop	[at 'falʲa i'hʊp]
to fall down (vi)	att störta ner	[at 'støːʈa ner]
to cave in (ceiling, floor)	att störta in	[at 'støːʈa in]

| piece of debris | spillra (en) | ['spilʲra] |
| ash | aska (en) | ['aska] |

| to suffocate (die) | att kvävas | [at 'kvɛːvas] |
| to be killed (perish) | att omkomma | [at 'ɔm͵kɔma] |

HUMAN ACTIVITIES

Job. Business. Part 1

103. Office. Working in the office

office (company ~)	kontor (ett)	[kɔn'tʊr]
office (of director, etc.)	kontor (ett)	[kɔn'tʊr]
reception desk	reception (en)	[resɛp'ɧʊn]
secretary	sekreterare (en)	[sɛkrə'terarə]
secretary (fem.)	sekreterare (en)	[sɛkrə'terarə]

director	direktör (en)	[dirɛk'tø:r]
manager	manager (en)	['me:nijər]
accountant	bokförare (en)	['bʊkˌfø:rarə]
employee	anställd (en)	['anstɛlʲd]

furniture	möbel (en)	['mø:bəlʲ]
desk	bord (ett)	['bʊ:d]
desk chair	arbetsstol (en)	['arbetsˌstʊlʲ]
drawer unit	kassette,	[ka'sɛtə],
	skuffemodul (en)	['skufəˌmɔdul]
coat stand	klädhängare (en)	['klʲɛdˌhɛŋarə]

computer	dator (en)	['datʊr]
printer	skrivare (en)	['skrivarə]
fax machine	fax (en)	['faks]
photocopier	kopiator (en)	[kʊpi'atʊr]

paper	papper (ett)	['papər]
office supplies	kontorsmaterial (ett)	[kɔn'tʊ:ʂ mate'rjalʲ]
mouse pad	musmatta (en)	['mʉ:sˌmata]
sheet (of paper)	ark (ett)	['ark]
binder	mapp (en)	['map]

catalog	katalog (en)	[kata'lʲɔg]
phone directory	telefonkatalog (en)	[telʲe'fɔn kata'lʲɔg]
documentation	dokumentation (en)	[dɔkumənta'ɧʊn]
brochure	broschyr (en)	[brɔ'ɧyr]
(e.g., 12 pages ~)		
leaflet (promotional ~)	reklamblad (ett)	[rɛ'klʲamˌblʲad]
sample	prov (ett)	['prʊv]

training meeting	träning (en)	['trɛ:niŋ]
meeting (of managers)	möte (ett)	['mø:tə]

lunch time	lunchrast (en)	['lɵnɕˌrast]
to make a copy	att ta en kopia	[at ta en kʉ'pia]
to make multiple copies	att kopiera	[at kɔ'pjera]
to receive a fax	att ta emot fax	[at ta ɛmoːt 'faks]
to send a fax	att skicka fax	[at 'ɧika 'faks]

to call (by phone)	att ringa	[at 'riŋa]
to answer (vt)	att svara	[at 'svara]
to put through	att koppla till ...	[at 'koplʲa tilʲ ...]

to arrange, to set up	att arrangera	[at aran'ʃera]
to demonstrate (vt)	att demonstrera	[at demɔn'strera]
to be absent	att vara frånvarande	[at 'vara 'froːnˌvarandə]
absence	frånvaro (en)	['froːnˌvarʉ]

104. Business processes. Part 1

business	handel (en)	['handəlʲ]
occupation	yrke (ett)	['yrkə]
firm	firma (en)	['firma]
company	bolag, företag (ett)	['bʉlʲag], ['førəˌtag]
corporation	korporation (en)	[kɔrpʉra'ʄʉn]
enterprise	företag (ett)	['førəˌtag]
agency	agentur (en)	[agɛn'tʉːr]

agreement (contract)	avtal (ett)	['avtalʲ]
contract	kontrakt (ett)	[kɔn'trakt]
deal	affär (en)	[a'fæːr]
order (to place an ~)	beställning (en)	[bɛ'stɛlʲnin]
terms (of the contract)	villkor (ett)	['vilʲˌkor]

wholesale (adv)	en gros	[ɛn 'groː]
wholesale (adj)	grossist-, engros-	[grɔ'sist-], [ɛn'gro-]
wholesale (n)	grosshandel (en)	['grɔsˌhandəlʲ]
retail (adj)	detalj-	[de'talj-]
retail (n)	detaljhandel (en)	[de'taljˌhandəlʲ]

competitor	konkurrent (en)	[kɔŋku'rɛnt]
competition	konkurrens (en)	[kɔŋku'rɛns]
to compete (vi)	att konkurrera	[at kɔŋku'rera]

partner (associate)	partner (en)	['paːʈnər]
partnership	partnerskap (ett)	['paːʈnɛˌskap]

crisis	kris (en)	['kris]
bankruptcy	konkurs (en)	[kɔŋ'kuːʂ]
to go bankrupt	att göra konkurs	[at 'jøːra kɔŋ'kuːʂ]
difficulty	svårighet (en)	['svoːrigˌhet]
problem	problem (ett)	[prɔ'blʲem]
catastrophe	katastrof (en)	[kata'strɔf]

economy	ekonomi (en)	[εkʊnɔ'miː]
economic (~ growth)	ekonomisk	[εkʊ'nɔmisk]
economic recession	ekonomisk nedgång (en)	[εkʊ'nɔmisk 'ned͵gɔŋ]

| goal (aim) | mål (ett) | ['moːlʲ] |
| task | uppgift (en) | ['up͵gift] |

to trade (vi)	att handla	[at 'handlʲa]
network (distribution ~)	nätverk (ett)	['nε:t͵vεrk]
inventory (stock)	lager (ett)	['lʲagər]
range (assortment)	sortiment (ett)	[sɔ:ţi'mεnt]

leader (leading company)	ledare (en)	['lʲedarə]
large (~ company)	stor	['stʊr]
monopoly	monopol (en)	[mɔnɔ'polʲ]

theory	teori (en)	[teʊ'riː]
practice	praktik (en)	[prak'tik]
experience (in my ~)	erfarenhet (en)	['εrfarɛnhet]
trend (tendency)	tendens (en)	[tɛn'dɛns]
development	utveckling (en)	['ʉt͵vɛkliŋ]

105. Business processes. Part 2

| profit (foregone ~) | utbyte (ett), fördel (en) | ['ʉt͵bytə], ['føː͵del] |
| profitable (~ deal) | fördelaktig | [føːdəlʲ'aktig] |

delegation (group)	delegation (en)	[delʲega'ɦʊn]
salary	lön (en)	['lʲøːn]
to correct (an error)	att rätta	[at 'ræta]
business trip	affärsresa (en)	[a'fæː͵s͵resa]
commission	provision (en)	[prɔvi'ɦʊn]

to control (vt)	att kontrollera	[at kɔntrɔ'lʲera]
conference	konferens (en)	[kɔnfə'ræns]
license	licens (en)	[li'sɛns]
reliable (~ partner)	pålitlig	['po͵litlig]

initiative (undertaking)	initiativ (ett)	[initsja'tiv]
norm (standard)	norm (en)	['nɔrm]
circumstance	omständighet (en)	['ɔm͵stɛndighet]
duty (of employee)	plikt (en)	['plikt]

organization (company)	organisation (en)	[ɔrganisa'ɦʊn]
organization (process)	organisering (en)	[ɔrgani'seriŋ]
organized (adj)	organiserad	[ɔrgani'serad]
cancellation	annullering (en)	[anʉ'lʲeriŋ]
to cancel (call off)	att inställa, att annullera	[at in'stɛlʲa], [at anʉ'lʲera]
report (official ~)	rapport (en)	[ra'pɔːt]
patent	patent (ett)	[pa'tɛnt]

to patent (obtain patent)	**att patentera**	[at patɛn'tera]
to plan (vt)	**att planera**	[at plʲa'nera]
bonus (money)	**bonus, premie (en)**	['bʊnus], ['premiə]
professional (adj)	**professionell**	[prɔfeŋʊ'nɛlʲ]
procedure	**procedur (en)**	[prʊsə'dʉːr]
to examine (contract, etc.)	**att undersöka**	[at 'undəˌsøːka]
calculation	**beräkning (en)**	[be'rɛkniŋ]
reputation	**rykte (ett)**	['rʏktə]
risk	**risk (en)**	['risk]
to manage, to run	**att styra, att leda**	[at 'styra], [at 'lʲeda]
information	**upplysningar (pl)**	['upˌlysniŋar]
property	**egendom (en)**	['ɛgənˌdʊm]
union	**förbund (ett)**	['førˌbund]
life insurance	**livförsäkring (en)**	['livˌfœː'sɛkriŋ]
to insure (vt)	**att försäkra**	[at fœː'sɛkra]
insurance	**försäkring (en)**	[fœː'sɛkriŋ]
auction (~ sale)	**auktion (en)**	[auk'ŋun]
to notify (inform)	**att underrätta**	[at 'undəˌrɛta]
management (process)	**ledning (en)**	['lʲedniŋ]
service (~ industry)	**tjänst (en)**	['ɕɛnst]
forum	**forum (ett)**	['fʊrum]
to function (vi)	**att fungera**	[at fun'gera]
stage (phase)	**etapp (en)**	[ɛ'tap]
legal (~ services)	**juridisk**	[jʉ'ridisk]
lawyer (legal advisor)	**jurist (en)**	[jʉ'rist]

106. Production. Works

plant	**verk (ett)**	['vɛrk]
factory	**fabrik (en)**	[fab'rik]
workshop	**verkstad (en)**	['vɛrkˌstad]
works, production site	**produktionsplats (en)**	[prɔduk'ŋunˌplʲats]
industry (manufacturing)	**industri (en)**	[indu'striː]
industrial (adj)	**industriell**	[industri'ɛlʲ]
heavy industry	**tung industri (en)**	['tuŋ indu'striː]
light industry	**lätt industri (en)**	['lʲæt indu'striː]
products	**produktion (en)**	[prɔduk'ŋun]
to produce (vt)	**att producera**	[at prɔdʉ'sera]
raw materials	**råvaror (pl)**	['roːˌvarʊr]
foreman (construction ~)	**förman, bas (en)**	['førman], ['bas]
workers team (crew)	**arbetslag (ett)**	['arbetsˌlag]

worker	arbetare (en)	['ar‚betarə]
working day	arbetsdag (en)	['arbeʦ‚dag]
pause (rest break)	vilopaus (en)	['vilʲɔ‚paʊs]
meeting	möte (ett)	['møːtə]
to discuss (vt)	att dryfta, att diskutera	[at 'dryfta], [at diskʉ'tera]

plan	plan (en)	['plʲan]
to fulfill the plan	att uppfylla planen	[at 'up‚fylʲa 'planən]
rate of output	produktionsmål (ett)	[prɔduk'ʃʊn‚moːlʲ]
quality	kvalité (en)	[kvali'teː]
control (checking)	kontroll (en)	[kɔn'trolʲ]
quality control	kvalitetskontroll (en)	[kvali'teʦ kɔn'trolʲ]

workplace safety	arbetarskydd (ett)	['arbetaː‚ʃyd]
discipline	disciplin (en)	[disip'lin]
violation	brott (ett)	['brɔt]
(of safety rules, etc.)		
to violate (rules)	att bryta	[at 'bryta]

strike	strejk (en)	['strɛjk]
striker	strejkande (en)	['strɛjkandə]
to be on strike	att strejka	[at 'strɛjka]
labor union	fackförening (en)	['fakfø‚reniŋ]

to invent (machine, etc.)	att uppfinna	[at 'up‚fina]
invention	uppfinning (en)	['up‚finiŋ]
research	forskning (en)	['fɔːʂkniŋ]
to improve (make better)	att förbättra	[at før'bætra]
technology	teknologi (en)	[teknɔlʲɔ'giː]
technical drawing	teknisk ritning (en)	['tɛknisk 'ritniŋ]

load, cargo	last (en)	['lʲast]
loader (person)	lastare (en)	['lʲastarə]
to load (vehicle, etc.)	att lasta	[at 'lʲasta]
loading (process)	lastning (en)	['lʲastniŋ]
to unload (vi, vt)	att lasta av	[at 'lʲasta av]
unloading	avlastning (en)	['av‚lʲastniŋ]

transportation	transport (en)	[trans'pɔːt]
transportation company	transportföretag (ett)	[trans'pɔːt‚førə'tag]
to transport (vt)	att transportera	[at transpɔː'ʈera]

freight car	godsvagn (en)	['gʊds‚vagn]
tank (e.g., oil ~)	tank (en)	['taŋk]
truck	lastbil (en)	['lʲast‚bilʲ]

machine tool	verktygsmaskin (en)	['vɛrk‚tygs ma'ʃiːn]
mechanism	mekanism (en)	[meka'nism]

industrial waste	industriellt avfall (ett)	[industri'ɛlʲt 'avfalʲ]
packing (process)	packning (en)	['pakniŋ]
to pack (vt)	att packa	[at 'paka]

107. Contract. Agreement

contract	kontrakt (ett)	[kɔn'trakt]
agreement	avtal (ett)	['avtalʲ]
addendum	tillägg (ett), bilaga (en)	['tilˌlʲɛːg], ['biˌlʲaga]

to sign a contract	att ingå avtal	[at 'ingo: 'avtalʲ]
signature	signatur, underskrift (en)	[signa'tʉːr], ['undəˌskrift]
to sign (vt)	att underteckna	[at 'undəˌtɛkna]
seal (stamp)	stämpel (en)	['stɛmpəlʲ]

subject of contract	kontraktets föremål (ett)	[kɔn'traktets 'førəˌmoːlʲ]
clause	klausul (en)	[klau'sʉl]
parties (in contract)	parter (pl)	['paːtər]
legal address	juridisk adress (en)	[jʉ'ridisk a'drɛs]

to violate the contract	att bryta kontraktet	[at 'bryta kɔn'traktet]
commitment (obligation)	förpliktelse (en)	[før'pliktəlʲsə]
responsibility	ansvar (ett)	['anˌsvar]
force majeure	force majeure (en)	[ˌfɔrs ma'ʒøːr]
dispute	tvist (en)	['tvist]
penalties	straffavgifter (pl)	['strafˌav'jiftər]

108. Import & Export

import	import (en)	[im'pɔːt]
importer	importör (en)	[impɔː'tøːr]
to import (vt)	att importera	[at impɔː'tera]
import (as adj.)	import-	[im'pɔːt-]

export (exportation)	export (en)	['ɛkspɔːt]
exporter	exportör (en)	[ɛkspɔː'tøːr]
to export (vi, vt)	att exportera	[at ɛkspɔː'tera]
export (as adj.)	export-	['ɛkspɔːt-]

goods (merchandise)	vara (en)	['vara]
consignment, lot	parti (ett)	[pa:'tiː]

weight	vikt (en)	['vikt]
volume	volym (en)	[vɔ'lʲym]
cubic meter	kubikmeter (en)	[kʉ'bikˌmetər]

manufacturer	producent (en)	[prɔdʉ'sɛnt]
transportation company	transportföretag (ett)	[trans'pɔːtˌførə'tag]
container	container (en)	[kɔn'tɛjnər]

border	gräns (en)	['grɛns]
customs	tull (en)	['tulʲ]
customs duty	tullavgift (en)	['tulʲˌav'jift]

customs officer	tulltjänsteman (en)	['tulʲ 'ɕɛnstə‚man]
smuggling	smuggling (en)	['smuɡliŋ]
contraband (smuggled goods)	smuggelgods (ett)	['smuɡəlʲ‚ɡʊds]

109. Finances

stock (share)	aktie (en)	['aktsiə]
bond (certificate)	obligation (en)	[ɔbliɡa'fjʊn]
promissory note	växel (en)	['vɛksəlʲ]

| stock exchange | börs (en) | ['bøːʂ] |
| stock price | aktiekurs (en) | ['aktsiə‚kuːʂ] |

| to go down
(become cheaper) | att gå ner | [at 'ɡoː ‚ner] |
| to go up (become
more expensive) | att gå upp | [at 'ɡoː 'up] |

share	andel (en)	['an‚del]
controlling interest	aktiemajoritet (en)	['aktsiə majʊri'tet]
investment	investering (en)	[invə'steriŋ]
to invest (vt)	att investera	[at invə'stera]
percent	procent (en)	[prʊ'sɛnt]
interest (on investment)	ränta (en)	['rɛnta]
profit	vinst, förtjänst (en)	['vinst], [fœː'ɕɛːnst]
profitable (adj)	fördelaktig	[føːdəlʲ'aktiɡ]
tax	skatt (en)	['skat]

currency (foreign ~)	valuta (en)	[va'lʉːta]
national (adj)	nationell	[natfjʊ'nɛlʲ]
exchange (currency ~)	växling (en)	['vɛksliŋ]

| accountant | bokförare (en) | ['bʊk‚føːrarə] |
| accounting | bokföring (en) | ['bʊk‚føːriŋ] |

bankruptcy	konkurs (en)	[kɔŋ'kuːʂ]
collapse, crash	krasch (en)	['kraʃ]
ruin	ruin (en)	[rʉ'in]
to be ruined (financially)	att ruinera sig	[at rʉi'nera sɛj]
inflation	inflation (en)	[inflʲa'fjʊn]
devaluation	devalvering (en)	[devalʲ'veriŋ]

capital	kapital (ett)	[kapi'talʲ]
income	inkomst (en)	['iŋ‚kɔmst]
turnover	omsättning (en)	['ɔm‚sætniŋ]
resources	resurser (pl)	[re'suːʂər]
monetary resources	penningmedel (pl)	['pɛniŋ‚medəlʲ]
overhead	fasta utgifter (pl)	['fasta 'ʉtjiftər]
to reduce (expenses)	att reducera	[at redʉ'sera]

110. Marketing

marketing	**marknadsföring (en)**	['marknads,fø:riŋ]
market	**marknad (en)**	['marknad]
market segment	**marknadsegment (ett)**	['marknad seg'mɛnt]
product	**produkt (en)**	[prɔ'dukt]
goods (merchandise)	**vara (en)**	['vara]
brand	**varumärke (ett)**	['varɵ,mæ:rkə]
trademark	**varumärke (ett)**	['varɵ,mæ:rkə]
logotype	**firmamärke (ett)**	['firma,mæ:rkə]
logo	**logotyp (en)**	['lɔgɔtyp]
demand	**efterfrågan (en)**	['ɛftə,fro:gan]
supply	**utbud (ett)**	['ɵt,bɵd]
need	**behov (ett)**	[be'hɵv]
consumer	**konsument, förbrukare (en)**	[kɔnsu'mɛnt], [før'brɵ:karə]
analysis	**analys (en)**	[ana'lʲys]
to analyze (vt)	**att analysera**	[at analʲy'sera]
positioning	**positionering (en)**	[pɵsiŋɵ'neriŋ]
to position (vt)	**att positionera**	[at pɔsiŋɵ'nera]
price	**pris (ett)**	['pris]
pricing policy	**prispolitik (en)**	['pris pɵli'tik]
price formation	**prisbildning (en)**	['pris,bilʲdniŋ]

111. Advertising

advertising	**reklam (en)**	[rɛ'klʲam]
to advertise (vt)	**att reklamera**	[at rɛklʲa'mera]
budget	**budget (en)**	['budjet]
ad, advertisement	**annons (en)**	[a'nɔns]
TV advertising	**tv-reklam (ett)**	['teve rɛ'klʲam]
radio advertising	**radioreklam (en)**	['radiɵ rɛ'klʲam]
outdoor advertising	**utomhusreklam (en)**	['ɵtɔm,hɵs rɛ'klʲam]
mass media	**massmedier (pl)**	['mas,mediər]
periodical (n)	**tidskrift (en)**	['tid,skrift]
image (public appearance)	**image (en)**	['imidʒ]
slogan	**slogan (en)**	['slʲɔgan]
motto (maxim)	**motto (ett)**	['mɔtɵ]
campaign	**kampanj (en)**	[kam'panʲ]
advertising campaign	**reklamkampanj (en)**	[rɛ'klʲam kam'panʲ]
target group	**målgrupp (en)**	['mo:lʲ,grup]

business card	visitkort (ett)	[vi'sițkɔ:ț]
leaflet (promotional ~)	reklamblad (ett)	[rɛ'kl̦am̦bl̦ad]
brochure	broschyr (en)	[brɔ'ɧyr]
(e.g., 12 pages ~)		
pamphlet	folder (en)	['foldə]
newsletter	nyhetsbrev (ett)	['nyhetșbrev]

signboard (store sign, etc.)	skylt (en)	['ɧyl̦t]
poster	poster, löpsedel (en)	['pɔstər], ['løp̦sedəl̦]
billboard	reklamskylt (en)	[rɛ'kl̦am̦ɧyl̦t]

112. Banking

| bank | bank (en) | ['baŋk] |
| branch (of bank, etc.) | avdelning (en) | [av'dɛl̦niŋ] |

| bank clerk, consultant | konsulent (en) | [kɔnsu'l̦ɛnt] |
| manager (director) | föreståndare (en) | [førə'stɔndarə] |

bank account	bankkonto (ett)	['baŋk̦kɔntʊ]
account number	kontonummer (ett)	['kɔntʊ̦numər]
checking account	checkkonto (ett)	['ɕɛk̦kɔntʊ]
savings account	sparkonto (ett)	['spar̦kɔntʊ]

to open an account	att öppna ett konto	[at 'øpna ɛt 'kɔntʊ]
to close the account	att avsluta kontot	[at 'av̦slʉ:ta 'kɔntʊt]
to deposit into the account	att sätta in på kontot	[at 'sæta in pɔ 'kɔntʊt]
to withdraw (vt)	att ta ut från kontot	[at ta ʉt frɔn 'kɔntʊt]

deposit	insats (en)	['in̦sats]
to make a deposit	att sätta in	[at 'sæta in]
wire transfer	överföring (en)	['ø:və̦fø:riŋ]
to wire, to transfer	att överföra	[at ø:və̦føra]

| sum | summa (en) | ['suma] |
| How much? | Hur mycket? | [hʉr 'mʏkə] |

| signature | signatur, underskrift (en) | [signa'tʉ:r], ['undə̦skrift] |
| to sign (vt) | att underteckna | [at 'undə̦tɛkna] |

credit card	kreditkort (ett)	[kre'dițkɔ:ț]
code (PIN code)	kod (en)	['kɔd]
credit card number	kreditkortsnummer (ett)	[kre'dițkɔ:ts 'numər]
ATM	bankomat (en)	[baŋkʊ'mat]

check	check (en)	['ɕɛk]
to write a check	att skriva en check	[at 'skriva en 'ɕɛk]
checkbook	checkbok (en)	['ɕɛk̦bʊk]
loan (bank ~)	lån (ett)	['l̦o:n]
to apply for a loan	att ansöka om lån	[at 'an̦sø:ka ɔm 'l̦o:n]

to get a loan	**att få ett lån**	[at fo: et 'lʲoːn]
to give a loan	**att ge ett lån**	[at je: et 'lʲoːn]
guarantee	**garanti (en)**	[garan'tiː]

113. Telephone. Phone conversation

telephone	**telefon (en)**	[telʲe'fɔn]
cell phone	**mobiltelefon (en)**	[mɔ'bilʲ telʲe'fɔn]
answering machine	**telefonsvarare (en)**	[telʲe'fɔnˌsvararə]
to call (by phone)	**att ringa**	[at 'riŋa]
phone call	**telefonsamtal (en)**	[telʲe'fɔnˌsamtalʲ]
to dial a number	**att slå nummer**	[at 'slʲoː 'numər]
Hello!	**Hallå!**	[ha'lʲoː]
to ask (vt)	**att fråga**	[at 'froːga]
to answer (vi, vt)	**att svara**	[at 'svara]
to hear (vt)	**att höra**	[at 'høːra]
well (adv)	**gott, bra**	['gɔt], ['bra]
not well (adv)	**dåligt**	['doːlit]
noises (interference)	**bruser, störningar** (pl)	['bruːsər], ['støːˌɳiŋar]
receiver	**telefonlur (en)**	[telʲe'fɔnˌlʉːr]
to pick up (~ the phone)	**att lyfta telefonluren**	[at 'lʲyfta telʲe'fɔn 'lʉːrən]
to hang up (~ the phone)	**att lägga på**	[at 'lʲɛga pɔ]
busy (engaged)	**upptagen**	['upˌtagən]
to ring (ab. phone)	**att ringa**	[at 'riŋa]
telephone book	**telefonkatalog (en)**	[telʲe'fɔn kata'lʲɔg]
local (adj)	**lokal-**	[lʲɔ'kalʲ-]
local call	**lokalsamtal (ett)**	[lʲɔ'kalʲˌsamtalʲ]
long distance (~ call)	**riks-**	['riks-]
long-distance call	**rikssamtal (ett)**	['riksˌsamtalʲ]
international (adj)	**internationell**	['intɛˌɳatʂʉˌnɛlʲ]
international call	**internationell samtal (ett)**	['intɛˌɳatʂʉˌnɛlʲ 'samtalʲ]

114. Cell phone

cell phone	**mobiltelefon (en)**	[mɔ'bilʲ telʲe'fɔn]
display	**skärm (en)**	['ʃæːrm]
button	**knapp (en)**	['knap]
SIM card	**SIM-kort (ett)**	['simˌkɔːt]
battery	**batteri (ett)**	[batɛ'riː]
to be dead (battery)	**att bli urladdad**	[at bli 'ʉːˌlʲadad]
charger	**laddare (en)**	['lʲadarə]

menu	meny (en)	[me'ny]
settings	inställningar (pl)	['inˌstɛlʲniŋar]
tune (melody)	melodi (en)	[melʲɔ'diː]
to select (vt)	att välja	[at 'vɛlja]

calculator	kalkylator (en)	[kalʲky'lʲatʊr]
voice mail	telefonsvarare (en)	[telʲe'fɔnˌsvararə]
alarm clock	väckarklocka, alarm (en)	['vɛkarˌklʲɔka], [a'lʲarm]
contacts	kontakter (pl)	[kɔn'taktər]

| SMS (text message) | SMS meddelande (ett) | [ɛsɛ'mɛs me'delʲandə] |
| subscriber | abonnent (en) | [abɔ'nɛnt] |

115. Stationery

| ballpoint pen | kulspetspenna (en) | ['kʉlʲspetsˌpɛna] |
| fountain pen | reservoarpenna (en) | [resɛrvʊ'arˌpɛna] |

pencil	blyertspenna (en)	['blʲyɛːʦˌpɛna]
highlighter	märkpenna (en)	['mœrkˌpɛna]
felt-tip pen	tuschpenna (en)	['tuːʃˌpɛna]

| notepad | block (ett) | ['blʲɔk] |
| agenda (diary) | dagbok (en) | ['dagˌbʊk] |

ruler	linjal (en)	[li'njalʲ]
calculator	kalkylator (en)	[kalʲky'lʲatʊr]
eraser	suddgummi (ett)	['sudˌgumi]
thumbtack	häftstift (ett)	['hɛftˌstift]
paper clip	gem (ett)	['gem]

glue	lim (ett)	['lʲim]
stapler	häftapparat (en)	['hɛft apaˌrat]
hole punch	hålslag (ett)	['hoːlʲˌslʲag]
pencil sharpener	pennvässare (en)	['pɛnˌvɛsarə]

116. Various kinds of documents

account (report)	rapport (en)	[ra'pɔːt]
agreement	avtal (ett)	['avtalʲ]
application form	ansökningsblankett (en)	['anˌsœkniŋs blaŋ'ket]
authentic (adj)	äckta	['ɛkta]
badge (identity tag)	bricka (en)	['brika]
business card	visitkort (ett)	[vi'sitˌkoːt]

certificate (~ of quality)	certifikat (ett)	[sɛːʦifi'kat]
check (e.g., draw a ~)	check (en)	['ɕɛk]
check (in restaurant)	nota (en)	['nʊta]

constitution	konstitution (en)	[kɔnstitu'ʃʊn]
contract (agreement)	avtal (ett)	['avtalʲ]
copy	kopia (en)	[kʊ'pia]
copy (of contract, etc.)	exemplar (ett)	[ɛksɛmp'lʲar]
customs declaration	tulldeklaration (en)	['tulʲ‚dɛklʲara'ʃʊn]
document	dokument (ett)	[dɔku'mɛnt]
driver's license	körkort (ett)	['ɕøːr‚kɔːt]
addendum	tillägg (ett), bilaga (en)	['til‚lʲɛːg], ['bi‚lʲaga]
form	formulär (ett)	[fɔrmʉ'lʲæːr]
ID card (e.g., FBI ~)	legitimation (en)	[lʲegitima'ʃʊn]
inquiry (request)	förfrågan (en)	['før‚froːgan]
invitation card	inbjudningskort (ett)	[in'bjʉːdniŋs‚kɔːt]
invoice	faktura (en)	[fak'tʉra]
law	lag (en)	['lʲag]
letter (mail)	brev (ett)	['brev]
letterhead	brevpapper (ett)	['brev‚papər]
list (of names, etc.)	lista (en)	['lista]
manuscript	manuskript (ett)	[manu'skript]
newsletter	nyhetsbrev (ett)	['nyhets‚brev]
note (short letter)	lapp (en)	['lʲap]
pass (for worker, visitor)	passerkort (ett)	[pa'sər‚kɔːt]
passport	pass (ett)	['pas]
permit	tillåtelse (en)	['til‚lʲoːtəlʲsə]
résumé	meritförteckning (en)	[me'rit‚fœː'ʈɛkniŋ]
debt note, IOU	skuldebrev (ett)	['skʉlʲdə‚brev]
receipt (for purchase)	kvitto (ett)	['kvitʊ]
sales slip, receipt	kvitto (ett)	['kvitʊ]
report (mil.)	rapport (en)	[ra'pɔːt]
to show (ID, etc.)	att visa	[at 'visa]
to sign (vt)	att underteckna	[at 'undə‚tɛkna]
signature	signatur, underskrift (en)	[signa'tʉːr], ['undə‚skrift]
seal (stamp)	stämpel (en)	['stɛmpəlʲ]
text	text (en)	['tɛkst]
ticket (for entry)	biljett (en)	[bi'lʲet]
to cross out	att stryka ut	[at 'stryka ʉt]
to fill out (~ a form)	att fylla i	[at 'fylʲa 'i]
waybill (shipping invoice)	fraktsedel (en)	['frakt‚sedəlʲ]
will (testament)	testamente (ett)	[tɛsta'mɛntə]

117. Kinds of business

accounting services	bokföringstjänster (en)	['bʊk‚føːriŋ 'ɕɛnstər]
advertising	reklam (en)	[rɛ'klʲam]

advertising agency	reklambyrå (en)	[rɛ'klʲamby,ro:]
air-conditioners	luftkonditionering (en)	['lɵft,kɔndiɧʊ'neriŋ]
airline	flygbolag (ett)	['flʲyg,bʉlʲag]
alcoholic beverages	alkoholhaltiga drycker (pl)	[alʲkʊ'holʲ,halʲtiga 'drʏkər]
antiques (antique dealers)	antikviteter (pl)	[antikvi'tetər]
art gallery (contemporary ~)	konstgalleri (ett)	['kɔnst galʲe'ri:]
audit services	revisiontjänster (pl)	[revi'ɧʉn,ɕɛnstər]
banking industry	bankaffärer (pl)	['baŋk a'fæ:rər]
bar	bar (en)	['bar]
beauty parlor	skönhetssalong (en)	['ɧø:nhets sa'lʲɔŋ]
bookstore	bokhandel (en)	['bʊk,handəlʲ]
brewery	bryggeri (ett)	[brʏge'ri:]
business center	affärscentrum (ett)	[a'fæ:ʂ,sɛntrum]
business school	affärsskola (en)	[a'fæ:ʂ,skʊlʲa]
casino	kasino (ett)	[ka'sinʊ]
construction	byggbranch (en)	['bʏgbranɕ]
consulting	konsulttjänster (pl)	[kɔn'sulʲt,ɕɛnstər]
dental clinic	tandklinik (en)	['tand kli'nik]
design	design (en)	[de'sajn]
drugstore, pharmacy	apotek (ett)	[apʊ'tek]
dry cleaners	kemtvätt (en)	['ɕemtvæt]
employment agency	arbetsförmedling (en)	['arbets,før'medliŋ]
financial services	finansiella tjänster (pl)	[finan'sjɛlʲa 'ɕɛnstər]
food products	matvaror (pl)	['mat,varʊr]
funeral home	begravningsbyrå (en)	[be'gravniŋs,byro:]
furniture (e.g., house ~)	möbel (en)	['mø:bəlʲ]
clothing, garment	kläder (pl)	['klʲɛ:dər]
hotel	hotell (ett)	[hʊ'tɛlʲ]
ice-cream	glass (en)	['glʲas]
industry (manufacturing)	industri (en)	[indu'stri:]
insurance	försäkring (en)	[fœ:'ʂɛkriŋ]
Internet	Internet	['intɛ:,ɳɛt]
investments (finance)	investering (en)	[invə'steriŋ]
jeweler	juvelerare (en)	[jɵvə'lʲe:rarə]
jewelry	smycken (pl)	['smʏkən]
laundry (shop)	tvätteri (ett)	[tvæte'ri:]
legal advisor	juridisk rådgivare (pl)	[jɵ'ridisk 'ro:djivarə]
light industry	lätt industri (en)	[lʲæt indu'stri:]
magazine	tidskrift (en)	['tid,skrift]
mail-order selling	postorderförsäljning (en)	['pɔst,ɔ:dər fœ:'ʂɛljniŋ]
medicine	medicin (en)	[medi'sin]
movie theater	biograf (en)	[biʊ'graf]

museum	museum (ett)	[mʉ'seum]
news agency	nyhetsbyrå (en)	['nyhets by'roː]
newspaper	tidning (en)	['tidniŋ]
nightclub	nattklubb (en)	['natˌklʉb]
oil (petroleum)	olja (en)	['ɔlja]
courier services	budtjänst (en)	['bʉːtˌɕɛnst]
pharmaceutics	farmaci (en)	[farma'siː]
printing (industry)	tryckeri (ett)	[trʏke'riː]
publishing house	förlag (ett)	[fœː'lʲag]
radio (~ station)	radio (en)	['radiʉ]
real estate	fastighet (en)	['fastigˌhet]
restaurant	restaurang (en)	[rɛstɔ'raŋ]
security company	säkerhetsbyrå (en)	['sɛːkərhetsˌby'roː]
sports	sport (en)	['spɔːt]
stock exchange	börs (en)	['bøːʂ]
store	affär, butik (en)	[a'fæːr], [bu'tik]
supermarket	snabbköp (ett)	['snabˌɕøːp]
swimming pool (public ~)	simbassäng (en)	['simbaˌsɛŋ]
tailor shop	skrädderi (ett)	[skrɛde'riː]
television	television (en)	[telʲevi'ʃʉn]
theater	teater (en)	[te'atər]
trade (commerce)	handel (en)	['handəlʲ]
transportation	transport (en)	[trans'pɔːt]
travel	turism (en)	[tu'rism]
veterinarian	veterinär (en)	[vetəri'næːr]
warehouse	lager (en)	['lʲagər]
waste collection	avfallshantering (en)	['avfalʲsˌhanteriŋ]

Job. Business. Part 2

118. Show. Exhibition

exhibition, show	mässa (en)	['mɛsa]
trade show	handelsmässa (en)	['handəlˡsˌmɛsa]
participation	deltagande (ett)	['delˡˌtagandə]
to participate (vi)	att delta	[at 'dɛlˡta]
participant (exhibitor)	deltagare (en)	['delˡˌtagarə]
director	direktör (en)	[dirɛk'tø:r]
organizers' office	arrangörskontor (ett)	[aran'ŋør kɔn'tʊr]
organizer	arrangör (en)	[aran'jø:r]
to organize (vt)	att organisera	[at ɔrgani'sera]
participation form	deltagarformulär (ett)	['delˡtagarˌfɔrmu'lˡæ:r]
to fill out (vt)	att fylla i	[at 'fylˡa 'i]
details	detaljer (pl)	[de'taljər]
information	information (en)	[infɔrma'ɧʊn]
price (cost, rate)	pris (ett)	['pris]
including	inklusive	['iŋklʉˌsivə]
to include (vt)	att inkludera	[at iŋklʉ'dera]
to pay (vi, vt)	att betala	[at be'talˡa]
registration fee	registreringsavgift (en)	[reji'streriŋs 'avˌjift]
entrance	ingång (en)	['inˌgɔŋ]
pavilion, hall	paviljong (en)	[pavi'ljɔŋ]
to register (vt)	att registrera	[at regi'strera]
badge (identity tag)	bricka (en)	['brika]
booth, stand	monter (en)	['mɔntər]
to reserve, to book	att reservera	[at resɛr'vera]
display case	glasmonter (en)	['glˡasˌmɔntər]
spotlight	spotlight (en)	['spotˌlajt]
design	design (en)	[de'sajn]
to place (put, set)	att placera	[at plˡa'sera]
to be placed	att bli placerat	[at bli plˡa'serat]
distributor	distributör (en)	[distribʉ'tø:r]
supplier	leverantör (en)	[lˡevəran'tø:r]
to supply (vt)	att förse, att leverera	[at fœ:'ʂə], [at lˡeve'rera]
country	land (ett)	['lˡand]
foreign (adj)	utländsk	['ʉtˌlˡɛŋsk]

product	produkt (en)	[prɔ'dukt]
association	förening (en)	[fø'reniŋ]
conference hall	konferenssal (en)	[kɔnfe'ræns‚salʲ]
congress	kongress (en)	[kɔŋ'grɛs]
contest (competition)	tävling (en)	['tɛvlʲiŋ]

visitor (attendee)	besökare (en)	[be'sø:karə]
to visit (attend)	att besöka	[at be'sø:ka]
customer	kund, beställare (en)	['kund], [be'stɛlʲarə]

119. Mass Media

newspaper	tidning (en)	['tidniŋ]
magazine	tidskrift (en)	['tid‚skrift]
press (printed media)	press (en)	['prɛs]
radio	radio (en)	['radiʊ]
radio station	radiostation (en)	['radiʊ sta'ʂʊn]
television	television (en)	[telʲevi'ʂʊn]

presenter, host	programledare (en)	[prɔ'gram‚lʲedarə]
newscaster	uppläsare (en)	['up‚lʲɛ:sarə]
commentator	kommentator (en)	[kɔmɛn'tatʊr]

journalist	journalist (en)	[ʂʊɳa'list]
correspondent (reporter)	korrespondent (en)	[kɔrɛspɔn'dɛnt]
press photographer	pressfotograf (en)	['prɛs fʊtʊ'graf]
reporter	reporter (en)	[re'pɔ:tər]

editor	redaktör (en)	[redak'tø:r]
editor-in-chief	chefredaktör (en)	['ʃef‚redak'tø:r]

to subscribe (to …)	att prenumerera	[at prenume'rera]
subscription	prenumeration (en)	[prenumera'ʂʊn]
subscriber	prenumerant (en)	[prenume'rant]
to read (vi, vt)	att läsa	[at 'lʲɛ:sa]
reader	läsare (en)	['lʲɛ:sarə]

circulation (of newspaper)	upplaga (en)	['up‚lʲaga]
monthly (adj)	månatlig	[mo'natlig]
weekly (adj)	vecko-	['vɛkɔ-]
issue (edition)	nummer (ett)	['numər]
new (~ issue)	ny, färsk	['ny], [fæ:ʂk]

headline	rubrik (en)	[ru'brik]
short article	notis (en)	[nʊ'tis]
column (regular article)	rubrik (en)	[ru'brik]
article	artikel (en)	[a'tikəlʲ]
page	sida (en)	['sida]
reportage, report	reportage (ett)	[repɔ:'ta:ʃ]
event (happening)	händelse (en)	['hɛndəlʲsə]

sensation (news)	sensation (en)	[sɛnsa'ʃʊn]
scandal	skandal (en)	[skan'dalʲ]
scandalous (adj)	skandalös	[skanda'lʲøs]
great (~ scandal)	stor	['stʊr]

show (e.g., cooking ~)	program (ett)	[prɔ'gram]
interview	intervju (en)	[intɛr'vjɯ:]
live broadcast	direktsändning (en)	[di'rɛkt‚sɛndniŋ]
channel	kanal (en)	[ka'nalʲ]

120. Agriculture

agriculture	jordbruk (ett)	['jʊ:d‚brʉk]
peasant (masc.)	bonde (en)	['bʊndə]
peasant (fem.)	bondkvinna (en)	['bʊnd‚kvina]
farmer	lantbrukare, bonde (en)	['lʲant‚brʉ:karə], ['bʊndə]

| tractor (farm ~) | traktor (en) | ['traktʊr] |
| combine, harvester | skördetröska (en) | ['ʃø:dɛ‚trœska] |

plow	plog (en)	['plʊg]
to plow (vi, vt)	att ploga	[at 'plʲʊga]
plowland	plöjd åker (en)	['plʲœjd 'o:kər]
furrow (in field)	fåra (en)	['fo:ra]

to sow (vi, vt)	att så	[at so:]
seeder	såmaskin (en)	['so:‚ma'ʃi:n]
sowing (process)	såning (en)	['so:niŋ]

| scythe | lie (en) | ['li:e] |
| to mow, to scythe | att meja, att slå | [at 'meja], [at 'slʲo:] |

| spade (tool) | spade (en) | ['spadə] |
| to till (vt) | att gräva | [at 'grɛ:va] |

hoe	hacka (en)	['haka]
to hoe, to weed	att hacka	[at 'haka]
weed (plant)	ogräs (ett)	[ʊ'grɛ:s]

watering can	vattenkanna (en)	['vatən‚kana]
to water (plants)	att vattna	[at 'vatna]
watering (act)	vattning (en)	['vatniŋ]

| pitchfork | grep (en) | ['grep] |
| rake | kratta (en) | ['krata] |

fertilizer	gödsel (en)	['jøsəlʲ]
to fertilize (vt)	att gödsla	[at 'jøslʲa]
manure (fertilizer)	dynga (en)	['dɤŋa]
field	åker (en)	['o:kər]

meadow	äng (en)	['ɛŋ]
vegetable garden	koksträdgård (en)	['kʊksˌtrɛ'goːd̪]
orchard (e.g., apple ~)	fruktträdgård (en)	['frʉktˌtrɛ'goːd̪]

to graze (vt)	att beta	[at 'beta]
herder (herdsman)	herde (en)	['hɛːd̪ə]
pasture	betesmark (en)	['betəsˌmark]

| cattle breeding | boskapsskötsel (en) | ['bʊskapsˌføːtsəlʲ] |
| sheep farming | fåravel (en) | ['foːrˌavəlʲ] |

plantation	plantage (en)	[plʲan'taːʃ]
row (garden bed ~s)	rad (en)	['rad]
hothouse	drivhus (ett)	['drivˌhʉs]

| drought (lack of rain) | torka (en) | ['torka] |
| dry (~ summer) | torr | ['tor] |

grain	korn, spannmål (ett)	['kʊːn], ['spanˌmoːlʲ]
cereal crops	sädesslag (en)	['sɛdəsˌslʲag]
to harvest, to gather	att inhösta	[at in'høsta]

miller (person)	mjölnare (en)	['mjœlʲnarə]
mill (e.g., gristmill)	kvarn (en)	[kvaːŋ]
to grind (grain)	att mala	[at 'malʲa]
flour	mjöl (ett)	['mjøːlʲ]
straw	halm (en)	['halʲm]

121. Building. Building process

construction site	byggplats (en)	['bʏgˌplʲats]
to build (vt)	att bygga	[at 'bʏga]
construction worker	byggarbetare (en)	['bʏgˌar'betarə]

project	projekt (ett)	[prʊ'fɛkt]
architect	arkitekt (en)	[arki'tɛkt]
worker	arbetare (en)	['arˌbetarə]

foundation (of a building)	fundament (ett)	[funda'mɛnt]
roof	tak (ett)	['tak]
foundation pile	påle (en)	['poːlʲe]
wall	mur, vägg (en)	['mʉːr], [vɛg]

| reinforcing bars | armeringsjärn (ett) | [ar'meriŋsˌjæːŋ] |
| scaffolding | ställningar (pl) | ['stɛlʲniŋar] |

concrete	betong (en)	[be'tɔŋ]
granite	granit (en)	[gra'nit]
stone	sten (en)	['sten]
brick	tegel, mursten (en)	['tegəlʲ], ['mʉːˌsten]

sand	sand (en)	['sand]
cement	cement (en)	[se'mɛnt]
plaster (for walls)	puts (en)	['pʉts]
to plaster (vt)	att putsa	[at 'putsa]
paint	färg (en)	['fæːrj]
to paint (~ a wall)	att måla	[at 'moːlʲa]
barrel	tunna (en)	['tuna]

crane	lyftkran (en)	['lʲyft‚kran]
to lift, to hoist (vt)	att lyfta	[at 'lʲyfta]
to lower (vt)	att sänka	[at 'sɛŋka]

bulldozer	bulldozer (en)	['bulʲ‚dɔːsər]
excavator	grävmaskin (en)	['grɛv‚ma'ɦiːn]
scoop, bucket	skopa (en)	['skʉpa]
to dig (excavate)	att gräva	[at 'grɛːva]
hard hat	hjälm (en)	['jɛlʲm]

122. Science. Research. Scientists

science	vetenskap (en)	['vetən‚skap]
scientific (adj)	vetenskaplig	['vetən‚skaplig]
scientist	vetenskapsman (en)	['vetənskaps‚man]
theory	teori (en)	[teʉ'riː]

axiom	axiom (ett)	[aksi'ɔm]
analysis	analys (en)	[ana'lʲys]
to analyze (vt)	att analysera	[at analʲy'sera]
argument (strong ~)	argument (ett)	[argʉ'mɛnt]
substance (matter)	stoff (ett), substans (en)	['stof], ['sʉbstans]

hypothesis	hypotes (en)	[hypɔ'tɛs]
dilemma	dilemma (ett)	['dilʲema]
dissertation	avhandling (en)	['av‚handliŋ]
dogma	dogm (en)	['dɔgm]

doctrine	doktrin (en)	[dɔk'trin]
research	forskning (en)	['fɔːʂkniŋ]
to research (vt)	att forska	[at 'fɔːʂka]
tests (laboratory ~)	test (ett)	['tɛst]
laboratory	laboratorium (ett)	[lʲabɔra'tɔrium]

method	metod (en)	[me'tɔd]
molecule	molekyl (en)	[mɔlʲe'kylʲ]
monitoring	övervakning (en)	['øːvə‚vakniŋ]
discovery (act, event)	upptäckt (en)	['up‚tɛkt]

postulate	postulat (ett)	[pɔstʉ'lʲat]
principle	princip (en)	[prin'sip]
forecast	prognos (en)	[prɔ'gnɔs]

to forecast (vt)	**att prognostisera**	[at prɔŋɔsti'sera]
synthesis	**syntes (en)**	[sʏn'tes]
trend (tendency)	**tendens (en)**	[tɛn'dɛns]
theorem	**teorém (ett)**	[teʊ're:m]
teachings	**läran (pl)**	['lʲæ:ran]
fact	**faktum (ett)**	['faktʊm]
expedition	**expedition (en)**	[ɛkspedi'ɧʊn]
experiment	**experiment (ett)**	[ɛksperi'mɛnt]
academician	**akademiker (en)**	[aka'demikər]
bachelor (e.g., ~ of Arts)	**bachelor (en)**	[baɕelor]
doctor (PhD)	**doktor (en)**	['dɔktʊr]
Associate Professor	**docent (en)**	[dɔ'sɛnt]
Master (e.g., ~ of Arts)	**magister (en)**	[ma'jistər]
professor	**professor (en)**	[prɔ'fɛsʊr]

Professions and occupations

123. Job search. Dismissal

job	**arbete, jobb (ett)**	['arbetə], ['jɔb]
staff (work force)	**personal, stab (en)**	[pɛʂʊ'nalʲ], ['stab]
personnel	**personal (en)**	[pɛʂʊ'nalʲ]
career	**karriär (en)**	[kari'æːr]
prospects (chances)	**utsikter** (pl)	['ʉtˌsiktər]
skills (mastery)	**mästerskap (ett)**	['mɛstəˌʂkap]
selection (screening)	**urval (ett)**	['ʉːrˌvalʲ]
employment agency	**arbetsförmedling (en)**	['arbetsˌfør'medliŋ]
résumé	**meritförteckning (en)**	[me'ritˌfœː'tɛkniŋ]
job interview	**jobbsamtal (ett)**	['jɔbˌsamtalʲ]
vacancy, opening	**vakans (en)**	['vakans]
salary, pay	**lön (en)**	['lʲøːn]
fixed salary	**fast lön (en)**	['fast ˌlʲøːn]
pay, compensation	**betalning (en)**	[be'talʲniŋ]
position (job)	**ställning (en)**	['stɛlʲniŋ]
duty (of employee)	**plikt (en)**	['plikt]
range of duties	**arbetsplikter** (pl)	['arbetsˌpliktər]
busy (I'm ~)	**upptagen**	['upˌtagən]
to fire (dismiss)	**att avskeda**	[at 'avˌɧeda]
dismissal	**avsked (ett)**	['avɧed]
unemployment	**arbetslöshet (en)**	['arbetsˌlʲøːshet]
unemployed (n)	**arbetslös (en)**	['arbetsˌlʲøːs]
retirement	**pension (en)**	[pan'ɧʊn]
to retire (from job)	**att gå i pension**	[at 'goː i pan'ɧʊn]

124. Business people

director	**direktör (en)**	[dirɛk'tøːr]
manager (director)	**föreståndare (en)**	[førə'stɔndarə]
boss	**boss (en)**	['bɔs]
superior	**överordnad (en)**	['øːvərˌɔːdnat]
superiors	**överordnade** (pl)	['øːvərˌɔːdnadə]
president	**president (en)**	[prɛsi'dɛnt]

chairman	ordförande (en)	['ʊːdˌførandə]
deputy (substitute)	ställföreträdare (en)	['stɛlˌfœre'trɛːdarə]
assistant	assistent (en)	[asi'stɛnt]
secretary	sekreterare (en)	[sɛkrə'terarə]
personal assistant	privatsekreterare (en)	[pri'vat sɛkrə'terarə]

businessman	affärsman (en)	[a'fæːʂˌman]
entrepreneur	entreprenör (en)	[æntepre'nøːr]
founder	grundläggare (en)	['grʉndˌlˡɛgarə]
to found (vt)	att grunda	[at 'grʉnda]

incorporator	stiftare (en)	['stiftarə]
partner	partner (en)	['paːʈnər]
stockholder	aktieägare (en)	['aktsiəˌɛːgarə]

millionaire	miljonär (en)	[miljʊ'næːr]
billionaire	miljardär (en)	[milja:'ɖæːr]
owner, proprietor	ägare (en)	['ɛːgarə]
landowner	jordägare (en)	['jʊːdˌɛːgarə]

client	kund (en)	['kund]
regular client	stamkund (en)	['stamˌkund]
buyer (customer)	köpare (en)	['ɕøːparə]
visitor	besökare (en)	[be'søːkarə]

professional (n)	yrkesman (en)	['yrkəsˌman]
expert	expert (en)	[ɛks'pɛːʈ]
specialist	specialist (en)	[spesia'list]

banker	bankir (en)	[baŋ'kir]
broker	mäklare (en)	['mɛklˡarə]

cashier, teller	kassör (en)	[ka'søːr]
accountant	bokförare (en)	['bʊkˌføːrarə]
security guard	säkerhetsvakt (en)	['sɛːkərhetsˌvakt]

investor	investerare (en)	[invɛ'sterarə]
debtor	gäldenär (en)	[jɛlˡdɛ'næːr]
creditor	kreditor (en)	[kre'ditʊr]
borrower	låntagare (en)	['lˡoːnˌtagarə]

importer	importör (en)	[impɔ:'tøːr]
exporter	exportör (en)	[ɛkspɔ:'tøːr]

manufacturer	producent (en)	[prodʉ'sɛnt]
distributor	distributör (en)	[distribʉ'tøːr]
middleman	mellanhand (en)	['mɛlˡanˌhand]

consultant	konsulent (en)	[kɔnsu'lˡɛnt]
sales representative	representant (en)	[represən'tant]
agent	agent (en)	[a'gɛnt]
insurance agent	försäkringsagent (en)	[fœ:'ʂɛkriŋs a'gɛnt]

125. Service professions

cook	**kock (en)**	['kɔk]
chef (kitchen chef)	**kökschef (en)**	['ɕœks͵ʃef]
baker	**bagare (en)**	['bagarə]
bartender	**bartender (en)**	['ba:͵tɛndər]
waiter	**servitör (en)**	[sɛrvi'tø:r]
waitress	**servitris (en)**	[sɛrvi'tris]
lawyer, attorney	**advokat (en)**	[advʊ'kat]
lawyer (legal expert)	**jurist (en)**	[jʉ'rist]
notary	**notarius publicus (en)**	[nʊ'tariʊs 'publikʉs]
electrician	**elektriker (en)**	[ɛ'lʲektrikər]
plumber	**rörmokare (en)**	['rø:r͵mɔkarə]
carpenter	**timmerman (en)**	['timər͵man]
masseur	**massör (en)**	[ma'sø:r]
masseuse	**massös (en)**	[ma'sø:s]
doctor	**läkare (en)**	['lʲɛ:karə]
taxi driver	**taxichaufför (en)**	['taksi ʃɔ'fø:r]
driver	**chaufför (en)**	[ʃɔ'fø:r]
delivery man	**bud (en)**	['bʉ:d]
chambermaid	**städerska (en)**	['stɛ:dɛʂka]
security guard	**säkerhetsvakt (en)**	['sɛ:kərhets͵vakt]
flight attendant (fem.)	**flygvärdinna (en)**	['flʲyg͵væ:dʲina]
schoolteacher	**lärare (en)**	['lʲæ:rarə]
librarian	**bibliotekarie (en)**	[bibliʊte'kariə]
translator	**översättare (en)**	['ø:və͵sætarə]
interpreter	**tolk (en)**	['tɔlʲk]
guide	**guide (en)**	['gajd]
hairdresser	**frisör (en)**	[fri'sø:r]
mailman	**brevbärare (en)**	['brev͵bæ:rarə]
salesman (store staff)	**försäljare (en)**	[fœ:'ʂɛljarə]
gardener	**trädgårdsmästare (en)**	['trɛ:go:ɖs 'mɛstarə]
domestic servant	**tjänare (en)**	['ɕɛ:narə]
maid (female servant)	**tjänarinna (en)**	[ɕɛ:na'rina]
cleaner (cleaning lady)	**städerska (en)**	['stɛ:dɛʂka]

126. Military professions and ranks

private	**menig (en)**	['menig]
sergeant	**sergeant (en)**	[sɛr'ʃant]

| lieutenant | löjtnant (en) | ['lʲœjtˌnant] |
| captain | kapten (en) | [kap'ten] |

major	major (en)	[ma'juːr]
colonel	överste (en)	['øːvəʂtə]
general	general (en)	[jeneˈralʲ]
marshal	marskalk (en)	[maːˈʂalʲk]
admiral	amiral (en)	[amiˈralʲ]

military (n)	militär (en)	[miliˈtæːr]
soldier	soldat (en)	[sʊlʲ'dat]
officer	officer (en)	[ɔfi'seːr]
commander	befälhavare (en)	[be'fɛl ˌhavarə]

border guard	gränsvakt (en)	['grɛnsˌvakt]
radio operator	radiooperatör (en)	['radiʊ ɔpera'tør]
scout (searcher)	spaningssoldat (en)	['spaniŋs sʊlʲ'dat]
pioneer (sapper)	pionjär (en)	[piʊ'njæːr]
marksman	skytt (en)	['ʃʏt]
navigator	styrman (en)	['styrˌman]

127. Officials. Priests

| king | kung (en) | ['kuŋ] |
| queen | drottning (en) | ['drɔtniŋ] |

| prince | prins (en) | ['prins] |
| princess | prinsessa (en) | [prin'sɛsa] |

| czar | tsar (en) | ['tsar] |
| czarina | tsarinna (en) | [tsa'rina] |

president	president (en)	[prɛsi'dɛnt] .
Secretary (minister)	minister (en)	[mi'nistər]
prime minister	statsminister (en)	['stats mi'nistər]
senator	senator (en)	[se'natʊr]

diplomat	diplomat (en)	[diplʲo'mat]
consul	konsul (en)	['kɔnsulʲ]
ambassador	ambassadör (en)	[ambasa'døːr]
counsilor (diplomatic officer)	rådgivare (en)	['roːdjivarə]

| official, functionary (civil servant) | tjänsteman (en) | ['ɕɛnstəˌman] |

prefect	prefekt (en)	[pre'fɛkt]
mayor	borgmästare (en)	['bɔrjˌmɛstarə]
judge	domare (en)	['dʊmarə]
prosecutor (e.g., district attorney)	åklagare (en)	[ɔ'klʲagarə]

missionary	missionär (en)	[miɲʊ'næ:r]
monk	munk (en)	['muŋk]
abbot	abbé (en)	[a'be:]
rabbi	rabbin (en)	[ra'bin]

vizier	vesir (en)	[ve'syr]
shah	schah (en)	['ʃa:]
sheikh	schejk (en)	['ʃɛjk]

128. Agricultural professions

beekeeper	biodlare (en)	['bi‚ʊdlʲarə]
herder, shepherd	herde (en)	['hɛ:də]
agronomist	agronom (en)	[agrʊ'nɔm]
cattle breeder	boskapsskötare (en)	['bʊskaps‚ɧø:tarə]
veterinarian	veterinär (en)	[vetəri'næ:r]

farmer	lantbrukare, bonde (en)	['lʲant‚brʉ:karə], ['bʊndə]
winemaker	vinodlare (en)	['vin‚ʊdlʲarə]
zoologist	zoolog (en)	[sʊɔ'lʲɔg]
cowboy	cowboy (en)	['kaʊ‚bɔj]

129. Art professions

| actor | skådespelare (en) | ['sko:də‚spelʲarə] |
| actress | skådespelerska (en) | ['sko:də‚spelʲeʂka] |

| singer (masc.) | sångare (en) | ['sɔŋarə] |
| singer (fem.) | sångerska (en) | ['sɔŋɛʂka] |

| dancer (masc.) | dansör (en) | [dan'sø:r] |
| dancer (fem.) | dansös (en) | [dan'sø:s] |

| performer (masc.) | skådespelare (en) | ['sko:də‚spelʲarə] |
| performer (fem.) | skådespelerska (en) | ['sko:də‚spelʲeʂka] |

musician	musiker (en)	['mʉsikər]
pianist	pianist (en)	[pia'nist]
guitar player	gitarrspelare (en)	[ji'tar‚spelʲarə]

conductor (orchestra ~)	dirigent (en)	[diri'ɧɛnt]
composer	komponist (en)	[kɔmpo'nist]
impresario	impressario (en)	[imprɛ'sariʊ]

film director	regissör (en)	[reɧi'sø:r]
producer	producent (en)	[prɔdʉ'sɛnt]
scriptwriter	manusförfattare (en)	['manus‚før'fatarə]
critic	kritiker (en)	['kritikər]

writer	författare (en)	[før'fatarə]
poet	poet (en)	[pʊ'et]
sculptor	skulptör (en)	[skɵlʲp'tøːr]
artist (painter)	konstnär (en)	['kɔnstnæːr]

juggler	jonglör (en)	[jɔng'lʲøːr]
clown	clown (en)	['klʲawn]
acrobat	akrobat (en)	[akrʊ'bat]
magician	trollkonstnär (en)	['trɔlʲˌkɔnstnæːr]

130. Various professions

doctor	läkare (en)	['lʲɛːkarə]
nurse	sjuksköterska (en)	['fʉ:kˌɦøːtɛʂka]
psychiatrist	psykiater (en)	[syki'atər]
dentist	tandläkare (en)	['tandˌlʲɛːkarə]
surgeon	kirurg (en)	[ɕi'rɵrg]

astronaut	astronaut (en)	[astrʊ'naʊt]
astronomer	astronom (en)	[astrʊ'nɔm]

driver (of taxi, etc.)	förare (en)	['føːrarə]
engineer (train driver)	lokförare (en)	['lʲʊkˌføːrarə]
mechanic	mekaniker (en)	[me'kanikər]

miner	gruvarbetare (en)	['grɵːvˌarbetarə]
worker	arbetare (en)	['arˌbetarə]
locksmith	låssmed (en)	['lʲɔsˌsmed]
joiner (carpenter)	snickare (en)	['snikarə]
turner (lathe machine operator)	svarvare (en)	['svarvarə]
construction worker	byggarbetare (en)	['bʏgˌar'betarə]
welder	svetsare (en)	['svɛtsarə]

professor (title)	professor (en)	[prɔ'fɛsʊr]
architect	arkitekt (en)	[arki'tɛkt]
historian	historiker (en)	[hi'stʊrikər]
scientist	vetenskapsman (en)	['vetənskapsˌman]
physicist	fysiker (en)	['fysikər]
chemist (scientist)	kemist (en)	[ɕe'mist]

archeologist	arkeolog (en)	[ˌarkeʊ'lʲɔg]
geologist	geolog (en)	[jeʊ'lʲɔg]
researcher (scientist)	forskare (en)	['fɔːʂkarə]

babysitter	barnflicka (en)	['baːɳˌflika]
teacher, educator	pedagog (en)	[peda'gɔg]

editor	redaktör (en)	[redak'tøːr]
editor-in-chief	chefredaktör (en)	['ɦefˌredak'tøːr]

| correspondent | korrespondent (en) | [kɔrɛspɔn'dɛnt] |
| typist (fem.) | maskinskriverska (en) | [ma'ɧiːn 'skrivɛʂka] |

designer	designer (en)	[de'sajnər]
computer expert	dataexpert (en)	['data ɛks'pɛːt]
programmer	programmerare (en)	[prɔgra'merarə]
engineer (designer)	ingenjör (en)	[inɧə'njøːr]

sailor	sjöman (en)	['ɧøː,man]
seaman	matros (en)	[ma'trʊs]
rescuer	räddare (en)	['rɛdarə]

fireman	brandman (en)	['brand,man]
police officer	polis (en)	[pʊ'lis]
watchman	nattvakt, väktare (en)	['nat,vakt], ['vɛktarə]
detective	detektiv (en)	[detɛk'tiv]

customs officer	tulltjänsteman (en)	['tulʲ 'ɕɛnstə,man]
bodyguard	livvakt (en)	['liːv,vakt]
prison guard	fångvaktare (en)	['fɔɳ,vaktarə]
inspector	inspektör (en)	[inspɛk'tøːr]

sportsman	idrottsman (en)	['idrɔts,man]
trainer, coach	tränare (en)	['trɛːnarə]
butcher	slaktare (en)	['slʲaktarə]
cobbler (shoe repairer)	skomakare (en)	['skʊ,makarə]
merchant	handelsman (en)	['handəlʲs,man]
loader (person)	lastare (en)	['lʲastarə]

| fashion designer | modedesigner (en) | ['mʊdə de'sajnər] |
| model (fem.) | modell, mannekäng (en) | [mʊ'dɛlʲ], ['manekɛŋ] |

131. Occupations. Social status

| schoolboy | skolbarn (ett) | ['skʊlʲ,baːɳ] |
| student (college ~) | student (en) | [stu'dɛnt] |

philosopher	filosof (en)	[filʲɔ'sɔf]
economist	ekonom (en)	[ɛkʊ'nɔm]
inventor	uppfinnare (en)	['up,finarə]

unemployed (n)	arbetslös (en)	['arbets,lʲøːs]
retiree	pensionär (en)	[panɧʊ'næːr]
spy, secret agent	spion (en)	[spi'ʊn]

prisoner	fånge (en)	['fɔŋə]
striker	strejkande (en)	['strɛjkandə]
bureaucrat	byråkrat (en)	['byrɔ,krat]
traveler (globetrotter)	resenär (en)	[rese'næːr]
gay, homosexual (n)	homosexuell (en)	['hɔmɔsɛksu,ɛlʲ]

hacker	hackare (en)	['hakarə]
hippie	hippie (en)	['hipi]
bandit	bandit (en)	[ban'dit]
hit man, killer	legomördare (en)	['lʲegʊˌmøːdarə]
drug addict	narkoman (en)	[narkʊ'man]
drug dealer	droglangare (en)	['drʊgˌlʲaɳarə]
prostitute (fem.)	prostituerad (en)	[prɔstitɵ'ɛrad]
pimp	hallik (en)	['halik]

sorcerer	trollkarl (en)	['trɔlʲˌkar]
sorceress (evil ~)	trollkvinna (en)	['trɔlʲˌkvina]
pirate	pirat, sjörövare (en)	[pi'rat], ['ɧøːˌrøːvarə]
slave	slav (en)	['slʲav]
samurai	samuraj (en)	[samu'raj]
savage (primitive)	vilde (en)	['vilʲdə]

Sports

132. Kinds of sports. Sportspersons

sportsman	**idrottsman (en)**	['idrɔts̩man]
kind of sports	**idrottsgren (en)**	['idrɔts̩gren]
basketball	**basket (en)**	['basket]
basketball player	**basketspelare (en)**	['basketˌspelʲarə]
baseball	**baseboll (en)**	['bɛjsbɔlʲ]
baseball player	**basebollspelare (en)**	['bɛjsbɔlʲˌspelʲarə]
soccer	**fotboll (en)**	['futbɔlʲ]
soccer player	**fotbollsspelare (en)**	['futbɔlʲs 'spelʲarə]
goalkeeper	**målvakt (en)**	['mɔːlʲˌvakt]
hockey	**ishockey (en)**	['isˌhɔki]
hockey player	**ishockeyspelare (en)**	['isˌhɔki 'spelʲarə]
volleyball	**volleyboll (en)**	['vɔliˌbɔlʲ]
volleyball player	**volleybollspelare (en)**	['vɔlibɔlʲ 'spelʲarə]
boxing	**boxning (en)**	['bʊksniŋ]
boxer	**boxare (en)**	['bʊksarə]
wrestling	**brottning (en)**	['brɔtniŋ]
wrestler	**brottare (en)**	['brɔtarə]
karate	**karate (en)**	[ka'ratə]
karate fighter	**karateutövare (en)**	[ka'ratəˌʉ'tøːvarə]
judo	**judo (en)**	['jʉdɔ]
judo athlete	**judobrottare (en)**	['jʉdɔˌbrɔtarə]
tennis	**tennis (en)**	['tɛnis]
tennis player	**tennisspelare (en)**	['tɛnisˌspelʲarə]
swimming	**simning (en)**	['simniŋ]
swimmer	**simmare (en)**	['simarə]
fencing	**fäktning (en)**	['fɛktniŋ]
fencer	**fäktare (en)**	['fɛktarə]
chess	**schack (ett)**	['ʃak]
chess player	**schackspelare (en)**	['ʃakˌspelʲarə]

| alpinism | alpinism (en) | ['alˈpiˌnizm] |
| alpinist | alpinist (en) | ['alˈpiˌnist] |

| running | löpning (en) | ['lˈœpniŋ] |
| runner | löpare (en) | ['lˈøːparə] |

| athletics | friidrott (en) | ['fri: 'iˌdrɔt] |
| athlete | atlet (en) | [at'lˈet] |

| horseback riding | ridsport (en) | ['ridˌspɔ:t] |
| horse rider | ryttare (en) | ['rʏtarə] |

figure skating	konståkning (en)	['kɔnˌstoːkniŋ]
figure skater (masc.)	konståkare (en)	['kɔnˌstoːkarə]
figure skater (fem.)	konståkerska (en)	['kɔnˌstoːkɛşka]

powerlifting	tyngdlyftning (en)	['tʏŋdˌlˈyftniŋ]
powerlifter	tyngdlyftare (en)	['tʏŋdˌlˈyftarə]
car racing	biltävling (en)	['bilˈˌtɛvliŋ]
racing driver	racerförare (en)	['rejsˌføːrarə]

| cycling | cykelsport (en) | ['sykəlˈˌspɔ:t] |
| cyclist | cyklist (en) | [sʏk'list] |

broad jump	längdhopp (ett)	['lˈɛŋdˌhɔp]
pole vault	stavhopp (ett)	['stavˌhɔp]
jumper	hoppare (en)	['hɔparə]

133. Kinds of sports. Miscellaneous

football	amerikansk fotboll (en)	[ameri'kansk 'fʊtbɔlˈ]
badminton	badminton (en)	['bɛdmintɔn]
biathlon	skidskytte (ett)	['ɧidˌɧʏtə]
billiards	biljard (en)	[bi'ljaːd̦]

bobsled	bobsleigh (en)	[bɔb'slˈej]
bodybuilding	kroppsbyggande (ett)	['krɔpsˌbʏgandə]
water polo	vattenpolo (ett)	['vatənˌpʊlˈʊ]
handball	handboll (en)	['handˌbɔlˈ]
golf	golf (en)	['gɔlˈf]
rowing, crew	rodd (en)	['rʊd]
scuba diving	dykning (en)	['dʏkniŋ]
cross-country skiing	skidåkning (en)	['ɧi:ˌdɔkniŋ]
table tennis (ping-pong)	bordtennis (en)	['bʊ:d̦ˌtɛnis]

sailing	segelsport (en)	['segəlˈˌspɔ:t]
rally racing	rally (ett)	['ralˈi]
rugby	rugby (en)	['rugbi]
snowboarding	snowboard (en)	['snɔwˌbɔ:d̦]
archery	bågskjutning (ett)	['bo:gˌɧɵ:tniŋ]

134. Gym

| barbell | skivstång (en) | ['ʂiv̩ˌstɔŋ] |
| dumbbells | hantlar (pl) | ['hantˌlʲar] |

training machine	träningsmaskin (en)	['trɛːniŋs ma'ʂiːn]
exercise bicycle	motioncykel (en)	[mɔt'ɧʊnˌsykəlʲ]
treadmill	löpband (ett)	['lʲøːpˌband]

horizontal bar	räcke (ett)	['rɛkə]
parallel bars	barr (en)	['bar]
vault (vaulting horse)	hoppbord (en)	['hɔpˌbuːd̪]
mat (exercise ~)	matta (en)	['mata]

jump rope	hopprep (ett)	['hɔprep]
aerobics	aerobics	[aɛ'robiks]
yoga	yoga (en)	['joga]

135. Hockey

hockey	ishockey (en)	['isˌhɔki]
hockey player	ishockeyspelare (en)	['isˌhɔki 'spelʲarə]
to play hockey	att spela ishockey	[at 'spelʲa 'isˌhɔki]
ice	is (en)	['is]

puck	puck (en)	['puk]
hockey stick	klubba (en)	['klʉba]
ice skates	skridskor (pl)	['skriˌskʊr]

| board (ice hockey rink ~) | sarg (en) | ['sarj] |
| shot | skott (ett) | ['skɔt] |

goaltender	målvakt (en)	['moːlʲˌvakt]
goal (score)	mål (ett)	['moːlʲ]
to score a goal	att göra mål	[at 'jøːra ˌmoːlʲ]

period	period (en)	[peri'ʊd]
second period	andra period (en)	['andra peri'ʊd]
substitutes bench	reservbänk (en)	[re'sɛrvˌbɛŋk]

136. Soccer

soccer	fotboll (en)	['fʊtbɔlʲ]
soccer player	fotbollsspelare (en)	['fʊtbɔlʲs 'spelʲarə]
to play soccer	att spela fotboll	[at 'spelʲa 'fʊtbɔlʲ]
major league	högsta liga (en)	['hœgsta 'liga]
soccer club	fotbollsklubb (en)	['fʊtbɔlʲs ˌklʉb]

| coach | tränare (en) | ['trɛ:narə] |
| owner, proprietor | ägare (en) | ['ɛ:garə] |

team	lag (ett)	['lʲag]
team captain	lagkapten (en)	['lʲag kap'ten]
player	spelare (en)	['spelʲarə]
substitute	reserv, avbytare (en)	[re'sɛrv], ['av‚bytarə]

forward	anfallsspelare (en)	['anfalʲs‚spelʲarə]
center forward	central anfallsspelare (en)	[sɛn'tralʲ 'anfalʲs‚spelʲarə]
scorer	målgörare (en)	['mo:lʲ‚jø:rarə]
defender, back	försvarare, back (en)	[fœ:'ṣvararə], ['bak]
midfielder, halfback	halvback (en)	['halʲv‚bak]

match	match (en)	['matʃ]
to meet (vi, vt)	att mötas	[at 'mø:tas]
final	final (en)	[fi'nalʲ]
semi-final	semifinal (en)	['semifi‚nalʲ]
championship	mästerskap (ett)	['mɛstə‚ṣkap]

period, half	halvlek (en)	['halʲv‚lʲek]
first period	den första perioden	[dɛn 'fœ:ṣta peri'ʊdən]
half-time	halvtid (en)	['halʲv‚tid]

goal	mål (ett)	['mo:lʲ]
goalkeeper	målvakt (en)	['mo:lʲ‚vakt]
goalpost	stolpe (en)	['stɔlʲpə]
crossbar	ribba (en)	['riba]
net	nät (ett)	['nɛ:t]
to concede a goal	att släppa in ett mål	[at 'slʲepa in ɛt 'mo:lʲ]

ball	boll (en)	['bɔlʲ]
pass	passning (en)	['pasniŋ]
kick	spark (ett)	['spark]
to kick (~ the ball)	att sparka	[at 'sparka]
free kick (direct ~)	frispark (en)	['fri‚spark]
corner kick	hörna (en)	['hø:ṇa]

attack	angrepp (ett)	['an‚grɛp]
counterattack	kontring, motattack (en)	['kɔntriŋ], ['mot a'tak]
combination	kombination (en)	[kɔmbina'ɧʊn]

referee	domare (en)	['dʊmarə]
to blow the whistle	att blåsa i visselpipan	[at 'blʲo:sa i 'visəlʲ‚pipan]
whistle (sound)	vissling (en)	['visliŋ]
foul, misconduct	regelbrott (ett)	['regəlʲ‚brɔt]
to commit a foul	att begå en förseelse	[at be'go en fœ:'ṣeəlʲsə]
to send off	att utvisa	[at 'ʉt‚visa]

| yellow card | gult kort (ett) | ['gʉlʲt 'kɔ:t] |
| red card | rött kort (ett) | ['rœt 'kɔ:t] |

137

| disqualification | diskvalificering (en) | [diskvalifi'seriŋ] |
| to disqualify (vt) | att diskvalificera | [at diskvalifi'sera] |

penalty kick	straffspark (en)	['straf‚spark]
wall	mur (en)	['mʉːr]
to score (vi, vt)	att göra mål	[at 'jøːra ‚moːlʲ]
goal (score)	mål (ett)	['moːlʲ]
to score a goal	att göra mål	[at 'jøːra ‚moːlʲ]

substitution	byte (ett)	['bytə]
to replace (a player)	att byta ut	[at 'byta ʉt]
rules	regler (pl)	['rɛglʲər]
tactics	taktik (en)	[tak'tik]

stadium	stadion (ett)	['stadiʊn]
stand (bleachers)	läktare (en)	['lʲɛktarə]
fan, supporter	fan (ett)	['fan]
to shout (vi)	att skrika	[at 'skrika]

| scoreboard | resultattavla (en) | [resulʲ'tat‚tavlʲa] |
| score | resultat (ett) | [resulʲ'tat] |

| defeat | nederlag (ett) | ['nedə:‚lʲag] |
| to lose (not win) | att förlora | [at fœː'lʲʊra] |

| tie | oavgjort (ett) | [ʊːav'jʊːt] |
| to tie (vi) | att spela oavgjort | [at 'spelʲa ʊːav'jʊːt] |

| victory | seger (en) | ['segər] |
| to win (vi, vt) | att vinna | [at 'vina] |

champion	mästare (en)	['mɛstarə]
best (adj)	bäst	['bɛst]
to congratulate (vt)	att gratulera	[at gratʉ'lʲera]

commentator	kommentator (en)	[kɔmɛn'tatʊr]
to commentate (vt)	att kommentera	[at kɔmɛn'tɛra]
broadcast	sändning (en)	['sɛndniŋ]

137. Alpine skiing

| skis | skidor (pl) | ['fjidʊr] |
| to ski (vi) | att åka skidor | [at 'oːka 'fjidʊr] |

| mountain-ski resort | skidort (en) | ['fjidoːt] |
| ski lift | skidlift (en) | ['fjid‚lift] |

ski poles	skidstavar (en)	['fjid‚staːvar]
slope	sluttning (en)	['slʉːtniŋ]
slalom	slalom (en)	['slʲalʲom]

138. Tennis. Golf

golf	golf (en)	['gɔlʲf]
golf club	golfklubb (en)	['gɔlʲf‚klʉb]
golfer	golfspelare (en)	['gɔlʲf‚spelʲarə]
hole	hål (ett)	['hoːlʲ]
club	klubba (en)	['klʉba]
golf trolley	golfvagn (en)	['gɔlʲf‚vagn]
tennis	tennis (en)	['tɛnis]
tennis court	tennisbana (en)	['tɛnis‚bana]
serve	serve (en)	['sɛrvə]
to serve (vt)	att serva	[at 'sɛrva]
racket	racket (en)	['raket]
net	nät (en)	['nɛːt]
ball	boll (en)	['bɔlʲ]

139. Chess

chess	schack (ett)	['ʃak]
chessmen	schackpjäser (pl)	['ʃak‚pjæːsər]
chess player	schackspelare (en)	['ʃak‚spelʲarə]
chessboard	schackbräde (ett)	['ʃak‚brɛːdə]
chessman	schackpjäs (en)	['ʃak‚pjæːs]
White (white pieces)	vita pjäser (pl)	['vita ‚pjæːsər]
Black (black pieces)	svarta pjäser (pl)	['svaːʈa 'pjæːsər]
pawn	bonde (en)	['bʉndə]
bishop	löpare (en)	['lʲøːparə]
knight	springare (en)	['spriŋarə]
rook	torn (ett)	['tʉːn]
queen	drottning, dam (en)	['drɔtniŋ], [dam]
king	kung (en)	['kuŋ]
move	drag (ett)	['drag]
to move (vi, vt)	att flytta	[at 'flʲyta]
to sacrifice (vt)	att offra	[at 'ɔfra]
castling	rockad (en)	[rʉ'kad]
check	schack (ett)	['ʃak]
checkmate	matt (en)	['mat]
chess tournament	schackturnering (en)	['ʃak tu:'ŋeriŋ]
Grand Master	stormästare (en)	['stʉr‚mɛstarə]
combination	kombination (en)	[kɔmbina'ʃʊn]
game (in chess)	parti (ett)	[pa:'ʈiː]
checkers	damspel (ett)	['dam‚spelʲ]

140. Boxing

boxing	boxning (en)	['bʊksniŋ]
fight (bout)	match (en)	['matʃ]
boxing match	boxningsmatch (en)	['bʊksniŋˌmatʃ]
round (in boxing)	rond (en)	['rɔnd]

| ring | ring (en) | ['riŋ] |
| gong | gong (en) | ['gɔŋ] |

punch	slag (ett)	['slʲag]
knockdown	knockdown (en)	['nɔkˌdawn]
knockout	knockout (en)	[nɔk'aʊt]
to knock out	att slå ut	[at 'slʲoː ʉt]

| boxing glove | boxhandske (en) | ['bʊksˌhanskə] |
| referee | domare (en) | ['dʊmarə] |

lightweight	lättvikt (en)	['lʲætˌvikt]
middleweight	mellanvikt (en)	['mɛlʲanˌvikt]
heavyweight	tungvikt (en)	['tuŋˌvikt]

141. Sports. Miscellaneous

Olympic Games	de olympiska spelen	[de ʊ'limpiska 'spelʲən]
winner	segrare (en)	['sɛgˌrarə]
to be winning	att vinna, att segra	[at 'vina], [at 'sɛgra]
to win (vi)	att vinna	[at 'vina]

| leader | ledare (en) | ['lʲedarə] |
| to lead (vi) | att leda | [at 'lʲeda] |

first place	förstaplats (en)	['fœːʂta plʲats]
second place	andraplats (en)	['andraˌplʲats]
third place	tredjeplats (en)	['trɛdjəˌplʲats]

medal	medalj (en)	[me'dalj]
trophy	trofé (en)	['trʊfeː]
prize cup (trophy)	pokal (en)	[pɔ'kalʲ]
prize (in game)	pris (ett)	['pris]
main prize	huvudpris (ett)	['hʉːvʉdˌpris]

| record | rekord (ett) | [re'kɔːd] |
| to set a record | att sätta rekord | [at 'sæta re'kɔːd] |

final	final (en)	[fi'nalʲ]
final (adj)	final-	[fi'nalʲ-]
champion	mästare (en)	['mɛstarə]
championship	mästerskap (ett)	['mɛstəˌskap]

stadium	stadion (ett)	['stadiʊn]
stand (bleachers)	läktare (en)	['lʲɛktarə]
fan, supporter	fan (ett)	['fan]
opponent, rival	motståndare (en)	['mʊtˌstɔndarə]

| start (start line) | start (en) | ['staːt] |
| finish line | mål (ett), mållinje (en) | ['moːlʲ], ['moːlʲˌlinjə] |

| defeat | nederlag (ett) | ['nedə:ˌlʲag] |
| to lose (not win) | att förlora | [at fœː'lʲʊra] |

referee	domare (en)	['dʊmarə]
jury (judges)	jury (en)	['jɵri]
score	resultat (ett)	[resulʲ'tat]
tie	oavgjort (ett)	[ʊːav'jʊːt]
to tie (vi)	att spela oavgjort	[at 'spelʲa ʊːav'jʊːt]
point	poäng (en)	[pʊ'ɛŋ]
result (final score)	resultat (ett)	[resulʲ'tat]

period	period (en)	[peri'ʊd]
half-time	halvtid (en)	['halʲvˌtid]
doping	dopning (en)	['dɔpniŋ]
to penalize (vt)	att straffa	[at 'strafa]
to disqualify (vt)	att diskvalificera	[at diskvalifi'sera]

apparatus	redskap (ett)	['rɛdˌskap]
javelin	spjut (ett)	['spjɵːt]
shot (metal ball)	kula (en)	['kɵːlʲa]
ball (snooker, etc.)	boll (en)	['bɔlʲ]

aim (target)	mål (ett)	['moːlʲ]
target	måltavla (en)	['moːlʲˌtavlʲa]
to shoot (vi)	att skjuta	[at 'ʃɵːta]
accurate (~ shot)	fullträff	['fulʲˌtrɛf]

trainer, coach	tränare (en)	['trɛːnarə]
to train (sb)	att träna	[at 'trɛːna]
to train (vi)	att träna	[at 'trɛːna]
training	träning (en)	['trɛːniŋ]

gym	idrottshall (en)	['idrɔtsˌhalʲ]
exercise (physical)	övning (en)	['øvniŋ]
warm-up (athlete ~)	uppvärmning (en)	['upˌværmniŋ]

Education

142. School

school	skola (en)	['skʊlʲa]
principal (headmaster)	rektor (en)	['rɛktʊr]
pupil (boy)	elev (en)	[ɛ'lʲev]
pupil (girl)	elev (en)	[ɛ'lʲev]
schoolboy	skolbarn (ett)	['skʊlʲˌbaːŋ]
schoolgirl	skolflicka (en)	['skʊlʲˌflika]
to teach (sb)	att undervisa	[at 'undəˌvisa]
to learn (language, etc.)	att lära sig	[at 'lʲæːra sɛj]
to learn by heart	att lära sig utantill	[at 'læːra sɛj 'ʉːtanˌtilʲ]
to learn (~ to count, etc.)	att lära sig	[at 'lʲæːra sɛj]
to be in school	att gå i skolan	[at 'goː i 'skʊlʲan]
to go to school	att gå till skolan	[at 'goː tilʲ 'skʊlʲan]
alphabet	alfabet (ett)	['alʲfabet]
subject (at school)	ämne (ett)	['ɛmnə]
classroom	klassrum (ett)	['klʲasˌruːm]
lesson	timme (en)	['timə]
recess	rast (en)	['rast]
school bell	skolklocka (en)	['skʊlʲˌklʲɔka]
school desk	skolbänk (en)	['skʊlʲˌbɛŋk]
chalkboard	tavla (en)	['tavlʲa]
grade	betyg (ett)	[be'tyg]
good grade	bra betyg (ett)	[bra be'tyg]
bad grade	dåligt betyg (ett)	['doːlit be'tyg]
to give a grade	att betygsätta	[at be'tygsæta]
mistake, error	fel (ett)	['felʲ]
to make mistakes	att göra misstag	[at 'jøːra 'mistag]
to correct (an error)	att rätta	[at 'ræta]
cheat sheet	fusklapp (en)	['fuskˌlʲap]
homework	läxor (pl)	['lʲɛːksʊr]
exercise (in education)	övning (en)	['øvniŋ]
to be present	att vara närvarande	[at 'vara 'næːrˌvarandə]
to be absent	att vara frånvarande	[at 'vara 'froːnˌvarandə]
to miss school	att missa skolan	[at 'misa 'skʊlʲan]

to punish (vt)	**att straffa**	[at 'strafa]
punishment	**straff (ett)**	['straf]
conduct (behavior)	**uppförande (ett)**	['upˌførandə]

report card	**betyg, omdöme (ett)**	[be'tyg], ['ɔmˌdø:mə]
pencil	**blyertspenna (en)**	['bliyɛ:tsˌpɛna]
eraser	**suddgummi (ett)**	['sudˌgumi]
chalk	**krita (en)**	['krita]
pencil case	**pennfodral (ett)**	['pɛnfʊdˌralʲ]

schoolbag	**skolväska (en)**	['skʊlʲˌvɛska]
pen	**penna (en)**	['pɛna]
school notebook	**övningsbok (en)**	['øvniŋsˌbʊk]
textbook	**lärobok (en)**	['lʲæ:rʊˌbʊk]
compasses	**passare (en)**	['pasarə]

to make technical drawings	**att rita**	[at 'rita]
technical drawing	**teknisk ritning (en)**	['tɛknisk 'ritniŋ]

poem	**dikt (en)**	['dikt]
by heart (adv)	**utantill**	['u:tanˌtilʲ]
to learn by heart	**att lära sig utantill**	[at 'lʲæ:ra sɛj 'ʉ:tanˌtilʲ]

school vacation	**skollov (ett)**	['skʊlˌlʲɔv]
to be on vacation	**att ha lov**	[at ha 'lʲɔv]
to spend one's vacation	**att tillbringa skollovet**	[at 'tilʲˌbriŋa 'skʊˌlʲɔvet]

test (written math ~)	**prov (ett)**	['prʊv]
essay (composition)	**uppsats (en)**	['upsats]
dictation	**diktamen (en)**	[dik'tamən]
exam (examination)	**examen (en)**	[ɛk'samən]
to take an exam	**att ta en examen**	[at ta en ɛk'samən]
experiment (e.g., chemistry ~)	**försök (ett)**	['fœːˌʂøːk]

143. College. University

academy	**akademi (en)**	[akade'mi:]
university	**universitet (ett)**	[univɛʂi'tet]
faculty (e.g., ~ of Medicine)	**fakultet (en)**	[fakulʲ'tet]

student (masc.)	**student (en)**	[stu'dɛnt]
student (fem.)	**kvinnlig student (en)**	['kvinlig stu'dɛnt]
lecturer (teacher)	**lärare, föreläsare (en)**	['lʲæ:rarə], ['førəˌlʲɛ:sarə]

lecture hall, room	**föreläsningssal (en)**	[førə'lʲɛsniŋˌsalʲ]
graduate	**alumn (en)**	[a'lʉmn]
diploma	**diplom (ett)**	[dip'lʲɔm]

143

dissertation	**avhandling (en)**	['avˌhandliŋ]
study (report)	**studie (en)**	['studiə]
laboratory	**laboratorium (ett)**	[lʲabora'tɔrium]

lecture	**föreläsning (en)**	['førəˌlʲɛsniŋ]
coursemate	**studiekompis (en)**	['studiəˌkɔmpis]
scholarship	**stipendium (ett)**	[sti'pɛndium]
academic degree	**akademisk grad (en)**	[aka'demisk grad]

144. Sciences. Disciplines

mathematics	**matematik (en)**	[matema'tik]
algebra	**algebra (en)**	['alʲgebra]
geometry	**geometri (en)**	[jeʊmə'tri:]

astronomy	**astronomi (en)**	[astrʊnɔ'mi:]
biology	**biologi (en)**	[biʊlʲɔ'gi:]
geography	**geografi (en)**	[jeʊgra'fi:]
geology	**geologi (en)**	[jeʊlʲɔ'gi:]
history	**historia (en)**	[hi'stʊria]

medicine	**medicin (en)**	[medi'sin]
pedagogy	**pedagogik (en)**	[pedagɔ'gik]
law	**rätt (en)**	['ræt]

physics	**fysik (en)**	[fy'zik]
chemistry	**kemi (en)**	[ɕe'mi:]
philosophy	**filosofi (en)**	[filʲɔsɔ'fi:]
psychology	**psykologi (en)**	[sykʊlʲɔ'gi:]

145. Writing system. Orthography

grammar	**grammatik (en)**	[grama'tik]
vocabulary	**ordförråd (ett)**	['ʊːdfœːˌroːd]
phonetics	**fonetik (en)**	[fone'tik]

noun	**substantiv (ett)**	['substanˌtiv]
adjective	**adjektiv (ett)**	['adjɛkˌtiv]
verb	**verb (ett)**	['vɛrb]
adverb	**adverb (ett)**	[ad'vɛrb]

pronoun	**pronomen (ett)**	[prʊ'nʊmən]
interjection	**interjektion (en)**	[intɛrjɛk'fjʊn]
preposition	**preposition (en)**	[prepʊsi'fjʊn]

root	**rot (en)**	['rʊt]
ending	**ändelse (en)**	['ɛndəlʲsə]
prefix	**prefix (ett)**	[prɛ'fiks]

| syllable | stavelse (en) | ['stavəlˈsə] |
| suffix | suffix (ett) | [suˈfiːks] |

| stress mark | betoning (en) | [beˈtʊniŋ] |
| apostrophe | apostrof (en) | [apʊˈstrɔf] |

period, dot	punkt (en)	['puŋkt]
comma	komma (ett)	['kɔma]
semicolon	semikolon (ett)	['semikʊˌlˈɔn]
colon	kolon (ett)	[kʊˈlˈɔn]
ellipsis	tre punkter (pl)	[trɛ 'puŋktər]

| question mark | frågetecken (ett) | ['froːgəˌtɛkən] |
| exclamation point | utropstecken (ett) | ['ʉtrʊpsˌtɛkən] |

quotation marks	anföringstecken (pl)	[anˈfœriŋsˌtɛkən]
in quotation marks	inom anföringstecken	['inɔm anˈfœriŋsˌtɛkən]
parenthesis	parentes (en)	[parɛnˈtes]
in parenthesis	inom parentes	['inɔm parɛnˈtes]

hyphen	bindestreck (ett)	['bindəˌstrɛk]
dash	tankstreck (ett)	['taŋkˌstrɛk]
space (between words)	mellanrum (ett)	['mɛlˈanˌruːm]

| letter | bokstav (en) | ['bʊkstav] |
| capital letter | stor bokstav (en) | ['stʊr 'bʊkstav] |

| vowel (n) | vokal (en) | [vʊˈkalˈ] |
| consonant (n) | konsonant (en) | [kɔnsɔˈnant] |

sentence	mening, sats (en)	['meniŋ], ['sats]
subject	subjekt (ett)	[subˈjɛːkt]
predicate	predikat (ett)	[prediˈkat]

line	rad (en)	['rad]
on a new line	på ny rad	[pɔ ny 'rad]
paragraph	stycke (ett)	['stʏkə]

word	ord (ett)	['ʊːd]
group of words	ordkombination (en)	['ʊːdˌkɔmbinaˈɧʊn]
expression	uttryck (ett)	['ʉtˌtrʏk]
synonym	synonym (en)	[synɔˈnym]
antonym	antonym, motsats (en)	[antɔˈnʏm], ['mʊtsats]

rule	regel (en)	['regəlˈ]
exception	undantag (ett)	['undanˌtaːg]
correct (adj)	riktig	['riktig]

conjugation	böjning (en)	['bœjniŋ]
declension	böjning (en)	['bœjniŋ]
nominal case	kasus (ett)	['kasus]
question	fråga (en)	['froːga]

| to underline (vt) | att understryka | [at 'undə‚stryka] |
| dotted line | pricklinje (en) | ['prik‚linjə] |

146. Foreign languages

language	språk (ett)	['spro:k]
foreign (adj)	främmande	['frɛmandə]
foreign language	främmande språk (ett)	['frɛmandə spro:k]
to study (vt)	att studera	[at stu'dera]
to learn (language, etc.)	att lära sig	[at 'lʲæ:ra sɛj]

to read (vi, vt)	att läsa	[at 'lʲɛ:sa]
to speak (vi, vt)	att tala	[at 'talʲa]
to understand (vt)	att förstå	[at fœ:'ʂto:]
to write (vt)	att skriva	[at 'skriva]

fast (adv)	snabbt	['snabt]
slowly (adv)	långsamt	['lʲɔŋ‚samt]
fluently (adv)	flytande	['flʲytandə]

rules	regler (pl)	['rɛglʲər]
grammar	grammatik (en)	[grama'tik]
vocabulary	ordförråd (ett)	['ʊːdfœ:‚ro:d]
phonetics	fonetik (en)	[fɔne'tik]

textbook	lärobok (en)	['lʲæ:rʊ‚bʊk]
dictionary	ordbok (en)	['ʊːd‚bʊk]
teach-yourself book	självinstruerande lärobok (en)	['ɧɛlʲv instrʉ'ɛrandə 'lʲæ:rʊ‚bʊk]
phrasebook	parlör (en)	[pa:'lʲø:r]

cassette, tape	kassett (en)	[ka'sɛt]
videotape	videokassett (en)	['videʊ ka'sɛt]
CD, compact disc	cd-skiva (en)	['sede ‚ɧiva]
DVD	dvd (en)	[deve'de:]

alphabet	alfabet (ett)	['alʲfabet]
to spell (vt)	att stava	[at 'stava]
pronunciation	uttal (ett)	['ʉt‚talʲ]

accent	brytning (en)	['brʏtniŋ]
with an accent	med brytning	[me 'brʏtniŋ]
without an accent	utan brytning	['ʉtan 'brʏtniŋ]

| word | ord (ett) | ['ʊːd] |
| meaning | betydelse (en) | [be'tydəlʲsə] |

course (e.g., a French ~)	kurs (en)	['ku:ʂ]
to sign up	att anmäla sig	[at 'an‚mɛ:lʲa sɛj]
teacher	lärare (en)	['lʲæ:rarə]

translation (process)	översättning (en)	['øːvəˌsætniŋ]
translation (text, etc.)	översättning (en)	['øːvəˌsætniŋ]
translator	översättare (en)	['øːvəˌsætərə]
interpreter	tolk (en)	['tolʲk]

polyglot	polyglott (en)	[pulʲy'glʲɔt]
memory	minne (ett)	['minə]

147. Fairy tale characters

Santa Claus	Jultomten	['julʲˌtɔmtən]
Cinderella	Askungen	['askuŋən]
mermaid	havsfru (en)	['havsˌfrʉː]
Neptune	Neptunus	[nep'tʉnus]

magician, wizard	trollkarl (en)	['trɔlʲˌkar]
fairy	fe (en)	['fe]
magic (adj)	troll-, magisk	['trɔlʲ-], ['magisk]
magic wand	trollspö (ett)	['trɔlʲˌspøː]

fairy tale	saga (en)	['saga]
miracle	mirakel (ett)	[mi'rakəlʲ]
dwarf	gnom, dvärg (en)	[gnʊm], ['dværj]
to turn into ...	att förvandlas till ...	[at før'vandlas tilʲ ...]

ghost	spöke (ett)	['spøːkə]
phantom	fantom, vålnad (ett)	[fan'toːm], ['vɔlʲnad]
monster	monster (ett)	['mɔnstər]
dragon	drake (en)	['drakə]
giant	jätte (en)	['jætə]

148. Zodiac Signs

Aries	Väduren	['vɛdʉrən]
Taurus	Oxen	['uksən]
Gemini	Tvillingarna	['tviliŋaːŋa]
Cancer	Kräftan	['krɛftan]
Leo	Lejonet	['lʲejɔnet]
Virgo	Jungfrun	['juŋfrʉn]

Libra	Vågen	['voːgən]
Scorpio	Skorpionen	[skɔrpi'unən]
Sagittarius	Skytten	['ʄytən]
Capricorn	Stenbocken	['stenˌbukən]
Aquarius	Vattumannen	['vatʉˌmanən]
Pisces	Fiskarna	['fiskaːŋa]
character	karaktär (en)	[karak'tæːr]
character traits	karaktärsdrag (ett)	[karak'tæːʂˌdrag]

behavior	**uppförande (ett)**	['up͵førandə]
to tell fortunes	**att spå**	[at spɔ]
fortune-teller	**spåkvinna (en)**	['spoː͵kvina]
horoscope	**horoskop (ett)**	[hʊrʊ'skɔp]

Arts

149. Theater

theater	teater (en)	[te'atər]
opera	opera (en)	['ʊpera]
operetta	operett (en)	[ʊpe'rɛt]
ballet	balett (en)	[ba'lʲet]
theater poster	affisch (en)	[a'fi:ʃ]
troupe	teatertrupp (en)	[te'atər‚trup]
(theatrical company)		
tour	turné (en)	[tur'ne:]
to be on tour	att vara på turné	[at 'vara pɔ tur'ne:]
to rehearse (vi, vt)	att repetera	[at repe'tera]
rehearsal	repetition (en)	[repeti'fʊn]
repertoire	repertoar (en)	[repɛːtʊ'aːr]
performance	föreställning (en)	['førə‚stɛlʲniŋ]
theatrical show	teaterstycke (ett)	[te'atər‚stʏkə]
play	skådespel (ett), pjäs (en)	['skoːdə‚spelʲ], [pjæːs]
ticket	biljett (en)	[bi'lʲet]
box office (ticket booth)	biljettkassa (en)	[bi'lʲet‚kasa]
lobby, foyer	lobby (en)	['lʲɔbi]
coat check (cloakroom)	garderob (en)	[gaːdə'rɔːb]
coat check tag	nummerbricka (en)	['numər‚brika]
binoculars	kikare (en)	['ɕikarə]
usher	platsanvisare (en)	['plʲats‚an'visarə]
orchestra seats	parkett (en)	[par'ket]
balcony	balkong (en)	[balʲ'kɔŋ]
dress circle	första raden (en)	['fœːʂta 'radən]
box	loge (en)	['lʲɔgə]
row	rad (en)	['rad]
seat	plats (en)	['plʲats]
audience	publik (en)	[pub'lik]
spectator	åskådare (en)	['ɔs‚koːdarə]
to clap (vi, vt)	att klappa	[at 'klʲapa]
applause	applåd (en)	[ap'lʲoːd]
ovation	bifall (ett)	['bi‚falʲ]
stage	scen (en)	['seːn]
curtain	ridå (en)	[ri'doː]
scenery	dekoration (en)	[dekɔra'fʊn]

backstage	kulisser (pl)	[kʉ'lisər]
scene (e.g., the last ~)	scen (en)	['se:n]
act	akt (en)	['akt]
intermission	mellanakt (en)	['mɛlʲanˌakt]

150. Cinema

| actor | skådespelare (en) | ['sko:dəˌspelʲarə] |
| actress | skådespelerska (en) | ['sko:dəˌspelʲeʂka] |

movies (industry)	filmindustri (en)	['filʲmˌindu'stri:]
movie	film (en)	['filʲm]
episode	del (en)	['delʲ]

detective movie	kriminalfilm (en)	[krimi'nalʲˌfilʲm]
action movie	actionfilm (en)	['ɛkʃənˌfilʲm]
adventure movie	äventyrsfilm (en)	['ɛ:vɛnˌtyʂ 'filʲm]
science fiction movie	science fiction film (en)	['sajəns ˌfikʃən 'filʲm]
horror movie	skräckfilm (en)	['skrɛkˌfilʲm]

comedy movie	komedi (en), lustspel (ett)	[kɔme'di:], [lʉ:stˌspel]
melodrama	melodram (en)	[melʲɔ'dram]
drama	drama (ett)	['drama]

fictional movie	spelfilm (en)	['spelʲˌfilʲm]
documentary	dokumentärfilm (en)	[dɔkumen'tæ:rˌfilʲm]
cartoon	tecknad film (en)	['tɛknad 'filʲm]
silent movies	stumfilm (en)	['stumˌfilʲm]

role (part)	roll (en)	['rɔlʲ]
leading role	huvudroll (en)	['hʉ:vʉdˌrɔlʲ]
to play (vi, vt)	att spela	[at 'spelʲa]

movie star	filmstjärna (en)	['filʲmˌɧæ:ɳa]
well-known (adj)	välkänd	[vɛlʲ'ɕɛnd]
famous (adj)	berömd	[be'rœmd]
popular (adj)	populär	[popʉ'lʲæ:r]

script (screenplay)	manus (ett)	['manus]
scriptwriter	manusförfattare (en)	['manusˌfør'fatarə]
movie director	regissör (en)	[reɧi'sø:r]
producer	producent (en)	[prɔdʉ'sɛnt]
assistant	assistent (en)	[asi'stɛnt]
cameraman	kameraman (en)	['kameraˌman]
stuntman	stuntman (en)	['stuntˌman]
double (stuntman)	ersättare (en)	[æ:'sætarə]

| to shoot a movie | att spela in en film | [at 'spelʲa in en 'filʲm] |
| audition, screen test | provspelning (en) | ['prʊvˌspɛlʲniŋ] |

shooting	inspelning (en)	['in,spɛlʲniŋ]
movie crew	filmteam (ett)	['filʲm,tim]
movie set	inspelningsplats (en)	['inspɛlʲniŋ,plʲats]
camera	filmkamera (en)	['filʲm,kamera]

movie theater	biograf (en)	[biʊ'graf]
screen (e.g., big ~)	filmduk (en)	['filʲm,dɵ:k]
to show a movie	att visa en film	[at 'visa en filʲm]

soundtrack	ljudspår (ett)	['jɵ:d,spo:r]
special effects	specialeffekter (pl)	[spesi'alʲ ɛ'fɛktər]
subtitles	undertexter (pl)	['undə,tɛkstər]
credits	eftertext (ett)	['ɛftə,tɛkst]
translation	översättning (en)	['ø:və,sætniŋ]

151. Painting

art	konst (en)	['kɔnst]
fine arts	de sköna konsterna	[de 'ʃø:na 'kɔnstɛ:ŋa]
art gallery	konstgalleri (ett)	['kɔnst galʲe'ri:]
art exhibition	konst utställning (en)	['kɔnst 'ɵt,stɛlʲniŋ]

painting (art)	måleri (ett)	[mo:lʲe'ri:]
graphic art	grafik (en)	[gra'fik]
abstract art	abstrakt konst (en)	[ab'strakt 'kɔnst]
impressionism	impressionism (en)	[imprɛʃʊ'nism]

picture (painting)	tavla (en)	['tavlʲa]
drawing	teckning (en)	['tɛkniŋ]
poster	poster, löpsedel (en)	['pɔstər], ['løp,sedəlʲ]

illustration (picture)	illustration (en)	[ilɵstra'ʃʊn]
miniature	miniatyr (en)	[minia'tyr]
copy (of painting, etc.)	kopia (en)	[kʊ'pia]
reproduction	reproduktion (en)	[rɛprɔduk'ʃʊn]

mosaic	mosaik (en)	[mʊsa'ik]
stained glass window	glasmålning (en)	['glʲas,mo:lʲniŋ]
fresco	fresk (en)	['frɛsk]
engraving	gravyr (en)	[gra'vyr]

bust (sculpture)	byst (en)	['bʏst]
sculpture	skulptur (en)	[skɵlʲp'tɵ:r]
statue	staty (en)	[sta'ty]
plaster of Paris	gips (en)	['jips]
plaster (as adj)	gips-	['jips-]

portrait	porträtt (en)	[pɔ:'ʈræt]
self-portrait	självporträtt (en)	['ɧɛlʲv,pɔ:'ʈræt]
landscape painting	landskapsmålning (en)	['lʲaŋ,skaps 'mo:lʲniŋ]

still life	**stilleben (ett)**	['stil‚lʲebən]
caricature	**karikatyr (en)**	[karika'tyr]
sketch	**skiss (en)**	['skis]
paint	**färg (en)**	['fæ:rj]
watercolor paint	**akvarell (en)**	[akva'rɛlʲ]
oil (paint)	**olja (en)**	['ɔlja]
pencil	**blyertspenna (en)**	['blʲyɛːts‚pɛna]
India ink	**tusch (en)**	['tu:ʃ]
charcoal	**kol (ett)**	['kɔlʲ]
to draw (vi, vt)	**att teckna**	[at 'tɛkna]
to paint (vi, vt)	**att måla**	[at 'mo:lʲa]
to pose (vi)	**att posera**	[at pʊ'sera]
artist's model (masc.)	**modell (en)**	[mʊ'dɛlʲ]
artist's model (fem.)	**modell (en)**	[mʊ'dɛlʲ]
artist (painter)	**konstnär (en)**	['kɔnstnæ:r]
work of art	**konstverk (ett)**	['kɔnst‚vɛrk]
masterpiece	**mästerverk (ett)**	['mɛstər‚vɛrk]
studio (artist's workroom)	**ateljé (en)**	[ate'ljeː]
canvas (cloth)	**kanvas, duk (en)**	['kanvas], [dʉ:k]
easel	**staffli (ett)**	[staf'li:]
palette	**palett (en)**	[pa'lʲet]
frame (picture ~, etc.)	**ram (en)**	['ram]
restoration	**restaurering (en)**	[rɛstɔ'reriŋ]
to restore (vt)	**att restaurera**	[at rɛstɔ'rera]

152. Literature & Poetry

literature	**litteratur (en)**	[litera'tʉ:r]
author (writer)	**författare (en)**	[før'fatarə]
pseudonym	**pseudonym (en)**	[sydɔ'nym]
book	**bok (en)**	['bʊk]
volume	**volym (en)**	[vɔ'lʲym]
table of contents	**innehållsförteckning (en)**	['inəhoːlʲs fœ:'tɛkniŋ]
page	**sida (en)**	['sida]
main character	**huvudperson (en)**	['hʉːvʉd‚pɛ'ʂʊn]
autograph	**autograf (en)**	[atɔ'graf]
short story	**novell (en)**	[nʊ'vɛlʲ]
story (novella)	**kortroman (en)**	['kɔ:t rʊ'man]
novel	**roman (en)**	[rʊ'man]
work (writing)	**verk (ett)**	['vɛrk]
fable	**fabel (en)**	['fabəlʲ]
detective novel	**kriminalroman (en)**	[krimi'nalʲ rʊ'man]

poem (verse)	dikt (en)	['dikt]
poetry	poesi (en)	[pue'si:]
poem (epic, ballad)	epos (ett)	['ɛpɔs]
poet	poet (en)	[pu'et]

fiction	skönlitteratur (en)	['fjø:n litera'tʉ:r]
science fiction	science fiction	['sajəns ˌfikʃən]
adventures	äventyr (pl)	['ɛ:vɛnˌtyr]
educational literature	undervisnings-litteratur (en)	['undəˌvisniŋ litera'tʉ:r]
children's literature	barnlitteratur (en)	['ba:nˌlitera'tʉ:r]

153. Circus

circus	cirkus (en)	['sirkʉs]
traveling circus	ambulerande cirkus (en)	['ambuˌlerandə 'sirkʉs]
program	program (ett)	[prɔ'gram]
performance	föreställning (en)	['førəˌstɛlʲniŋ]

| act (circus ~) | nummer (ett) | ['numər] |
| circus ring | arena (en) | [a'rena] |

pantomime (act)	pantomim (en)	[pantɔ'mim]
clown	clown (en)	['klʲawn]
acrobat	akrobat (en)	[akrʊ'bat]
acrobatics	akrobatik (en)	[akrʊba'tik]
gymnast	gymnast (en)	[jym'nast]
gymnastics	gymnastik (en)	[jymna'stik]
somersault	salto (en)	['salʲtʊ]

athlete (strongman)	atlet (en)	[at'lʲet]
tamer (e.g., lion ~)	djur-tämjare (en)	['jʉ:r ˌtɛmjarə]
rider (circus horse ~)	ryttare (en)	['rʏtarə]
assistant	assistent (en)	[asi'stɛnt]
stunt	trick (ett)	['trik]
magic trick	magitrick (ett)	[ma'giˌtrik]
conjurer, magician	trollkarl (en)	['trɔlʲˌkar]

juggler	jonglör (en)	[jong'lʲø:r]
to juggle (vi, vt)	att jonglera	[at jong'lʲera]
animal trainer	dressör (en)	[drɛ'sø:r]
animal training	dressyr (en)	[drɛ'syr]
to train (animals)	att dressera	[at drɛ'sera]

154. Music. Pop music

| music | musik (en) | [mʉ'si:k] |
| musician | musiker (en) | ['mʉsikər] |

musical instrument	musikinstrument (ett)	[mʉ'si:k instru'mɛnt]
to play ...	att spela ...	[at 'spelʲa ...]
guitar	gitarr (en)	[ji'tar]
violin	fiol, violin (en)	[fi'ʊlʲ], [viɔ'lin]
cello	cello (en)	['sɛlʲʊ]
double bass	kontrabas (en)	['kɔntraˌbas]
harp	harpa (en)	['harpa]
piano	piano (ett)	[pi'anʊ]
grand piano	flygel (en)	['flʲygəlʲ]
organ	orgel (en)	['ɔrjəlʲ]
wind instruments	blåsinstrumenter (pl)	['blʲo:sˌinstru'mɛntər]
oboe	oboe (en)	[ɔb'ɔ:]
saxophone	saxofon (en)	[saksʊ'fɔn]
clarinet	klarinett (en)	[klʲari'net]
flute	flöjt (en)	['flʲøjt]
trumpet	trumpet (en)	[trum'pet]
accordion	dragspel (ett)	['dragˌspelʲ]
drum	trumma (en)	['truma]
duo	duo (en)	['dʉ:ɔ]
trio	trio (en)	['tri:ɔ]
quartet	kvartett (en)	[kva'tɛt]
choir	kör (en)	['ɕø:r]
orchestra	orkester (en)	[ɔr'kɛstər]
pop music	popmusik (en)	['pɔp mʉ'si:k]
rock music	rockmusik (en)	['rɔk mʉ'si:k]
rock group	rockband (ett)	['rɔkˌband]
jazz	jazz (en)	['jas]
idol	idol (en)	[i'dɔlʲ]
admirer, fan	beundrare (en)	[be'undrarə]
concert	konsert (en)	[kɔn'sɛ:r]
symphony	symfoni (en)	[sʏmfʊ'ni:]
composition	komposition (en)	[kɔmpʊsi'ɧʊn]
to compose (write)	att komponera	[at kɔmpʊ'nera]
singing (n)	sång (en)	['sɔŋ]
song	sång (en)	['sɔŋ]
tune (melody)	melodi (en)	[melʲɔ'di:]
rhythm	rytm (en)	['rʏtm]
blues	blues (en)	['blʉs]
sheet music	noter (pl)	['nʊtər]
baton	taktpinne (en)	['taktˌpinə]
bow	stråke (en)	['stro:kə]
string	sträng (en)	['strɛŋ]
case (e.g., guitar ~)	fodral (ett)	[fʊd'ralʲ]

Rest. Entertainment. Travel

155. Trip. Travel

tourism, travel	turism (en)	[tu'rism]
tourist	turist (en)	[tu'rist]
trip, voyage	resa (en)	['resa]
adventure	äventyr (ett)	['ɛːvɛnˌtyr]
trip, journey	tripp (en)	['trip]
vacation	semester (en)	[se'mɛstər]
to be on vacation	att ha semester	[at ha se'mɛstər]
rest	uppehåll (ett), vila (en)	['upə'hoːlʲ], ['vilʲa]
train	tåg (ett)	['toːg]
by train	med tåg	[me 'toːg]
airplane	flygplan (ett)	['flʲygplʲan]
by airplane	med flygplan	[me 'flʲygplʲan]
by car	med bil	[me 'bilʲ]
by ship	med båt	[me 'boːt]
luggage	bagage (ett)	[ba'gaːʃ]
suitcase	resväska (en)	['rɛsˌvɛska]
luggage cart	bagagevagn (en)	[ba'gaːʃ ˌvagn]
passport	pass (ett)	['pas]
visa	visum (ett)	['viːsum]
ticket	biljett (en)	[bi'lʲet]
air ticket	flygbiljett (en)	['flʲyg biˌlʲet]
guidebook	reseguidebok (en)	['reseˌgajdbʊk]
map (tourist ~)	karta (en)	['kaːʈa]
area (rural ~)	område (ett)	['ɔmˌroːdə]
place, site	plats (en)	['plʲats]
exotica (n)	(det) exotiska	[ɛ'ksɔtiska]
exotic (adj)	exotisk	[ɛk'sɔtisk]
amazing (adj)	förunderlig	[fø'rundelig]
group	grupp (en)	['grup]
excursion, sightseeing tour	utflykt (en)	['ʉtˌflʲykt]
guide (person)	guide (en)	['gajd]

156. Hotel

hotel	hotell (ett)	[hʊ'tɛlʲ]
motel	motell (ett)	[mʊ'tɛlʲ]
three-star (~ hotel)	trestjärnigt	['tre͵ɧæːɲit]
five-star	femstjärnigt	[fɛm͵ɧæːɲit]
to stay (in a hotel, etc.)	att bo	[at 'bʊː]
room	rum (ett)	['ruːm]
single room	enkelrum (ett)	['ɛŋkəlʲ͵ruːm]
double room	dubbelrum (ett)	['dubəlʲ͵ruːm]
to book a room	att boka rum	[at 'bʊka 'ruːm]
half board	halvpension (en)	['halʲv͵panˈɧʊn]
full board	helpension (en)	['helʲ͵panˈɧʊn]
with bath	med badkar	[me 'bad͵kar]
with shower	med dusch	[me 'duʃ]
satellite television	satellit-TV (en)	[satɛ'liːt 'teve]
air-conditioner	luftkonditionerare (en)	['lʉft͵kɔndiɧʊ'nerarə]
towel	handduk (en)	['hand͵dʉːk]
key	nyckel (en)	['nʏkəlʲ]
administrator	administratör (en)	[administra'tør]
chambermaid	städerska (en)	['stɛːdɛʂka]
porter, bellboy	bärare (en)	['bæːrarə]
doorman	portier (en)	[pɔːˈtʲeː]
restaurant	restaurang (en)	[rɛstɔ'raŋ]
pub, bar	bar (en)	['bar]
breakfast	frukost (en)	['frʉːkɔst]
dinner	kvällsmat (en)	['kvɛlʲs͵mat]
buffet	buffet (en)	[bu'fet]
lobby	lobby (en)	['lʲɔbi]
elevator	hiss (en)	['his]
DO NOT DISTURB	STÖR EJ!	['støːr ɛj]
NO SMOKING	RÖKNING FÖRBJUDEN	['rœkniŋ før'bjʉːdən]

157. Books. Reading

book	bok (en)	['bʊk]
author	författare (en)	[før'fatarə]
writer	författare (en)	[før'fatarə]
to write (~ a book)	att skriva	[at 'skriva]
reader	läsare (en)	['lʲɛːsarə]
to read (vi, vt)	att läsa	[at 'lʲɛːsa]

reading (activity)	**läsning (en)**	['lʲɛsniŋ]
silently (to oneself)	**för sig själv**	[før ˌsɛj 'hɛlʲv]
aloud (adv)	**högt**	['hœgt]

to publish (vt)	**att publicera**	[at publi'sera]
publishing (process)	**publicering (en)**	[publi'seriŋ]
publisher	**förläggare (en)**	['fœːˌlʲɛgarə]
publishing house	**förlag (ett)**	[fœː'lʲag]

to come out (be released)	**att komma ut**	[at 'kɔma ʉt]
release (of a book)	**utgåva (en)**	['ʉtˌgoːva]
print run	**upplaga (en)**	['upˌlʲaga]

bookstore	**bokhandel (en)**	['bʊkˌhandəlʲ]
library	**bibliotek (ett)**	[bibliʊ'tek]

story (novella)	**kortroman (en)**	['kɔːʈ rʊ'man]
short story	**novell (en)**	[nʊ'vɛlʲ]
novel	**roman (en)**	[rʊ'man]
detective novel	**kriminalroman (en)**	[krimi'nalʲ rʊ'man]

memoirs	**memoarer (pl)**	[memʊ'arər]
legend	**legend (en)**	[lʲe'gɛnd]
myth	**myt (en)**	['myt]

poetry, poems	**dikter (pl)**	['diktər]
autobiography	**självbiografi (en)**	['hɛlʲv biʊgra'fiː]
selected works	**utvalda verk (pl)**	['ʉtˌvalʲda vɛrk]
science fiction	**science fiction**	['sajəns ˌfikʃən]

title	**titel (en)**	['titəlʲ]
introduction	**inledning (en)**	['inˌlʲedniŋ]
title page	**titelsida (en)**	['titəlʲˌsida]

chapter	**kapitel (ett)**	[ka'pitəlʲ]
extract	**utdrag (ett)**	['ʉtˌdrag]
episode	**episod (en)**	[ɛpi'sʊd]

plot (storyline)	**handling (en)**	['handliŋ]
contents	**innehåll (ett)**	['ineˌhoːlʲ]
table of contents	**innehållsförteckning (en)**	['ineho:lʲs fœː'ʈɛkniŋ]
main character	**huvudperson (en)**	['hʉːvʉdˌpɛ'ʂʊn]

volume	**volym (en)**	[vɔ'lʲym]
cover	**omslag (ett)**	['ɔmˌslʲag]
binding	**bokband (ett)**	['bʊkˌband]
bookmark	**bokmärke (ett)**	['bʊkˌmæːrkə]
page	**sida (en)**	['sida]
to page through	**att bläddra**	[at 'blʲɛdra]
margins	**marginaler (pl)**	[margi'nalʲər]
annotation	**annotering (ett)**	[anɔ'tɛriŋ]
(marginal note, etc.)		

footnote	anmärkning (en)	['an͵mæːrkniŋ]
text	text (en)	['tɛkst]
type, font	typsnitt (ett)	['typsnit]
misprint, typo	tryckfel (ett)	['trʏk͵felʲ]

translation	översättning (en)	['øːvə͵sætniŋ]
to translate (vt)	att översätta	[at 'øːvə͵sæta]
original (n)	original (ett)	[ɔrigiʹnalʲ]

famous (adj)	berömd	[beʹrœmd]
unknown (not famous)	okänd	[ʊːʹɕɛnd]
interesting (adj)	intressant	[intrɛʹsant]
bestseller	bestseller (en)	['bɛst͵sɛːlʲər]

dictionary	ordbok (en)	['ʊːd͵bʊk]
textbook	lärobok (en)	['lʲæːrʊ͵bʊk]
encyclopedia	encyklopedi (en)	[ɛnsʏklʲɔpeʹdiː]

158. Hunting. Fishing

hunting	jakt (en)	['jakt]
to hunt (vi, vt)	att jaga	[at 'jaga]
hunter	jägare (en)	['jɛːgarə]

to shoot (vi)	att skjuta	[at 'ɧʉːta]
rifle	gevär (ett)	[jeʹvæːr]
bullet (shell)	patron (en)	[paʹtrʊn]
shot (lead balls)	hagel (ett)	['hagəlʲ]

steel trap	sax (en)	['saks]
snare (for birds, etc.)	fälla (en)	['fɛlʲa]
to fall into the steel trap	att fångas i fälla	[at 'fɔŋas i 'fɛlʲa]
to lay a steel trap	att gillra en fälla	[at 'jilʲra en 'fɛlʲa]

poacher	tjuvskytt (en)	['ɕʉːv͵ɧʏt]
game (in hunting)	vilt (ett)	['vilʲt]
hound dog	jakthund (en)	['jakt͵hund]
safari	safari (en)	[saʹfari]
mounted animal	uppstoppat djur (ett)	['up͵stɔpat jʉːr]

fisherman, angler	fiskare (en)	['fiskarə]
fishing (angling)	fiske (ett)	['fiskə]
to fish (vi)	att fiska	[at 'fiska]

fishing rod	fiskespö (ett)	['fiskə͵spøː]
fishing line	fiskelina (en)	['fiskə͵lina]
hook	krok (en)	['krʊk]
float, bobber	flöte (ett)	['flʲøːtə]
bait	agn (en)	['agn]
to cast a line	att kasta ut	[at 'kasta ʉt]

to bite (ab. fish)	att nappa	[at 'napa]
catch (of fish)	fångst (en)	['fɔŋst]
ice-hole	hål (ett) i isen	['hoːlʲ i 'isən]

fishing net	nät (ett)	['nɛːt]
boat	båt (en)	['boːt]
to net (to fish with a net)	att fiska med nät	[at 'fiska me 'nɛːt]
to cast[throw] the net	att kasta nätet	[at 'kasta 'nɛːtət]
to haul the net in	att dra upp nätet	[at 'dra up 'nɛːtət]
to fall into the net	att bli fångad i nätet	[at bli foːŋad i 'nɛːtət]

whaler (person)	valfångare (en)	['valʲˌfɔŋarə]
whaleboat	valfångstbåt (ett)	['valʲfɔŋstˌboːt]
harpoon	harpun (en)	[har'puːn]

159. Games. Billiards

billiards	biljard (en)	[bi'ljaːɖ]
billiard room, hall	biljardsalong (en)	[bi'ljaːɖ sa'lɔŋ]
ball (snooker, etc.)	biljardboll (en)	[bi'ljaːɖˌbɔlʲ]

to pocket a ball	att sänka en boll	[at 'sɛŋka en 'bɔlʲ]
cue	kö (en)	['køː]
pocket	hål (ett)	['hoːlʲ]

160. Games. Playing cards

diamonds	ruter (pl)	['ruːtər]
spades	spader (pl)	['spadər]
hearts	hjärter	['jæːtər]
clubs	klöver (pl)	['klʲøːvər]

ace	äss (ett)	['ɛs]
king	kung (en)	['kuŋ]
queen	dam (en)	['dam]
jack, knave	knekt (en)	['knɛkt]

| playing card | kort (ett) | ['kɔːt] |
| cards | kort (pl) | ['kɔːt] |

| trump | trumf (en) | ['trumf] |
| deck of cards | kortlek (en) | ['kɔːtˌlʲek] |

point	poäng (en)	[pu'ɛŋ]
to deal (vi, vt)	att ge, att dela ut	[at jeː], [at 'delʲa ut]
to shuffle (cards)	att blanda	[at 'blʲanda]
lead, turn (n)	utspel (ett)	['utspelʲ]
cardsharp	falskspelare (en)	['falʲskˌspelʲarə]

161. Casino. Roulette

casino	kasino (ett)	[ka'sinʊ]
roulette (game)	roulett (ett)	[ru'lʲet]
bet	insats (en)	['in‚sats]
to place bets	att satsa	[at 'satsa]

red	röd (en)	['røːd]
black	svart (en)	['svaːt]
to bet on red	att satsa på rött	[at 'satsa pɔ 'rœt]
to bet on black	att satsa på svart	[at 'satsa pɔ 'svaːt]

croupier (dealer)	croupier (en)	[krʊ'pjeː]
to spin the wheel	att snurra hjulet	[at 'snura 'jʉːlʲet]
rules (of game)	spelregler (pl)	['spelʲ‚rɛglʲər]
chip	spelmark (en)	['spelʲmark]

| to win (vi, vt) | att vinna | [at 'vina] |
| win (winnings) | vinst (en) | ['vinst] |

| to lose (~ 100 dollars) | att förlora | [at fœː'lʲʊra] |
| loss (losses) | förlust (en) | [fœː'lʲʉːst] |

player	spelare (en)	['spelʲarə]
blackjack (card game)	blackjack (ett)	['blʲɛkʃɛk]
craps (dice game)	tärningsspel (ett)	['tæːɳiɲs‚spelʲ]
dice (a pair of ~)	tärningar (pl)	['tɛɳiɲar]
slot machine	spelautomat (en)	['spelʲ autʊ'mat]

162. Rest. Games. Miscellaneous

to stroll (vi, vt)	att promenera, att ströva	[at prʊme'nera], [at 'strøːva]
stroll (leisurely walk)	promenad (en)	[prʊme'nad]
car ride	utflykt, biltur (en)	['ʉtˌflʲykt], ['bilʲˌtʉr]
adventure	äventyr (ett)	['ɛːvɛnˌtyr]
picnic	picknick (en)	['piknik]

game (chess, etc.)	spel (ett)	['spelʲ]
player	spelare (en)	['spelʲarə]
game (one ~ of chess)	parti (ett)	[paː'ʈiː]

collector (e.g., philatelist)	samlare (en)	['samlʲarə]
to collect (stamps, etc.)	att samla	[at 'samlʲa]
collection	samling (en)	['samliŋ]

| crossword puzzle | korsord (ett) | ['kɔːʂˌʊːd] |
| racetrack (horse racing venue) | galoppbana (en) | [ga'lʲɔpˌbana] |

disco (discotheque)	diskotek (ett)	[disko'tek]
sauna	sauna (en)	['sauna]
lottery	lotteri (ett)	[lʲote'riː]

camping trip	campingresa (en)	['kampiŋˌresa]
camp	läger (ett)	['lʲɛːgər]
tent (for camping)	tält (ett)	['tɛlʲt]
compass	kompass (en)	[kɔm'pas]
camper	campare (en)	['kamparə]

to watch (movie, etc.)	att se på	[at 'seː pɔ]
viewer	tv-tittare (en)	['teveˌtitarə]
TV show (TV program)	tv-show (ett)	['teveʃɔw]

163. Photography

| camera (photo) | kamera (en) | ['kamera] |
| photo, picture | foto, fotografi (ett) | ['futʊ], [fʊtʊgra'fiː] |

photographer	fotograf (en)	[fʊtʊ'graf]
photo studio	fotoateljé (en)	['fʊtʊ atəˌljeː]
photo album	fotoalbum (ett)	['fʊtʊ ˌalʲbum]

camera lens	objektiv (ett)	[ɔbjɛk'tiv]
telephoto lens	teleobjektiv (ett)	['telʲe ɔbjɛk'tiv]
filter	filter (ett)	['filʲtər]
lens	lins (en)	['lins]

optics (high-quality ~)	optik (en)	[ɔp'tik]
diaphragm (aperture)	bländare (en)	['blʲɛndarə]
exposure time (shutter speed)	exponeringstid (en)	[ɛkspʊ'neriŋsˌtid]
viewfinder	sökare (en)	['søːkarə]

digital camera	digitalkamera (en)	[digi'talʲ ˌkamera]
tripod	stativ (ett)	[sta'tiv]
flash	blixt (en)	['blikst]

to photograph (vt)	att fotografera	[at fʊtʊgra'fera]
to take pictures	att ta bilder	[at ta 'bilʲdər]
to have one's picture taken	att bli fotograferad	[at bli fʊtʊgra'ferad]

focus	skärpa (en)	['ʃærpa]
to focus	att ställa in skärpan	[at 'stɛlʲa in 'ʃærpan]
sharp, in focus (adj)	skarp	['skarp]
sharpness	skärpa (en)	['ʃærpa]

contrast	kontrast (en)	[kɔn'trast]
contrast (as adj)	kontrast-	[kɔn'trast-]
picture (photo)	bild (en)	['bilʲd]

161

negative (n)	negativ (ett)	['nega,tiv]
film (a roll of ~)	film (en)	['filʲm]
frame (still)	bild, kort (en)	['bilʲd], ['kɔ:t]
to print (photos)	att skriva ut	[at 'skriva ʉt]

164. Beach. Swimming

beach	badstrand (en)	['bad,strand]
sand	sand (en)	['sand]
deserted (beach)	öde	['ø:də]

suntan	solbränna (en)	['sʊlʲ,brɛna]
to get a tan	att sola sig	[at 'sʊlʲa: sɛj]
tan (adj)	solbränd	['sʊlʲ,brɛnd]
sunscreen	solkräm (en)	['sʊlʲ,krɛm]

bikini	bikini (en)	[bi'kini]
bathing suit	baddräkt (en)	['bad,drɛkt]
swim trunks	simbyxor (pl)	['sim,byksʊr]

swimming pool	simbassäng (en)	['simba,sɛŋ]
to swim (vi)	att simma	[at 'sima]
shower	dusch (en)	['duʃ]
to change (one's clothes)	att klä om sig	[at 'klʲɛ ɔm sɛj]
towel	handduk (en)	['hand,dʉ:k]

boat	båt (en)	['bo:t]
motorboat	motorbåt (en)	['mʊtʊr,bo:t]

water ski	vattenskidor (pl)	['vatən,ʃidʊr]
paddle boat	vattencykel (en)	['vatən,sykəlʲ]
surfing	surfing (en)	['su:rfiŋ]
surfer	surfare (en)	['su:rfarə]

scuba set	dykapparat (en)	['dyk,apa'rat]
flippers (swim fins)	simfenor (pl)	['sim,fœnʊr]
mask (diving ~)	mask (en)	['mask]
diver	dykare (en)	['dykarə]
to dive (vi)	att dyka	[at 'dyka]
underwater (adv)	under vatten	['undə,vatən]

beach umbrella	parasoll (en)	[para'solʲ]
sunbed (lounger)	liggstol (en)	['lig,stʊlʲ]
sunglasses	solglasögon (pl)	['sʊlʲglʲas,ø:gɔn]
air mattress	luftmadrass (en)	['lʉft,mad'ras]

to play (amuse oneself)	att leka	[at 'lʲeka]
to go for a swim	att bada	[at 'bada]
beach ball	boll (en)	['bɔlʲ]
to inflate (vt)	att blåsa upp	[at 'blʲo:sa up]

inflatable, air (adj)	uppblåsbar	['up,bl⁺oːsbar]
wave	våg (en)	['voːg]
buoy (line of ~s)	boj (en)	['bɔj]
to drown (ab. person)	att drunkna	[at 'drʉŋkna]

to save, to rescue	att rädda	[at 'rɛda]
life vest	räddningsväst (en)	['rɛdniŋ,vɛst]
to observe, to watch	att observera	[at ɔbsɛr'vera]
lifeguard	badvakt (en)	['bad,vakt]

TECHNICAL EQUIPMENT. TRANSPORTATION

Technical equipment

165. Computer

computer	dator (en)	['datʊr]
notebook, laptop	bärbar dator (en)	['bærbar 'datʊr]
to turn on	att slå på	[at 'slʲoː pɔ]
to turn off	att slå av	[at 'slʲoː 'av]
keyboard	tangentbord (ett)	[tan'jent‚bʊːd]
key	tangent (en)	[tan'jent]
mouse	mus (en)	['mʉːs]
mouse pad	musmatta (en)	['mʉːs‚mata]
button	knapp (en)	['knap]
cursor	markör (en)	[marˈkøːr]
monitor	monitor, bildskärm (en)	[mɔniˈtor], ['bilʲdʃæːrm]
screen	skärm (en)	['ʃæːrm]
hard disk	hårddisk (en)	['hoːɖ‚disk]
hard disk capacity	hårddisk kapacitet (en)	['hoːɖ‚disk kapasiˈtet]
memory	minne (ett)	['minə]
random access memory	operativminne (ett)	[ɔperaˈtiv‚minə]
file	fil (en)	['filʲ]
folder	mapp (en)	['map]
to open (vt)	att öppna	[at 'øpna]
to close (vt)	att stänga	[at 'stɛŋa]
to save (vt)	att bevara	[at beˈvara]
to delete (vt)	att ta bort, att radera	[at ta 'bɔːt], [at raˈdera]
to copy (vt)	att kopiera	[at kɔˈpjera]
to sort (vt)	att sortera	[at sɔːˈtera]
to transfer (copy)	att överföra	[at øːvəˌføra]
program	program (ett)	[prɔˈgram]
software	programvara (en)	[prɔˈgram‚vara]
programmer	programmerare (en)	[prɔgraˈmerarə]
to program (vt)	att programmera	[at prɔgraˈmera]
hacker	hackare (en)	['hakarə]
password	lösenord (ett)	['lʲøːsənˌʊːd]

| virus | virus (ett) | ['vi:rʉs] |
| to find, to detect | att upptäcka | [at 'ʉp̩tɛka] |

| byte | byte (ett) | ['bajt] |
| megabyte | megabyte (en) | ['mega̩bajt] |

| data | data (pl) | ['data] |
| database | databas (en) | ['data̩bas] |

cable (USB, etc.)	kabel (en)	['kabəlʲ]
to disconnect (vt)	att koppla från	[at 'koplʲa frɔn]
to connect (sth to sth)	att koppla	[at 'koplʲa]

166. Internet. E-mail

Internet	Internet	['intɛ:̩nɛt]
browser	webbläsare (en)	['vɛb̩lʲɛ:sarə]
search engine	sökmotor (en)	['sø:k̩mʉtʊr]
provider	leverantör (en)	[lʲevəran'tø:r]

webmaster	webbmästare (en)	['vɛb̩mɛstarə]
website	webbplats (en)	['vɛb̩plʲats]
webpage	webbsida (en)	['vɛb̩sida]

| address (e-mail ~) | adress (en) | [a'drɛs] |
| address book | adressbok (en) | [a'drɛs̩bʊk] |

mailbox	brevlåda (en)	['brev̩lʲo:da]
mail	post (en)	['post]
full (adj)	full	['fulʲ]

message	meddelande (ett)	[me'delʲandə]
incoming messages	inkommande meddelanden	[in'komandə me'delʲandən]
outgoing messages	utgående meddelanden	['ʉt̩go:əndə me'delʲandən]
sender	avsändare (en)	['av̩sɛndarə]
to send (vt)	att skicka	[at 'ɧika]
sending (of mail)	avsändning (en)	['av̩sɛndniŋ]

| receiver | mottagare (en) | ['mot̩tagarə] |
| to receive (vt) | att ta emot | [at ta ɛmo:t] |

| correspondence | korrespondens (en) | [korɛspon'dɛns] |
| to correspond (vi) | att brevväxla | [at 'brev̩vɛkslʲa] |

file	fil (en)	['filʲ]
to download (vt)	att ladda ner	[at 'lʲada ner]
to create (vt)	att skapa	[at 'skapa]
to delete (vt)	att ta bort, att radera	[at ta 'bo:t], [at ra'dera]
deleted (adj)	borttagen	['bo:t̩ta:gən]

connection (ADSL, etc.)	förbindelse (en)	[før'bindəlˌsə]
speed	hastighet (en)	['hastigˌhet]
modem	modem (ett)	[mʊ'dem]
access	tillträde (ett)	· ['tilˌtrɛ:də]
port (e.g., input ~)	port (en)	['pɔ:t]

| connection (make a ~) | uppkoppling (en) | ['upˌkoplʲiŋ] |
| to connect to … (vi) | att ansluta | [at 'anˌslʉ:ta] |

| to select (vt) | att välja | [at 'vɛlja] |
| to search (for …) | att söka efter … | [at 'sø:ka ˌɛftər …] |

167. Electricity

electricity	elektricitet (en)	[ɛlʲektrisi'tet]
electric, electrical (adj)	elektrisk	[ɛ'lʲektrisk]
electric power plant	kraftverk (ett)	['kraftˌvɛrk]
energy	energi (en)	[ɛner'ɕi]
electric power	elkraft (en)	['ɛlʲˌkraft]

light bulb	glödlampa (en)	['glʲø:dˌlʲampa]
flashlight	ficklampa (en)	['fikˌlʲampa]
street light	gatlykta (en)	['gatˌlʲykta]

light	ljus (ett)	['jʉ:s]
to turn on	att slå på	[at 'slʲo: pɔ]
to turn off	att slå av	[at 'slʲo: 'av]
to turn off the light	att släcka ljuset	[at 'slʲɛka 'jʉ:sət]

to burn out (vi)	att brinna ut	[at 'brina ʉt]
short circuit	kortslutning (en)	['kɔ:tˌslʉ:tniŋ]
broken wire	kabelbrott (ett)	['kabəlʲˌbrɔt]
contact (electrical ~)	kontakt (en)	[kɔn'takt]

light switch	strömbrytare (en)	['strø:mˌbrytarə]
wall socket	eluttag (ett)	['ɛlʲˌʉ:'tag]
plug	stickkontakt (en)	['stik kɔn'takt]
extension cord	grenuttag (ett)	['grenʉ:ˌtag]

fuse	säkring (en)	['sɛkriŋ]
cable, wire	ledning (en)	['lʲedniŋ]
wiring	ledningsnät (ett)	['lʲedniŋsˌnɛ:t]

ampere	ampere (en)	[am'pɛr]
amperage	strömstyrka (en)	['strø:mˌstyrka]
volt	volt (en)	['vɔlʲt]
voltage	spänning (en)	['spɛniŋ]

| electrical device | elektrisk apparat (en) | [ɛ'lʲektrisk apa'rat] |
| indicator | indikator (en) | [indi'katʊr] |

electrician	elektriker (en)	[ɛ'lʲektrikər]
to solder (vt)	att löda	[at 'lʲøːda]
soldering iron	lödkolv (en)	['lʲøːd,kɔlʲv]
electric current	ström (en)	['strøːm]

168. Tools

tool, instrument	verktyg (ett)	['vɛrk,tyg]
tools	verktyg (pl)	['vɛrk,tyg]
equipment (factory ~)	utrustning (en)	['ʉ,trustniŋ]

hammer	hammare (en)	['hamarə]
screwdriver	skruvmejsel (en)	['skrʉːv,mɛjsəlʲ]
ax	yxa (en)	['yksa]

saw	såg (en)	['soːg]
to saw (vt)	att såga	[at 'soːga]
plane (tool)	hyvel (en)	['hyvəlʲ]
to plane (vt)	att hyvla	[at 'hʏvlʲa]
soldering iron	lödkolv (en)	['lʲøːd,kɔlʲv]
to solder (vt)	att löda	[at 'lʲøːda]

file (tool)	fil (en)	['filʲ]
carpenter pincers	kniptång (en)	['knip,tɔŋ]
lineman's pliers	flacktång (en)	['flʲak,tɔŋ]
chisel	stämjärn, huggjärn (ett)	['stɛm,jæːn], ['hug,jæːn]

drill bit	borr (en)	['bɔr]
electric drill	borrmaskin (en)	['bɔr,ma'ɧiːn]
to drill (vi, vt)	att borra	[at 'bɔra]

knife	kniv (en)	['kniv]
pocket knife	fickkniv (en)	['fik,kniv]
folding (~ knife)	fäll-	['fɛlʲ-]
blade	blad (ett)	['blʲad]

sharp (blade, etc.)	skarp	['skarp]
dull, blunt (adj)	slö	['slʲøː]
to get blunt (dull)	att bli slö	[at bli 'slʲøː]
to sharpen (vt)	att slipa, att vässa	[at 'slipa], [at 'vɛsa]

bolt	bult (en)	['bulʲt]
nut	mutter (en)	['mutər]
thread (of a screw)	gänga (en)	['jɛŋa]
wood screw	skruv (en)	['skrʉːv]

nail	spik (en)	['spik]
nailhead	spikhuvud (ett)	['spik,hʉːvʉd]
ruler (for measuring)	linjal (en)	[li'njalʲ]
tape measure	måttband (ett)	['mɔt,band]

| spirit level | vattenpass (ett) | ['vatən‚pas] |
| magnifying glass | lupp (en) | ['lʉp] |

measuring instrument	mätinstrument (ett)	['mɛ:t‚instru'mɛnt]
to measure (vt)	att mäta	[at 'mɛ:ta]
scale	skala (en)	['skalʲa]
(of thermometer, etc.)		
readings	avläsningar (pl)	['av‚lʲɛsniŋar]

| compressor | kompressor (en) | [kɔm'prɛsʊr] |
| microscope | mikroskop (ett) | [mikrʊ'skɔp] |

pump (e.g., water ~)	pump (en)	['pump]
robot	robot (en)	['rɔbɔt]
laser	laser (en)	['lʲasər]

wrench	skruvnyckel (en)	['skrʉ:v‚nʏkəlʲ]
adhesive tape	tejp (en)	['tɛjp]
glue	lim (ett)	['lim]

sandpaper	sandpapper (ett)	['sand‚papər]
spring	fjäder (en)	['fjɛ:dər]
magnet	magnet (en)	[mag'net]
gloves	handskar (pl)	['hanskar]

rope	rep (ett)	['rep]
cord	snör (ett)	['snø:r]
wire (e.g., telephone ~)	tråd, ledning (en)	['tro:d], ['lʲedniŋ]
cable	kabel (en)	['kabəlʲ]

sledgehammer	slägga (en)	['slʲɛga]
prybar	spett, järnspett (ett)	['spɛt], ['jæ:ɳ‚spɛt]
ladder	stege (en)	['stegə]
stepladder	trappstege (en)	['trap‚stegə]

to screw (tighten)	att skruva fast	[at 'skrʉ:va fast]
to unscrew (lid, filter, etc.)	att skruva av	[at 'skrʉ:va av]
to tighten	att klämma	[at 'klʲɛma]
(e.g., with a clamp)		
to glue, to stick	att klistra, att limma	[at 'klistra], [at 'lima]
to cut (vt)	att skära	[at 'ɧæ:ra]

malfunction (fault)	funktionsstörning (en)	[fuŋk'ɧʊns‚stø:ɳiŋ]
repair (mending)	reparation (en)	[repara'ɧʊn]
to repair, to fix (vt)	att reparera	[at repa'rera]
to adjust (machine, etc.)	att justera	[at ɧu'stera]

to check (to examine)	att checka	[at 'ɕɛka]
checking	kontroll (en)	[kɔn'trɔlʲ]
readings	avläsningar (pl)	['av‚lʲɛsniŋar]
reliable, solid (machine)	pålitlig	['po‚litlig]
complex (adj)	komplex	[kɔm'plʲeks]

to rust (get rusted)	**att rosta**	[at 'rɔsta]
rusty, rusted (adj)	**rostig**	['rɔstig]
rust	**rost (en)**	['rɔst]

Transportation

169. Airplane

airplane	flygplan (ett)	['flʲygplʲan]
air ticket	flygbiljett (en)	['flʲyg bi,lʲet]
airline	flygbolag (ett)	['flʲyg,bʊlʲag]
airport	flygplats (en)	['flʲyg,plʲats]
supersonic (adj)	överljuds-	['ø:vərˌjɵ:ds-]
captain	kapten (en)	[kap'ten]
crew	besättning (en)	[be'sætniŋ]
pilot	pilot (en)	[pi'lʲʊt]
flight attendant (fem.)	flygvärdinna (en)	['flʲyg,væ:dʲina]
navigator	styrman (en)	['styrˌman]
wings	vingar (pl)	['viŋar]
tail	stjärtfena (en)	['fjæ:t fe:na]
cockpit	cockpit, förarkabin (en)	['kɔkpit], ['fø:rarˌka'bin]
engine	motor (en)	['mʊtʊr]
undercarriage (landing gear)	landningsställ (ett)	['landniŋsˌstɛlʲ]
turbine	turbin (en)	[tur'bin]
propeller	propeller (en)	[prʊ'pɛlʲər]
black box	svart låda (en)	['sva:t ˈlʲo:da]
yoke (control column)	styrspak (ett)	['sty:ˌspak]
fuel	bränsle (ett)	['brɛnslʲe]
safety card	säkerhetsinstruktion (en)	['sɛ:kərhets instruk'fʊn]
oxygen mask	syremask (en)	['syreˌmask]
uniform	uniform (en)	[uni'fɔrm]
life vest	räddningsväst (en)	['rɛdniŋˌvɛst]
parachute	fallskärm (en)	['falʲˌfjæ:rm]
takeoff	start (en)	['sta:t]
to take off (vi)	att lyfta	[at 'lʲyfta]
runway	startbana (en)	['sta:tˌba:na]
visibility	siktbarhet (en)	['siktbarˌhet]
flight (act of flying)	flygning (en)	['flʲygniŋ]
altitude	höjd (en)	['hœjd]
air pocket	luftgrop (en)	['lʲuftˌgrʊp]
seat	plats (en)	['plʲats]
headphones	hörlurar (pl)	['hœ:ˌlʲɵ:rar]

folding tray (tray table)	utfällbart bord (ett)	['ʉtfɛlˌbart 'bʉːd]
airplane window	fönster (ett)	['fœnstər]
aisle	mittgång (en)	['mitˌɡɔŋ]

170. Train

train	tåg (ett)	['toːɡ]
commuter train	lokaltåg, pendeltåg (ett)	[lʰɔ'kalʲˌtoːɡ], ['pendəlˌtoːɡ],
express train	expresståg (ett)	[ɛks'prɛsˌtoːɡ]
diesel locomotive	diesellokomotiv (ett)	['disəlʲ lʲɔkɔmɔ'tiv]
steam locomotive	ånglokomotiv (en)	['ɔŋˌlʲɔkɔmɔ'tiv]

| passenger car | vagn (en) | ['vagn] |
| dining car | restaurangvagn (en) | [rɛstɔ'raŋˌvagn] |

rails	räls, rälsar (pl)	['rɛlʲs], ['rɛlʲsar]
railroad	järnväg (en)	['jæːnˌvɛːɡ]
railway tie	sliper (en)	['slipər]

platform (railway ~)	perrong (en)	[pɛ'rɔŋ]
track (~ 1, 2, etc.)	spår (ett)	['spoːr]
semaphore	semafor (en)	[sema'fɔr]
station	station (en)	[sta'ʃʉn]

engineer (train driver)	lokförare (en)	['lʰʊkˌføːrarə]
porter (of luggage)	bärare (en)	['bæːrarə]
car attendant	tågvärd (en)	['toːɡˌvæːd]
passenger	passagerare (en)	[pasa'ʃerarə]
conductor (ticket inspector)	kontrollant (en)	[kɔntrɔ'lʲant]

| corridor (in train) | korridor (en) | [kɔri'dɔːr] |
| emergency brake | nödbroms (en) | ['nøːdˌbrɔms] |

compartment	kupé (en)	[kʉ'peː]
berth	slaf, säng (en)	['slaf], ['sɛŋ]
upper berth	överslaf (en)	['øvəˌslaf]
lower berth	underslaf (en)	['undəˌslaf]
bed linen, bedding	sängkläder (pl)	['sɛŋˌklʲɛːdər]

ticket	biljett (en)	[bi'lʲet]
schedule	tidtabell (en)	['tid ta'bɛlʲ]
information display	informationstavla (en)	[infɔrma'ʃʉnsˌtavlʲa]

to leave, to depart	att avgå	[at 'avˌɡoː]
departure (of train)	avgång (en)	['avˌɡɔŋ]
to arrive (ab. train)	att ankomma	[at 'aŋˌkɔma]
arrival	ankomst (en)	['aŋˌkɔmst]
to arrive by train	att ankomma med tåget	[at 'aŋˌkɔma me 'toːɡət]
to get on the train	att stiga på tåget	[at 'stiga pɔ 'toːɡət]

to get off the train	att stiga av tåget	[at 'stiga av 'toːɡət]
train wreck	tågolycka (en)	['toːɡ ʊːˈlʲyka]
to derail (vi)	att spåra ur	[at 'spoːra ʉːr]
steam locomotive	ånglokomotiv (en)	['ɔŋˌlʲokɔmoˈtiv]
stoker, fireman	eldare (en)	['ɛlʲdarə]
firebox	eldstad (en)	['ɛlʲdˌstad]
coal	kol (ett)	['kɔlʲ]

171. Ship

ship	skepp (ett)	['ʃɛp]
vessel	fartyg (ett)	['faːˌtyɡ]
steamship	ångbåt (en)	['ɔŋˌboːt]
riverboat	flodbåt (en)	['flʲʊdˌboːt]
cruise ship	kryssningfartyg (ett)	['krysniŋˌfaːˈtyɡ]
cruiser	kryssare (en)	['krʏsarə]
yacht	jakt (en)	['jakt]
tugboat	bogserbåt (en)	['bʊksɛːrˌboːt]
barge	pråm (en)	['proːm]
ferry	färja (en)	['fæːrja]
sailing ship	segelbåt (en)	['seɡəlʲˌboːt]
brigantine	brigantin (en)	[brigan'tin]
ice breaker	isbrytare (en)	['isˌbrytarə]
submarine	ubåt (en)	[ʉːˈboːt]
boat (flat-bottomed ~)	båt (en)	['boːt]
dinghy	jolle (en)	['jɔlʲe]
lifeboat	livbåt (en)	['livˌboːt]
motorboat	motorbåt (en)	['mʊtʊrˌboːt]
captain	kapten (en)	[kap'ten]
seaman	matros (en)	[ma'trʊs]
sailor	sjöman (en)	['ʃøːˌman]
crew	besättning (en)	[be'sætniŋ]
boatswain	båtsman (en)	['botsman]
ship's boy	jungman (en)	['jʉŋˌman]
cook	kock (en)	['kɔk]
ship's doctor	skeppsläkare (en)	['ʃɛpˌlʲɛːkarə]
deck	däck (ett)	['dɛk]
mast	mast (en)	['mast]
sail	segel (ett)	['seɡəlʲ]
hold	lastrum (ett)	['lʲastˌruːm]
bow (prow)	bog (en)	['bʊɡ]

stern	akter (en)	['aktər]
oar	åra (en)	['oːra]
screw propeller	propeller (en)	[prʊ'pɛlʲər]

cabin	hytt (en)	['hʏt]
wardroom	officersmäss (en)	[ɔfi'seːrsˌmɛs]
engine room	maskinrum (ett)	[ma'ɧiːnˌruːm]
bridge	kommandobrygga (en)	[kɔm'andʊˌbrʏga]
radio room	radiohytt (en)	['radiʊˌhʏt]

| wave (radio) | våg (en) | ['voːg] |
| logbook | loggbok (en) | ['lʲɔgˌbʊk] |

spyglass	tubkikare (en)	['tʉbˌçikarə]
bell	klocka (en)	['klʲɔka]
flag	flagga (en)	['flʲaga]

| hawser (mooring ~) | tross (en) | ['trɔs] |
| knot (bowline, etc.) | knop, knut (en) | ['knʊp], ['knʉt] |

| deckrails | räcken (pl) | ['rɛkən] |
| gangway | landgång (en) | ['lʲandˌgɔŋ] |

| anchor | ankar (ett) | ['aŋkar] |
| to weigh anchor | att lätta ankar | [at 'lʲæta 'aŋkar] |

| to drop anchor | att kasta ankar | [at 'kasta 'aŋkar] |
| anchor chain | ankarkätting (en) | ['aŋkarˌçætiŋ] |

| port (harbor) | hamn (en) | ['hamn] |
| quay, wharf | kaj (en) | ['kaj] |

| to berth (moor) | att förtöja | [at fœː'ʈœːja] |
| to cast off | att kasta loss | [at 'kasta 'lʲɔs] |

| trip, voyage | resa (en) | ['resa] |
| cruise (sea trip) | kryssning (en) | ['krʏsniŋ] |

| course (route) | kurs (en) | ['kuːʂ] |
| route (itinerary) | rutt (en) | ['rut] |

| fairway (safe water channel) | farled, segelled (en) | ['faːlʲed], ['segəlˌled] |

| shallows | grund (ett) | ['grʉnd] |
| to run aground | att gå på grund | [at 'goː pɔ 'grʉnd] |

storm	storm (en)	['stɔrm]
signal	signal (en)	[sig'nalʲ]
to sink (vi)	att sjunka	[at 'ɧuŋka]
Man overboard!	Man överbord!	['man 'øːvəˌbʊːd]
SOS (distress signal)	SOS	[ɛso'ɛs]
ring buoy	livboj (en)	['livˌbɔj]

172. Airport

airport	**flygplats (en)**	['flʲyg‚plʲats]
airplane	**flygplan (ett)**	['flʲygplʲan]
airline	**flygbolag (ett)**	['flʲyg‚buʲlʲag]
air traffic controller	**flygledare (en)**	['flʲyg‚lʲedarə]
departure	**avgång (en)**	['av‚gɔŋ]
arrival	**ankomst (en)**	['aŋ‚kɔmst]
to arrive (by plane)	**att ankomma**	[at 'aŋ‚kɔma]
departure time	**avgångstid (en)**	['avgɔŋs‚tid]
arrival time	**ankomsttid (en)**	['aŋkɔmst‚tid]
to be delayed	**att bli försenad**	[at bli fœ:'ʂɛnad]
flight delay	**avgångsförsening (en)**	['avgɔŋs‚fœ:'ʂɛniŋ]
information board	**informationstavla (en)**	[infɔrma'ɧʊns‚tavlʲa]
information	**information (en)**	[infɔrma'ɧʊn]
to announce (vt)	**att meddela**	[at 'me‚delʲa]
flight (e.g., next ~)	**flyg (ett)**	['flʲyg]
customs	**tull (en)**	['tulʲ]
customs officer	**tulltjänsteman (en)**	['tulʲ 'ɕɛnstə‚man]
customs declaration	**tulldeklaration (en)**	['tulʲ‚dɛklʲara'ɧʊn]
to fill out (vt)	**att fylla i**	[at 'fylʲa 'i]
to fill out the declaration	**att fylla i en tulldeklaration**	[at 'fylʲa i en 'tulʲ‚dɛklʲara'ɧʊn]
passport control	**passkontroll (en)**	['paskɔn‚trolʲ]
luggage	**bagage (ett)**	[ba'ga:ʃ]
hand luggage	**handbagage (ett)**	['hand ba‚ga:ʃ]
luggage cart	**bagagevagn (en)**	[ba'ga:ʃ ‚vagn]
landing	**landning (en)**	['lʲandniŋ]
landing strip	**landningsbana (en)**	['lʲandniŋs‚bana]
to land (vi)	**att landa**	[at 'lʲanda]
airstairs	**trappa (en)**	['trapa]
check-in	**incheckning (en)**	['in‚ɕɛkniŋ]
check-in counter	**incheckningsdisk (en)**	['in‚ɕɛkniŋs 'disk]
to check-in (vi)	**att checka in**	[at 'ɕɛka in]
boarding pass	**boardingkort (ett)**	['bɔ:diŋ‚kɔ:t]
departure gate	**gate (en)**	['gejt]
transit	**transit (en)**	['transit]
to wait (vt)	**att vänta**	[at 'vɛnta]
departure lounge	**väntsal (en)**	['vɛnt‚salʲ]
to see off	**att vinka av**	[at 'viŋka av]
to say goodbye	**att säga adjö**	[at 'sɛ:ja a'jø:]

173. Bicycle. Motorcycle

bicycle	cykel (en)	['sykəlʲ]
scooter	scooter (en)	['skuːtər]
motorcycle, bike	motorcykel (en)	['mʊtʊrˌsykəlʲ]

to go by bicycle	att cykla	[at 'sʏklʲa]
handlebars	styre (ett)	['styrə]
pedal	pedal (en)	[pe'dalʲ]
brakes	bromsar (pl)	['brɔmsar]
bicycle seat (saddle)	sadel (en)	['sadəlʲ]

pump	pump (en)	['pump]
luggage rack	bagagehållare (en)	[ba'gaːʃ ˌhoːlʲarə]
front lamp	lykta (en)	['lʲykta]
helmet	hjälm (en)	['jɛlʲm]

wheel	hjul (ett)	['jʉːlʲ]
fender	stänkskärm (en)	['stɛŋkˌʃæːrm]
rim	fälg (en)	['fɛlj]
spoke	eker (en)	['ɛkər]

Cars

174. Types of cars

automobile, car	bil (en)	['biⁱ]
sports car	sportbil (en)	['spɔ:t̩biⁱ]
limousine	limousine (en)	[limu'si:n]
off-road vehicle	terrängbil (en)	[tɛ'rɛŋˌbiⁱ]
convertible (n)	cabriolet (en)	[kabriɔ'lⁱe:]
minibus	minibuss (en)	['miniˌbus]
ambulance	ambulans (en)	[ambɵ'lⁱans]
snowplow	snöplog (en)	['snø:ˌplⁱʊg]
truck	lastbil (en)	['lⁱastˌbiⁱ]
tanker truck	tankbil (en)	['taŋkˌbiⁱ]
van (small truck)	skåpbil (en)	['sko:pˌbiⁱ]
road tractor (trailer truck)	dragbil (en)	['dragˌbiⁱ]
trailer	släpvagn (en)	['slⁱɛpˌvagn]
comfortable (adj)	komfortabel	[kɔmfo't̩abəlⁱ]
used (adj)	begagnad	[be'gagnad]

175. Cars. Bodywork

hood	motorhuv (en)	['mʊtʊr hɵ:v]
fender	stänkskärm (en)	['stɛŋkˌɧæ:rm]
roof	tak (ett)	['tak]
windshield	vindruta (en)	['vindˌrɵta]
rear-view mirror	backspegel (en)	['bakˌspegəlⁱ]
windshield washer	vindrutespolar (en)	['vindrɵtəˌspʊlⁱar]
windshield wipers	vindrutetorkare (en)	['vindrɵtəˌtorkarə]
side window	sidoruta (en)	['sidʊˌrɵ:ta]
window lift (power window)	fönsterhiss (en)	['fœnstərˌhis]
antenna	antenn (en)	[an'tɛn]
sunroof	taklucka (en), soltak (ett)	['takˌlⁱɵka], ['sɔlˌtak]
bumper	stötfångare (en)	['stø:tˌfɔŋarə]
trunk	bagageutrymme (ett)	[ba'ga:ʃ 'ɵtˌrʏmə]
roof luggage rack	takräcke (ett)	['takˌrɛkə]
door	dörr (en)	['dœr]

| door handle | dörrhandtag (ett) | ['dœr,hantag] |
| door lock | dörrlås (ett) | ['dœr,ᶫo:s] |

| license plate | nummerplåt (en) | ['numər,plᶦo:t] |
| muffler | ljuddämpare (en) | ['jʉ:d,dɛmparə] |

| gas tank | bensintank (en) | [bɛn'sin,taŋk] |
| tailpipe | avgasrör (ett) | ['avgas,rø:r] |

gas, accelerator	gas (en)	['gas]
pedal	pedal (en)	[pe'dalᶦ]
gas pedal	gaspedal (en)	['gas pe'dalᶦ]

brake	broms (en)	['brɔms]
brake pedal	bromspedal (en)	['brɔms pe'dalᶦ]
to brake (use the brake)	att bromsa	[at 'brɔmsa]
parking brake	handbroms (en)	['hand,brɔms]

clutch	koppling (en)	['kɔpliŋ]
clutch pedal	kopplingspedal (en)	['kɔpliŋs pe'dalᶦ]
clutch disc	kopplingslamell (en)	['kɔpliŋs la'mɛlᶦ]
shock absorber	stötdämpare (en)	['stø:t,dɛmparə]

| wheel | hjul (ett) | ['jʉ:lᶦ] |
| spare tire | reservhjul (ett) | [re'sɛrv,jʉ:lᶦ] |

| tire | däck (ett) | ['dɛk] |
| hubcap | navkapsel (en) | ['nav,kapsəlᶦ] |

driving wheels	drivhjul (pl)	['driv,jʉ:lᶦ]
front-wheel drive (as adj)	framhjulsdriven	['framjʉ:lᶦs,drivən]
rear-wheel drive (as adj)	bakhjulsdriven	['bakjʉ:lᶦs,drivən]
all-wheel drive (as adj)	fyrahjulsdriven	['fyrajʉ:lᶦs,drivən]

gearbox	växellåda (en)	['vɛksəl,ᶫo:da]
automatic (adj)	automatisk	[autʉ'matisk]
mechanical (adj)	mekanisk	[me'kanisk]
gear shift	växelspak (en)	['vɛksəlᶦ,spak]

| headlight | strålkastare (en) | ['stro:lᶦ,kastarə] |
| headlights | strålkastare (pl) | ['stro:lᶦ,kastarə] |

low beam	halvljus (ett)	[halᶦvjʉ:s]
high beam	helljus (ett)	['hɛlᶦ:,jʉ:s]
brake light	stoppljus (ett)	['stɔpjʉ:s]

parking lights	positionsljus (ett)	[pʊsi'ʃʉns,jʉ:s]
hazard lights	nödljus (ett)	['nø:d,jʉ:s]
fog lights	dimlykta (en)	['dim,lᶦykta]

| turn signal | blinker (en) | ['bliŋkər] |
| back-up light | backljus (ett) | ['bak,jʉ:s] |

177

176. Cars. Passenger compartment

car inside (interior)	interiör, inredning (en)	[intɛ'rjøːr], ['in̩rednɪŋ]
leather (as adj)	läder-	['lʲɛːdər-]
velour (as adj)	velour-	[veˈlʉːr-]
upholstery	klädsel (en)	['klʲɛdsəlʲ]
instrument (gage)	instrument (ett)	[instruˈmɛnt]
dashboard	instrumentpanel (en)	[instruˈmɛnt paˈnəlʲ]
speedometer	hastighetsmätare (en)	['hastiɡhets̩mɛːtarə]
needle (pointer)	visare (en)	['visarə]
odometer	vägmätare (en)	['vɛːɡ̩mɛːtarə]
indicator (sensor)	indikator (en)	[indiˈkatʊr]
level	nivå (en)	[niˈvoː]
warning light	varningslampa (en)	['vaːnɪŋs ˌlʲampa]
steering wheel	ratt (en)	['rat]
horn	horn (ett)	['hʊːn]
button	knapp (en)	['knap]
switch	omskiftare (en)	['ɔm̩hiftarə]
seat	säte (ett)	['sɛtə]
backrest	ryggstöd (ett)	['rʏɡ̩støːd]
headrest	nackstöd (ett)	['nak̩støːd]
seat belt	säkerhetsbälte (ett)	['sɛːkərhets̩bɛlʲtə]
to fasten the belt	att sätta fast säkerhetsbältet	[at 'sæta fast 'sɛkərhets̩bɛlʲtət]
adjustment (of seats)	justering (en)	[ɦuˈsteːrɪŋ]
airbag	krockkudde (en)	['krɔk̩kudə]
air-conditioner	luftkonditionerare (en)	['lʉft̩kɔndiɦuˈnerarə]
radio	radio (en)	['radiʊ]
CD player	cd-spelare (en)	['sede ˌspelʲarə]
to turn on	att slå på	[at 'slʲoː pɔ]
antenna	antenn (en)	[anˈtɛn]
glove box	handskfack (ett)	['hansk̩fak]
ashtray	askkopp (en)	['askɔp]

177. Cars. Engine

engine, motor	motor (en)	['mʊtʊr]
diesel (as adj)	diesel-	['disəlʲ-]
gasoline (as adj)	bensin-	[bɛnˈsin-]
engine volume	motorvolym (en)	['mʊtʊr vɔˈlʲym]
power	styrka (en)	['styrka]
horsepower	hästkraft (en)	['hɛst̩kraft]

piston	kolv (en)	['kɔlʲv]
cylinder	cylinder (en)	[sy'lindər]
valve	ventil (en)	[vɛn'tilʲ]

injector	injektor (en)	[in'jɛktʊr]
generator (alternator)	generator (en)	[jene'ratʊr]
carburetor	förgasare (en)	[før'gasarə]
motor oil	motorolja (en)	['mʊtʊrˌɔlja]

radiator	kylare (en)	['çylʲarə]
coolant	kylvätska (en)	['çylʲˌvɛtska]
cooling fan	fläkt (en)	['flʲɛkt]

battery (accumulator)	batteri (ett)	[batɛ'ri:]
starter	starter, startmotor (en)	[sta:tə], ['sta:tˌmʊtʊr]
ignition	tändning (en)	['tɛndniŋ]
spark plug	tändstift (ett)	['tɛndˌstift]

terminal (of battery)	klämma (en)	['klʲɛma]
positive terminal	plusklämma (en)	['plʉsˌklʲɛma]
negative terminal	minusklämma (en)	['minusˌklʲɛma]
fuse	säkring (en)	['sɛkriŋ]

air filter	luftfilter (ett)	['lʉftˌfilʲtər]
oil filter	oljefilter (ett)	['ɔljəˌfilʲtər]
fuel filter	bränslefilter (ett)	['brɛnslʲeˌfilʲtər]

178. Cars. Crash. Repair

car crash	bilolycka (en)	['bilʲ ʊ:'lʲyka]
traffic accident	trafikolycka (en)	[tra'fik ʊ:'lʲyka]
to crash (into the wall, etc.)	att köra in i …	[at 'çø:ra in i …]

to get smashed up	att haverera	[at have'rera]
damage	skada (en)	['skada]
intact (unscathed)	oskadad	[ʊ:'skadad]

breakdown	haveri (ett)	[have'ri:]
to break down (vi)	att bryta ihop	[at 'bryta i'hʊp]
towrope	bogserlina (en)	['bʊksɛ:rˌlina]

puncture	punktering (en)	[puŋk'teriŋ]
to be flat	att vara punkterat	[at 'vara puŋk'terat]
to pump up	att pumpa upp	[at 'pumpa up]
pressure	tryck (ett)	['tryk]
to check (to examine)	att checka	[at 'ɕɛka]

repair	reparation (en)	[repara'ɧʊn]
auto repair shop	bilverkstad (en)	['bilʲvɛrkˌstad]
spare part	reservdel (en)	[re'sɛrvˌdelʲ]

part	del (en)	['delʲ]
bolt (with nut)	bult (en)	['bulʲt]
screw (fastener)	skruv (en)	['skrʉ:v]
nut	mutter (en)	['mutər]
washer	bricka (en)	['brika]
bearing	lager (ett)	['lʲagər]

tube	rör (ett)	['rø:r]
gasket (head ~)	tätning (en)	['tɛtniŋ]
cable, wire	ledning (en)	['lʲedniŋ]

jack	domkraft (en)	['dʊm‚kraft]
wrench	skruvnyckel (en)	['skrʉ:v‚nʏkəlʲ]
hammer	hammare (en)	['hamarə]
pump	pump (en)	['pump]
screwdriver	skruvmejsel (en)	['skrʉ:v‚mɛjsəlʲ]

fire extinguisher	brandsläckare (en)	['brand‚slʲɛkarə]
warning triangle	varningstriangel (en)	['va:ŋiŋs tri'aŋəlʲ]

to stall (vi)	att stanna	[at 'stana]
stall (n)	tjuvstopp (ett)	['ɕʉvstɔp]
to be broken	att vara trasig	[at 'vara ‚trasig]

to overheat (vi)	att bli överhettad	[at bli 'øvə‚hɛtad]
to be clogged up	att bli igensatt	[at bli 'ijɛnsat]
to freeze up (pipes, etc.)	att frysa	[at 'frysa]
to burst (vi, ab. tube)	att spricka, att brista	[at 'sprika], [at 'brista]

pressure	tryck (ett)	['trʏk]
level	nivå (en)	[ni'vo:]
slack (~ belt)	slak	['slʲak]

dent	buckla (en)	['buklʲa]
knocking noise (engine)	knackande ljud (ett)	['knakandə‚jʉ:d]
crack	spricka (en)	['sprika]
scratch	repa, skråma (en)	['repa], ['skroma]

179. Cars. Road

road	väg (en)	['vɛ:g]
highway	huvudväg (en)	['hʉ:vʉd‚vɛ:g]
freeway	motorväg (en)	['mʊtʊr‚vɛ:g]
direction (way)	riktning (en)	['riktniŋ]
distance	avstånd (ett)	['av‚stɔnd]
bridge	bro (en)	['brʊ]
parking lot	parkeringsplats (en)	[par'keriŋs‚plʲats]
square	torg (ett)	['tɔrj]
interchange	trafikplats,	[tra'fik‚plʲats],
	vägkorsning (en)	['vɛ:g‚kɔ:ʂniŋ]

tunnel	tunnel (en)	['tunəlʲ]
gas station	bensinstation (en)	[bɛn'sin‚sta'fʊn]
parking lot	parkeringsplats (en)	[par'keriŋs‚plʲats]
gas pump (fuel dispenser)	bensinpump (en)	[bɛn'sin‚pump]
auto repair shop	bilverkstad (en)	['bilʲvɛrk‚stad]
to get gas (to fill up)	att tanka	[at 'taŋka]
fuel	bränsle (ett)	['brɛnslʲe]
jerrycan	dunk (en)	['duːŋk]

asphalt	asfalt (en)	['asfalʲt]
road markings	vägmarkering (en)	['vɛːg‚mar'keriŋ]
curb	trottoarkant (en)	[trɔtʊ'ar‚kant]
guardrail	vägräcke (ett)	['vɛːg‚rɛkə]
ditch	vägdike (ett)	['vɛːg‚dikə]
roadside (shoulder)	vägkant (en)	['vɛːg‚kant]
lamppost	lyktstolpe (en)	['lʲyk‚stɔlʲpə]

to drive (a car)	att köra	[at 'çøːra]
to turn (e.g., ~ left)	att svänga	[at 'svɛŋa]
to make a U-turn	att göra en u-sväng	[at 'jøːra en 'ʉː‚svɛŋ]
reverse (~ gear)	backning (en)	['bakniŋ]

to honk (vi)	att tuta	[at 'tʉːta]
honk (sound)	tuta (en)	['tʉːta]
to get stuck (in the mud, etc.)	att köra fast	[at 'çøːra fast]
to spin the wheels	att spinna	[at 'spina]
to cut, to turn off (vt)	att stanna	[at 'stana]

speed	hastighet (en)	['hastig‚het]
to exceed the speed limit	att överstiga hastighetsgränsen	[at 'øːvə‚stiga 'hastighets‚grɛnsən]
to give a ticket	att bötfälla	[at 'bøt‚fɛlʲa]
traffic lights	trafikljus (ett)	[tra'fik‚jʉːs]
driver's license	körkort (ett)	['çøːr‚koːt]

grade crossing	överkörsväg (en)	['øːvə‚çøː‚svɛːg]
intersection	korsning (en)	['kɔː‚sniŋ]
crosswalk	övergångsställe (ett)	['øː‚vərgɔŋs‚stɛlʲe]
bend, curve	kurva, krök (en)	['kurva], ['krøːk]
pedestrian zone	gånggata (en)	['gɔŋ‚gata]

180. Traffic signs

rules of the road	trafiklag (en)	[tra'fik‚lag]
road sign (traffic sign)	vägmärke (ett)	['vɛːg‚mæːrkə]
passing (overtaking)	omkörning (en)	['ɔm‚çøː‚niŋ]
curve	krök, kurva (en)	['krøːk], ['kurva]
U-turn	U-sväng (en)	['ʉː‚svɛŋ]
traffic circle	rondell (en)	['rʊn‚dɛlʲ]

No entry	Förbud mot infart med fordon	[før'bjʉːd mʊt 'infaːt mɛ 'fuːdɔn]
No vehicles allowed	förbud mot fordonstrafik	[før'bjʉːd mʊt 'fuːdɔns tra'fik]
No passing	Förbud mot omkörning	[før'bjʉːd mʊt 'ɔm,çøːɳiŋ]
No parking	Förbud mot att parkera fordon	[før'bjʉːd mʊt at par'kera 'fuːdɔn]
No stopping	Förbud att stanna och parkera fordon	[før'bjʉːd at 'stana ɔ par'kera 'fuːdɔn]
dangerous bend	Farlig kurva	['faːlig ,kurva]
steep descent	Nedförslutning	['nɛdfør,slʉːtniŋ]
one-way traffic	Enkelriktad trafik	['ɛŋkəlʲ,riktad tra'fik]
crosswalk	övergångsställe (ett)	['øːvərgɔŋs,stɛlʲe]
slippery road	Slirig väg	['slirig vɛːg]
YIELD	Väjningsplikt	['vɛjniŋs,plikt]

PEOPLE. LIFE EVENTS

Life events

181. Holidays. Event

celebration, holiday	fest (en)	['fɛst]
national day	nationaldag (en)	[natʃʊ'nalʲˌdag]
public holiday	helgdag (en)	['hɛljˌdag]
to commemorate (vt)	att fira	[at 'fira]
event (happening)	begivenhet (en)	[be'jivənˌhet]
event (organized activity)	evenemang (ett)	[ɛvenə'maŋ]
banquet (party)	bankett (en)	[baŋ'ket]
reception (formal party)	reception (en)	[resɛp'ʃʊn]
feast	fest (en)	['fɛst]
anniversary	årsdag (en)	['oːʂˌdag]
jubilee	jubileum (ett)	[jʉbi'lʲeum]
to celebrate (vt)	att fira	[at 'fira]
New Year	nyår (ett)	['nyˌoːr]
Happy New Year!	Gott Nytt År!	[gɔt nʏt 'oːr]
Santa Claus	Jultomten	['julʲˌtomtən]
Christmas	jul (en)	['juːlʲ]
Merry Christmas!	God jul!	[ˌgʊd 'juːlʲ]
Christmas tree	julgran (en)	['julʲˌgran]
fireworks (fireworks show)	fyrverkeri (ett)	[fyrvɛrke'riː]
wedding	bröllop (ett)	['brœlʲɔp]
groom	brudgum (en)	['brʉːdˌguːm]
bride	brud (en)	['brʉːd]
to invite (vt)	att inbjuda, att invitera	[at in'bjʉːda], [at invi'tera]
invitation card	inbjudan (en)	[in'bjʉːdan]
guest	gäst (en)	['jɛst]
to visit	att besöka	[at be'søːka]
(~ your parents, etc.)		
to meet the guests	att hälsa på gästerna	[at 'hɛlʲsa pɔ 'jɛstena]
gift, present	gåva, present (en)	['goːva], [pre'sɛnt]
to give (sth as present)	att ge	[at jeː]
to receive gifts	att få presenter	[at foː pre'sɛntər]

bouquet (of flowers)	bukett (en)	[bʉ'kɛt]
congratulations	lyckönskning (en)	['lʲyk,øŋskniŋ]
to congratulate (vt)	att gratulera	[at gratʉ'lʲera]

greeting card	gratulationskort (ett)	[gratʉlʲa'ɧʊns,kɔ:t]
to send a postcard	att skicka vykort	[at 'ɧika 'vy,kɔ:t]
to get a postcard	att få vykort	[at fo: 'vy,kɔ:t]

toast	skål (en)	['sko:lʲ]
to offer (a drink, etc.)	att bjuda	[at 'bjʉ:da]
champagne	champagne (en)	[ɧam'panʲ]

to enjoy oneself	att ha roligt	[at ha 'rʊlit]
merriment (gaiety)	uppsluppenhet (en)	['up,slupənhet]
joy (emotion)	glädje (en)	['glʲɛdjə]

| dance | dans (en) | ['dans] |
| to dance (vi, vt) | att dansa | [at 'dansa] |

| waltz | vals (en) | ['valʲs] |
| tango | tango (en) | ['taŋgɔ] |

182. Funerals. Burial

cemetery	kyrkogård (en)	['ɕyrkʊ,go:d]
grave, tomb	grav (en)	['grav]
cross	kors (ett)	['kɔ:ʂ]
gravestone	gravsten (en)	['grav,sten]
fence	stängsel (ett)	['stɛŋsəlʲ]
chapel	kapell (ett)	[ka'pɛlʲ]

death	död (en)	['dø:d]
to die (vi)	att dö	[at 'dø:]
the deceased	den avlidne	[dɛn 'av,lidnə]
mourning	sorg (en)	['sɔrj]
to bury (vt)	att begrava	[at be'grava]
funeral home	begravningsbyrå (en)	[be'gravniŋs,byro:]
funeral	begravning (en)	[be'gravniŋ]

wreath	krans (en)	['krans]
casket, coffin	likkista (en)	['lik,ɕista]
hearse	likvagn (en)	['lik,vagn]
shroud	liksvepning (en)	['lik,svɛpniŋ]

funeral procession	begravningståg (ett)	[be'gravniŋs,to:g]
funerary urn	gravurna (en)	['grav,u:ɳa]
crematory	krematorium (ett)	[krema'tɔrium]
obituary	nekrolog (en)	[nɛkrʊ'lʲɔg]
to cry (weep)	att gråta	[at 'gro:ta]
to sob (vi)	att snyfta	[at 'snɤfta]

183. War. Soldiers

platoon	pluton (en)	[plʉ'tʊn]
company	kompani (ett)	[kɔmpa'ni:]
regiment	regemente (ett)	[rege'mɛntə]
army	här, armé (en)	['hæː r], [arʹmeː]
division	division (en)	[divi'ʃʊn]

| section, squad | trupp (en) | ['trup] |
| host (army) | här (en) | ['hæː r] |

| soldier | soldat (en) | [sʊlʲ'dat] |
| officer | officer (en) | [ɔfi'seː r] |

private	menig (en)	['menig]
sergeant	sergeant (en)	[sɛrʹʃant]
lieutenant	löjtnant (en)	['lʲœjtˌnant]
captain	kapten (en)	[kap'ten]
major	major (en)	[ma'jʊː r]
colonel	överste (en)	['øːvəʂtə]
general	general (en)	[jene'ralʲ]

sailor	sjöman (en)	['ʃøːˌman]
captain	kapten (en)	[kap'ten]
boatswain	båtsman (en)	['bɔtsman]

artilleryman	artillerist (en)	[aːʈilʲe'rist]
paratrooper	fallskärmsjägare (en)	['falʲʃæː rms jɛː garə]
pilot	flygare (en)	['flʲygarə]
navigator	styrman (en)	['styrˌman]
mechanic	mekaniker (en)	[me'kanikər]

pioneer (sapper)	pionjär (en)	[piʊ'njæː r]
parachutist	fallskärmshoppare (en)	['falʲʃæː rms ˌhɔparə]
reconnaissance scout	spaningssoldat (en)	['spaniŋs sʊlʲ'dat]
sniper	prickskytt (en)	['prikˌʃʏt]

patrol (group)	patrull (en)	[pat'rulʲ]
to patrol (vt)	att patrullera	[at patru'lʲera]
sentry, guard	vakt (en)	['vakt]

warrior	krigare (en)	['krigarə]
hero	hjälte (en)	['jɛlʲtə]
heroine	hjältinna (en)	['jɛlʲ tina]
patriot	patriot (en)	[patri'ʊt]

traitor	förrädare (en)	[fœ'rɛː darə]
to betray (vt)	att förråda	[at fœ'roːda]
deserter	desertör (en)	[desɛ'ʈøː r]
to desert (vi)	att desertera	[at desɛ'ʈera]
mercenary	legosoldat (en)	['lʲegʊ sʊlʲ'dat]

| recruit | rekryt (en) | [rɛk'ryt] |
| volunteer | frivillig (en) | ['fri͵vilig] |

dead (n)	döda (en)	['døːda]
wounded (n)	sårad (en)	['soːrad]
prisoner of war	fånge (en)	['fɔŋə]

184. War. Military actions. Part 1

war	krig (ett)	['krig]
to be at war	att vara i krig	[at 'vara i ͵krig]
civil war	inbördeskrig (ett)	['inbøːdɛs͵krig]

treacherously (adv)	lömsk, förrädisk	['lʲømsk], [fœ:'rɛdisk]
declaration of war	krigsförklaring (en)	['krigs͵før'klʲarin]
to declare (~ war)	att förklara	[at før'klʲara]
aggression	aggression (en)	[agrɛ'fŋun]
to attack (invade)	att angripa	[at 'an͵gripa]

to invade (vt)	att invadera	[at inva'dera]
invader	angripare (en)	['an͵griparə]
conqueror	erövrare (en)	[ɛ'rœvrarə]

defense	försvar (ett)	[fœ:'ʂvar]
to defend (a country, etc.)	att försvara	[at fœ:'ʂvara]
to defend (against …)	att försvara sig	[at fœ:'ʂvara sɛj]

enemy	fiende (en)	['fjɛndə]
foe, adversary	motståndare (en)	['mʊt͵stɔndarə]
enemy (as adj)	fientlig	['fjɛntlig]

| strategy | strategi (en) | [strate'ŋiː] |
| tactics | taktik (en) | [tak'tik] |

order	order (en)	['ɔːdər]
command (order)	order, kommando (en)	['ɔːdər], [kɔm'mandʊ]
to order (vt)	att beordra	[at be'oːdra]
mission	uppdrag (ett)	['updrag]
secret (adj)	hemlig	['hɛmlig]

battle	batalj (en)	[ba'talʲ]
battle	slag (ett)	['slʲag]
combat	kamp (en)	['kamp]

attack	angrepp (ett)	['an͵grɛp]
charge (assault)	stormning (en)	['stɔrmnin]
to storm (vt)	att storma	[at 'stɔrma]
siege (to be under ~)	belägring (en)	[be'lʲɛgrin]
offensive (n)	offensiv (en)	['ɔfɛn͵siːv]
to go on the offensive	att angripa	[at 'an͵gripa]

retreat	reträtt (en)	[rɛ'træt]
to retreat (vi)	att retirera	[at reti'rera]
encirclement	omringning (en)	['ɔm,riŋniŋ]
to encircle (vt)	att omringa	[at 'ɔm,riŋa]
bombing (by aircraft)	bombning (en)	['bɔmbniŋ]
to drop a bomb	att släppa en bomb	[at 'slʲepa en bɔmb]
to bomb (vt)	att bombardera	[at bɔmba'dera]
explosion	explosion (en)	[ɛksplʲɔ'ɧʊn]
shot	skott (ett)	['skɔt]
to fire (~ a shot)	att skjuta	[at 'ɧʉːta]
firing (burst of ~)	skjutande (ett)	['ɧʉːtandə]
to aim (to point a weapon)	att sikta på ...	[at 'sikta pɔ ...]
to point (a gun)	att rikta	[at 'rikta]
to hit (the target)	att träffa	[at 'trɛfa]
to sink (~ a ship)	att sänka	[at 'sɛŋka]
hole (in a ship)	hål (ett)	['hoːlʲ]
to founder, to sink (vi)	att sjunka	[at 'ɧuŋka]
front (war ~)	front (en)	['frɔnt]
evacuation	evakuering (en)	[ɛvakʉ'eːriŋ]
to evacuate (vt)	att evakuera	[at ɛvakʉ'eːra]
trench	skyttegrav (en)	['ɧʏtə,grav]
barbwire	taggtråd (en)	['tag,troːd]
barrier (anti tank ~)	avspärning (en)	['av,spɛrniŋ]
watchtower	vakttorn (ett)	['vakt,tʊːn]
military hospital	militärsjukhus (ett)	[mili'tæːrs,hʉs]
to wound (vt)	att såra	[at 'soːra]
wound	sår (ett)	['soːr]
wounded (n)	sårad (en)	['soːrad]
to be wounded	att bli sårad	[at bli 'soːrad]
serious (wound)	allvarlig	[alʲ'vaːlʲig]

185. War. Military actions. Part 2

captivity	fångenskap (en)	['fɔŋən,skap]
to take captive	att tillfångata	[at tilʲ'fɔŋata]
to be held captive	att vara i fångenskap	[at 'vara i 'fɔŋən,skap]
to be taken captive	att bli tagen till fånga	[at bli 'tagən tilʲ 'fɔŋa]
concentration camp	koncentrationsläger (ett)	[kɔnsentra'ɧʊns,lʲeːgər]
prisoner of war	fånge (en)	['fɔŋə]
to escape (vi)	att fly	[at flʲy]
to betray (vt)	att förråda	[at fœ'roːda]

| betrayer | förrädare (en) | [fœ:'rɛ:darə] |
| betrayal | förräderi (ett) | [fœ:rɛ:de'ri:] |

| to execute (by firing squad) | att arkebusera | [at 'arkebʉˌsera] |
| execution (by firing squad) | arkebusering (en) | ['arkebʉˌseriŋ] |

equipment (military gear)	mundering (en)	[mun'deriŋ]
shoulder board	axelklaff (en)	['aksɛlⁱˌklʲaf]
gas mask	gasmask (en)	['gasˌmask]

field radio	fältradio (en)	['fɛltˌradiʊ]
cipher, code	chiffer (ett)	['ɧifər]
secrecy	sekretess (en)	[sɛkre'tɛs]
password	lösenord (ett)	['lʲø:sənˌʊ:d]

land mine	mina (en)	['mina]
to mine (road, etc.)	att minera	[at mi'nera]
minefield	minfält (ett)	['minˌfɛlʲt]

air-raid warning	flyglarm (ett)	['flygˌlʲarm]
alarm (alert signal)	alarm (ett)	[a'lʲarm]
signal	signal (en)	[sig'nalʲ]
signal flare	signalraket (en)	[sig'nalʲˌraket]

headquarters	stab (en)	['stab]
reconnaissance	spaning (en)	['spaniŋ]
situation	situation (en)	[sitʉa'ɧʊn]
report	rapport (en)	[ra'pɔ:t]
ambush	bakhåll (ett)	['bakˌho:lʲ]
reinforcement (of army)	förstärkning (en)	[fœ:'stæ:kniŋ]

target	mål (ett)	['mo:lʲ]
proving ground	skjutbana (en)	['ɧʉ:tˌbana]
military exercise	manövrar (pl)	[ma'nœvrar]

panic	panik (en)	[pa'nik]
devastation	ödeläggelse (en)	['ø:dəˌlʲɛgəlʲsə]
destruction, ruins	ruiner (pl)	[rʉ'i:nər]
to destroy (vt)	att ödelägga	[at 'ødəˌlʲɛga]

to survive (vi, vt)	att överleva	[at 'ø:vəˌlʲeva]
to disarm (vt)	att avväpna	[at 'avˌvɛpna]
to handle (~ a gun)	att hantera	[at han'tera]

| Attention! | Givakt! | [ji'vakt] |
| At ease! | Lystring - STÄLL! Manöver! | ['lʲystriŋ - stɛlʲ], [ma'nøvər] |

act of courage	bedrift (en)	[be'drift]
oath (vow)	ed (en)	['ɛd]
to swear (an oath)	att svära	[at 'svæ:ra]

decoration (medal, etc.)	belöning (en)	[be'lʲøːniŋ]
to award (give medal to)	att belöna	[at be'lʲøːna]
medal	medalj (en)	[me'dalj]
order (e.g., ~ of Merit)	orden (en)	['ɔːdən]

victory	seger (en)	['segər]
defeat	nederlag (ett)	['nedəːˌlʲag]
armistice	vapenvila (en)	['vapənˌvilʲa]

standard (battle flag)	fana (en)	['fana]
glory (honor, fame)	berömmelse (en)	[be'rœməlʲsə]
parade	parad (en)	[pa'rad]
to march (on parade)	att marschera	[at mar'ʃera]

186. Weapons

weapons	vapen (ett)	['vapən]
firearms	skjutvapen (ett)	['ʃʉːtˌvapən]
cold weapons (knives, etc.)	blank vapen (ett)	['blʲaŋk 'vapən]

chemical weapons	kemiskt vapen (ett)	['ɕemiskt 'vapən]
nuclear (adj)	kärn-	['ɕæːŋ-]
nuclear weapons	kärnvapen (ett)	['ɕæːnˌvapən]

| bomb | bomb (en) | ['bɔmb] |
| atomic bomb | atombomb (en) | [a'tɔmˌbɔmb] |

pistol (gun)	pistol (en)	[pi'stʊlʲ]
rifle	gevär (ett)	[je'væːr]
submachine gun	maskinpistol (en)	[ma'ɧiːn pi'stʊlʲ]
machine gun	maskingevär (ett)	[ma'ɧiːn je'væːr]

muzzle	mynning (en)	['mʏniŋ]
barrel	lopp (ett)	['lʲɔp]
caliber	kaliber (en)	[ka'libər]

trigger	avtryckare (en)	['avˌtrʏkarə]
sight (aiming device)	sikte (ett)	['siktə]
magazine	magasin (ett)	[maga'sin]
butt (shoulder stock)	kolv (en)	['kɔlʲv]

| hand grenade | handgranat (en) | ['hand graˌnat] |
| explosive | sprängämne (ett) | ['sprɛŋˌɛmnə] |

bullet	kula (en)	['kʉːlʲa]
cartridge	patron (en)	[pa'trʊn]
charge	laddning (en)	['lʲadniŋ]
ammunition	ammunition (en)	[amʉni'ɧʊn]
bomber (aircraft)	bombplan (ett)	['bɔmbˌplʲan]

| fighter | jaktplan (ett) | ['jakt‚plʲan] |
| helicopter | helikopter (en) | [heli'kɔptər] |

anti-aircraft gun	luftvärnskanon (en)	['lʉftvæːŋs ka'nʊn]
tank	stridsvagn (en)	['strids‚vagn]
tank gun	kanon (en)	[ka'nʊn]

artillery	artilleri (ett)	[aːtʲilʲe'riː]
gun (cannon, howitzer)	kanon (en)	[ka'nʊn]
to lay (a gun)	att rikta in	[at 'rikta in]

shell (projectile)	projektil (en)	[prʊŋek'tilʲ]
mortar bomb	granat (en)	[gra'nat]
mortar	granatkastare (en)	[gra'nat‚kastarə]
splinter (shell fragment)	splitter (ett)	['splitər]

submarine	ubåt (en)	[ʉː'boːt]
torpedo	torped (en)	[tɔr'ped]
missile	robot, missil (en)	['rɔbɔt], [mi'silʲ]

to load (gun)	att ladda	[at 'lʲada]
to shoot (vi)	att skjuta	[at 'fʉːta]
to point at (the cannon)	att sikta på ...	[at 'sikta pɔ ...]
bayonet	bajonett (en)	[bajʊ'nɛt]

rapier	värja (en)	['væːrja]
saber (e.g., cavalry ~)	sabel (en)	['sabəlʲ]
spear (weapon)	spjut (ett)	['spjʉːt]
bow	båge (en)	['boːgə]
arrow	pil (en)	['pilʲ]
musket	musköt (en)	[mu'skøːt]
crossbow	armborst (ett)	['arm‚bɔːʂt]

187. Ancient people

primitive (prehistoric)	ur-	['ʉr-]
prehistoric (adj)	förhistorisk	['førhi‚stʊrisk]
ancient (~ civilization)	forntida, antikens	['fʊːɳ‚tida], [an'tikəns]

Stone Age	Stenåldern	['sten‚ɔːlʲdɛːɳ]
Bronze Age	bronsålder (en)	['brɔns‚oːlʲdər]
Ice Age	istid (en)	['is‚tid]

tribe	stam (en)	['stam]
cannibal	kannibal (en)	[kani'balʲ]
hunter	jägare (en)	['jɛːgarə]
to hunt (vi, vt)	att jaga	[at 'jaga]
mammoth	mammut (en)	[ma'mut]
cave	grotta (en)	['grɔta]
fire	eld (en)	['ɛlʲd]

| campfire | bål (ett) | ['boːlʲ] |
| cave painting | hällristning (en) | ['hɛlʲˌristniŋ] |

tool (e.g., stone ax)	redskap (ett)	['rɛdˌskap]
spear	spjut (ett)	['spjʉːt]
stone ax	stenyxa (en)	['stenˌyksa]
to be at war	att vara i krig	[at 'vara i ˌkrig]
to domesticate (vt)	att tämja	[at 'tɛmja]

idol	idol (en)	[i'dɔlʲ]
to worship (vt)	att dyrka	[at 'dyrka]
superstition	vidskepelse (en)	['vidˌhɛpəlʲsə]
rite	ritual (en)	[ritu'alʲ]

evolution	evolution (en)	[ɛvɔlʉ'hʊn]
development	utveckling (en)	['ʉtˌvɛkliŋ]
disappearance (extinction)	försvinnande (ett)	[fœː'ʂvinandə]
to adapt oneself	att anpassa sig	[at 'anˌpasa sɛj]

archeology	arkeologi (en)	[ˌarkeʉlʲɔ'giː]
archeologist	arkeolog (en)	[ˌarkeʉ'lʲɔg]
archeological (adj)	arkeologisk	[ˌarkeʉ'lʲɔgisk]

excavation site	utgrävningsplats (en)	['ʉtˌgrɛvniŋs 'plʲats]
excavations	utgrävningar (pl)	['ʉtˌgrɛvniŋar]
find (object)	fynd (ett)	['fʏnd]
fragment	fragment (ett)	[frag'mɛnt]

188. Middle Ages

people (ethnic group)	folk (ett)	['fɔlʲk]
peoples	folk (pl)	['fɔlʲk]
tribe	stam (en)	['stam]
tribes	stammar (pl)	['stamar]

barbarians	barbarer (pl)	[bar'barər]
Gauls	galler (pl)	['galʲer]
Goths	goter (pl)	['gʊtər]
Slavs	slavar (pl)	['slʲavar]
Vikings	vikingar (pl)	['vikiŋar]

| Romans | romare (pl) | ['rʊmarə] |
| Roman (adj) | romersk | ['rʊmɛʂk] |

Byzantines	bysantiner (pl)	[bysan'tinər]
Byzantium	Bysans	['bysans]
Byzantine (adj)	bysantinsk	[bysan'tinsk]

| emperor | kejsare (en) | ['ɕejsarə] |
| leader, chief (tribal ~) | hövding (en) | ['hœvdiŋ] |

191

powerful (~ king)	**mäktig, kraftfull**	['mɛktig], ['kraft̩fulʲ]
king	**kung (en)**	['kuŋ]
ruler (sovereign)	**härskare (en)**	['hæːʂkarə]
knight	**riddare (en)**	['ridarə]
feudal lord	**feodalherre (en)**	[feʊ'dalʲ̩hærə]
feudal (adj)	**feodal-**	[feʊ'dalʲ-]
vassal	**vasall (en)**	[va'salʲ]
duke	**hertig (en)**	['hɛːʈig]
earl	**greve (en)**	['grevə]
baron	**baron (en)**	[ba'rʊn]
bishop	**biskop (en)**	['biskɔp]
armor	**rustning (en)**	['rustniŋ]
shield	**sköld (en)**	['ɧœlʲd]
sword	**svärd (ett)**	['svæːd̩]
visor	**visir (ett)**	[vi'sir]
chainmail	**ringbrynja (en)**	['riŋˌbrʏnja]
Crusade	**korståg (ett)**	['kɔːʂˌtoːg]
crusader	**korsfarare (en)**	['kɔːʂˌfararə]
territory	**territorium (ett)**	[tɛri'tʊrium]
to attack (invade)	**att angripa**	[at 'anˌgripa]
to conquer (vt)	**att erövra**	[at ɛ'rœvra]
to occupy (invade)	**att ockupera**	[at ɔkɵp'era]
siege (to be under ~)	**belägring (en)**	[be'lʲɛgriŋ]
besieged (adj)	**belägrad**	[be'lʲɛgrad]
to besiege (vt)	**att belägra**	[at be'lʲɛgra]
inquisition	**inkvisition (en)**	[iŋkvisi'ɧʊn]
inquisitor	**inkvisitor (en)**	[iŋkvi'sitʊr]
torture	**tortyr (en)**	[tɔː'tyr]
cruel (adj)	**brutal**	[brɵ'talʲ]
heretic	**kättare (en)**	['ɕætarə]
heresy	**kätteri (ett)**	[ɕæte'riː]
seafaring	**sjöfart (en)**	['ɧøːˌfaːt]
pirate	**pirat, sjörövare (en)**	[pi'rat], ['ɧøːˌrøːvarə]
piracy	**sjöröveri (ett)**	['ɧøːˌrøːve'riː]
boarding (attack)	**äntring (en)**	['ɛntriŋ]
loot, booty	**byte (ett)**	['bytə]
treasures	**skatter (pl)**	['skatər]
discovery	**upptäckt (en)**	['upˌtɛkt]
to discover (new land, etc.)	**att upptäcka**	[at 'upˌtɛka]
expedition	**expedition (en)**	[ɛkspedi'ɧʊn]
musketeer	**musketör (en)**	[muskə'tøːr]
cardinal	**kardinal (en)**	[ka:dɪ'nalʲ]

| heraldry | heraldik (en) | [heralʲ'dik] |
| heraldic (adj) | heraldisk | [he'ralʲdisk] |

189. Leader. Chief. Authorities

king	kung (en)	['kuŋ]
queen	drottning (en)	['drɔtniŋ]
royal (adj)	kunglig	['kuŋlig]
kingdom	kungarike (ett)	['kuŋaˌrikə]
prince	prins (en)	['prins]
princess	prinsessa (en)	[prin'sɛsa]

president	president (en)	[prɛsi'dɛnt]
vice-president	vicepresident (en)	['visəˌprɛsi'dɛnt]
senator	senator (en)	[se'natʊr]

monarch	monark (en)	[mʊ'nark]
ruler (sovereign)	härskare (en)	['hæ:ʂkarə]
dictator	diktator (en)	[dik'tatʊr]
tyrant	tyrann (en)	[ty'ran]
magnate	magnat (en)	[mag'nat]

director	direktör (en)	[dirɛk'tø:r]
chief	chef (en)	['ʃef]
manager (director)	föreståndare (en)	[førə'stɔndarə]
boss	boss (en)	['bɔs]
owner	ägare (en)	['ɛ:garə]

leader	ledare (en)	['lʲedarə]
head (~ of delegation)	ledare (en)	['lʲedarə]
authorities	myndigheter (pl)	['mʏndiˌhetər]
superiors	överordnade (pl)	['ø:vərˌɔ:dnadə]

governor	guvernör (en)	[gʉvɛ:'ŋø:r]
consul	konsul (en)	['kɔnsulʲ]
diplomat	diplomat (en)	[diplʲo'mat]
mayor	borgmästare (en)	['bɔrjˌmɛstarə]
sheriff	sheriff (en)	[ʃe'rif]

emperor	kejsare (en)	['ɕejsarə]
tsar, czar	tsar (en)	['tsar]
pharaoh	farao (en)	['faraʊ]
khan	kan (en)	['kan]

190. Road. Way. Directions

| road | väg (en) | ['vɛ:g] |
| way (direction) | väg (en) | ['vɛ:g] |

freeway	motorväg (en)	['mʊtʊrˌvɛ:g]
highway	huvudväg (en)	['hʉ:vʉdˌvɛ:g]
interstate	riksväg (en)	['riksˌvɛ:g]

| main road | huvudväg (en) | ['hʉ:vʉdˌvɛ:g] |
| dirt road | byväg (en) | ['byˌvɛ:g] |

| pathway | stig (en) | ['stig] |
| footpath (troddenpath) | stig (en) | ['stig] |

Where?	Var?	['var]
Where (to)?	Vart?	['va:t]
From where?	Varifrån?	['varifro:n]

| direction (way) | riktning (en) | ['riktniŋ] |
| to point (~ the way) | att peka | [at 'peka] |

to the left	till vänster	[tilʲ 'vɛnstər]
to the right	till höger	[tilʲ 'hø:gər]
straight ahead (adv)	rakt fram	['rakt fram]
back (e.g., to turn ~)	tillbaka	[tilʲ'baka]

bend, curve	kurva, krök (en)	['kurva], ['krø:k]
to turn (e.g., ~ left)	att svänga	[at 'svɛŋa]
to make a U-turn	att göra en u-sväng	[at 'jø:ra en 'ʉ:ˌsvɛŋ]

to be visible	att vara synlig	[at 'vara 'synlig]
(mountains, castle, etc.)		
to appear (come into view)	att visa sig	[at 'visa sɛj]

stop, halt	uppehåll (ett)	['upəˌho:lʲ]
(e.g., during a trip)		
to rest, to pause (vi)	att vila	[at 'vilʲa]
rest (pause)	vila (en)	['vilʲa]

to lose one's way	att gå vilse	[at 'go: 'vilʲsə]
to lead to ... (ab. road)	att leda till ...	[at 'lʲeda tilʲ ...]
to come out	att komma ut ...	[at 'kɔma ʉt ...]
(e.g., on the highway)		
stretch (of road)	sträckning (en)	['strɛkning]

asphalt	asfalt (en)	['asfalʲt]
curb	trottoarkant (en)	[trɔtʊ'arˌkant]
ditch	vägdike (ett)	['vɛ:gˌdikə]
manhole	manlucka (en)	['manˌlʉka]
roadside (shoulder)	vägkant (en)	['vɛ:gˌkant]
pit, pothole	grop (en)	['grʊp]

to go (on foot)	att gå	[at 'go:]
to pass (overtake)	att passera	[at pa'sera]
step (footstep)	steg, fotsteg (ett)	['steg], ['fʊtˌsteg]
on foot (adv)	till fots	[tilʲ 'fʊts]

to block (road)	att spärra	[at 'spɛra]
boom gate	bom (en)	['bʊm]
dead end	återvändsgränd (en)	['oːtərvɛnsˌgrɛnd]

191. Breaking the law. Criminals. Part 1

bandit	bandit (en)	[ban'dit]
crime	brott (ett)	['brɔt]
criminal (person)	förbrytare (en)	[før'brytarə]

thief	tjuv (en)	['ɕʉːv]
to steal (vi, vt)	att stjäla	[at 'ɧɛːlʲa]
stealing (larceny)	tjuveri (ett)	[ɕʉveˈriː]
theft	stöld (en)	['stœlʲd]

to kidnap (vt)	att kidnappa	[at 'kidˌnapa]
kidnapping	kidnapping (en)	['kidˌnapiŋ]
kidnapper	kidnappare (en)	['kidˌnaparə]

ransom	lösesumma (en)	['lʲøːsəˌsuma]
to demand ransom	att kräva lösesumma	[at 'krɛːva 'lʲøːsəˌsuma]

to rob (vt)	att råna	[at 'roːna]
robbery	rån (ett)	['roːn]
robber	rånare (en)	['roːnarə]

to extort (vt)	att pressa ut	[at 'prɛsa ʉt]
extortionist	utpressare (en)	['ʉtˌprɛsarə]
extortion	utpressning (en)	['ʉtˌprɛsniŋ]

to murder, to kill	att mörda	[at 'møːɖa]
murder	mord (ett)	['mʊːɖ]
murderer	mördare (en)	['møːɖarə]

gunshot	skott (ett)	['skɔt]
to fire (~ a shot)	att skjuta	[at 'ɧʉːta]
to shoot to death	att skjuta ner	[at 'ɧʉːta ner]
to shoot (vi)	att skjuta	[at 'ɧʉːta]
shooting	skjutande (ett)	['ɧʉːtandə]

incident (fight, etc.)	händelse (en)	['hɛndəlʲsə]
fight, brawl	slagsmål (ett)	['slʲaksˌmoːlʲ]
Help!	Hjälp!	['jɛlʲp]
victim	offer (ett)	['ɔfər]

to damage (vt)	att skada	[at 'skada]
damage	skada (en)	['skada]
dead body, corpse	lik (ett)	['liːk]
grave (~ crime)	allvarligt	[alʲˈvaːlʲit]
to attack (vt)	att anfalla	[at 'anfalʲa]

to beat (to hit)	att slå	[at 'slʲoː]
to beat up	att prygla	[at 'prʏglʲa]
to take (rob of sth)	att beröva	[at be'røːva]
to stab to death	att skära ihjäl	[at 'ʃæːra i'jɛlʲ]
to maim (vt)	att lemlästa	[at 'lem,lɛsta]
to wound (vt)	att såra	[at 'soːra]

blackmail	utpressning (en)	['ʉt,prɛsniŋ]
to blackmail (vt)	att utpressa	[at 'ʉt,prɛsa]
blackmailer	utpressare (en)	['ʉt,prɛsarə]

protection racket	utpressning (en)	['ʉt,prɛsniŋ]
racketeer	utpressare (en)	['ʉt,prɛsarə]
gangster	gangster (en)	['gaŋstər]
mafia, Mob	maffia (en)	['mafia]

pickpocket	ficktjuv (en)	['fik,ɕʉːv]
burglar	inbrottstjuv (en)	['inbrɔts,ɕʉːv]
smuggling	smuggling (en)	['smugliŋ]
smuggler	smugglare (en)	['smuglʲarə]

forgery	förfalskning (en)	[før'falʲskniŋ]
to forge (counterfeit)	att förfalska	[at før'falʲska]
fake (forged)	falsk	['falʲsk]

192. Breaking the law. Criminals. Part 2

rape	våldtäkt (en)	['voːlʲ,tɛkt]
to rape (vt)	att våldta	[at 'voːlʲ,ta]
rapist	våldtäktsman (en)	['voːlʲtɛkts,man]
maniac	maniker (en)	['manikər]

prostitute (fem.)	prostituerad (en)	[prɔstitʉ'ɛrad]
prostitution	prostitution (en)	[prɔstitʉ'fjʉn]
pimp	hallik (en)	['halik]

| drug addict | narkoman (en) | [narkʉ'man] |
| drug dealer | droglangare (en) | ['drʉg,lʲaŋarə] |

to blow up (bomb)	att spränga	[at 'sprɛŋa]
explosion	explosion (en)	[ɛksplɔ'fjʉn]
to set fire	att sätta eld	[at 'sæta ,ɛlʲd]
arsonist	mordbrännare (en)	['mʉːd,brɛnarə]

terrorism	terrorism (en)	[tɛrʉ'rism]
terrorist	terrorist (en)	[tɛrʉ'rist]
hostage	gisslan (en)	['jislʲan]

| to swindle (deceive) | att bedra | [at be'dra] |
| swindle, deception | bedrägeri (en) | [bedrɛːge'riː] |

swindler	bedragare (en)	[be'dragarə]
to bribe (vt)	att muta, att besticka	[at 'mʉːta], [at be'stika]
bribery	muta (en)	['mʉːta]
bribe	muta (en)	['mʉːta]

poison	gift (en)	['jift]
to poison (vt)	att förgifta	[at før'jifta]
to poison oneself	att förgifta sig själv	[at før'jifta sɛj ɧɛlʲv]

| suicide (act) | självmord (ett) | ['ɧɛlʲvˌmʉːd] |
| suicide (person) | självmördare (en) | ['ɧɛlʲvˌmøːdarə] |

to threaten (vt)	att hota	[at 'hʊta]
threat	hot (ett)	['hʊt]
to make an attempt	att begå mordförsök	[at be'go 'mʉːdfœːˌsøːk]
attempt (attack)	mordförsök (ett)	['mʉːdfœːˌsøːk]

| to steal (a car) | att stjäla | [at 'ɧɛːlʲa] |
| to hijack (a plane) | att kapa | [at 'kapa] |

| revenge | hämnd (en) | ['hɛmnd] |
| to avenge (get revenge) | att hämnas | [at 'hɛmnas] |

to torture (vt)	att tortera	[at tɔː'ʈera]
torture	tortyr (en)	[tɔː'ʈyr]
to torment (vt)	att plåga	[at 'plʲoːga]

pirate	pirat, sjörövare (en)	[pi'rat], ['ɧøːˌrøːvarə]
hooligan	buse (en)	['bʉːsə]
armed (adj)	beväpnad	[be'vɛpnad]
violence	våld (ett)	['voːlʲd]
illegal (unlawful)	illegal	['ilʲeˌgalʲ]

| spying (espionage) | spioneri (ett) | [spiʊne'riː] |
| to spy (vi) | att spionera | [at spiʊ'nera] |

193. Police. Law. Part 1

| justice | rättvisa (en) | ['rætˌvisa] |
| court (see you in ~) | rättssal (en) | ['rætˌsalʲ] |

judge	domare (en)	['dʊmarə]
jurors	jurymedlemmer (pl)	['jʉriˌmedle'mər]
jury trial	juryrättegång (en)	['jʉriˌræte'goŋ]
to judge (vt)	att döma	[at 'døːma]

lawyer, attorney	advokat (en)	[advʊ'kat]
defendant	anklagad (en)	['aŋˌklʲagad]
dock	anklagades bänk (en)	['aŋˌklʲagadəs ˌbɛŋk]
charge	anklagelse (en)	['aŋˌklʲagəlʲsə]

accused	**den anklagade**	[dɛn 'aŋ̩klʲagadə]
sentence	**dom (en)**	['dɔm]
to sentence (vt)	**att döma**	[at 'dø:ma]
guilty (culprit)	**skyldig (en)**	['ɧylʲdig]
to punish (vt)	**att straffa**	[at 'strafa]
punishment	**straff (ett)**	['straf]
fine (penalty)	**bot (en)**	['bʊt]
life imprisonment	**livstids fängelse (ett)**	['livstids 'fɛŋəlʲsə]
death penalty	**dödsstraff (ett)**	['dø:dˌstraf]
electric chair	**elektrisk stol (en)**	[ɛ'lʲektrisk ˌstʊlʲ]
gallows	**galge (en)**	['galʲə]
to execute (vt)	**att avrätta**	[at 'avˌræta]
execution	**avrättning (en)**	['avˌrætniŋ]
prison, jail	**fängelse (ett)**	['fɛŋəlʲsə]
cell	**cell (en)**	['sɛlʲ]
escort	**eskort (en)**	[ɛs'kɔ:t]
prison guard	**fångvaktare (en)**	['fɔŋˌvaktarə]
prisoner	**fånge (en)**	['fɔŋə]
handcuffs	**handbojor** (pl)	['handˌbɔjʊr]
to handcuff (vt)	**att sätta handbojor**	[at 'sæta 'handˌbɔjʊr]
prison break	**flukt (en)**	['flʉkt]
to break out (vi)	**att rymma**	[at 'rʏma]
to disappear (vi)	**att försvinna**	[at fœ:'ʂvina]
to release (from prison)	**att frige**	[at 'frije]
amnesty	**amnesti (en)**	[amnɛs'ti:]
police	**polis (en)**	[pʊ'lis]
police officer	**polis (en)**	[pʊ'lis]
police station	**polisstation (en)**	[pʊ'lisˌsta'fjʊn]
billy club	**gummibatong (en)**	['gumibaˌtʊŋ]
bullhorn	**megafon (en)**	[mega'fɔn]
patrol car	**patrullbil (en)**	[pat'rulʲˌbil]
siren	**siren (en)**	[si'ren]
to turn on the siren	**att slå på sirenen**	[at slʲo: pɔ si'renən]
siren call	**siren tjut (ett)**	[si'ren ˌɕʉ:t]
crime scene	**brottsplats (en)**	['brɔts plʲats]
witness	**vittne (ett)**	['vitnə]
freedom	**frihet (en)**	['friˌhet]
accomplice	**medskyldig (en)**	['mɛdˌɧylʲdig]
to flee (vi)	**att fly**	[at flʲy]
trace (to leave a ~)	**spår (ett)**	['spo:r]

194. Police. Law. Part 2

search (investigation)	undersökning (en)	['undə‚sœkniŋ]
to look for ...	att söka efter ...	[at 'søːka ‚ɛftər ...]
suspicion	misstanke (en)	['mis‚taŋkə]
suspicious (e.g., ~ vehicle)	misstänksam	['mistɛŋksam]
to stop (cause to halt)	att stanna	[at 'stana]
to detain (keep in custody)	att anhålla	[at 'an‚hoːlʲa]

case (lawsuit)	sak, rättegång (en)	[sak], ['rætə‚goŋ]
investigation	undersökning (en)	['undə‚sœkniŋ]
detective	detektiv (en)	[detɛk'tiv]
investigator	undersökare (en)	['undə‚søːkarə]
hypothesis	version (en)	[vɛr'ʃʊn]

motive	motiv (ett)	[mʊ'tiv]
interrogation	förhör (ett)	[før'høːr]
to interrogate (vt)	att förhöra	[at før'høːra]
to question	att avhöra	[at 'av‚høːra]
(~ neighbors, etc.)		
check (identity ~)	kontroll (en)	[kɔn'trolʲ]

round-up	razzia (en)	['ratsia]
search (~ warrant)	rannsakan (en)	['ran‚sakan]
chase (pursuit)	jakt (en)	['jakt]
to pursue, to chase	att förfölja	[at før'følja]
to track (a criminal)	att spåra	[at 'spoːra]

arrest	arrest (en)	[a'rɛst]
to arrest (sb)	att arrestera	[at arɛ'stera]
to catch (thief, etc.)	att fånga	[at 'foŋa]
capture	gripande (en)	['gripandə]

document	dokument (ett)	[dɔku'mɛnt]
proof (evidence)	bevis (ett)	[be'vis]
to prove (vt)	att bevisa	[at be'visa]
footprint	fotspår (ett)	['fʊt‚spoːr]
fingerprints	fingeravtryck (pl)	['fiŋer‚avtrʏk]
piece of evidence	bevis (ett)	[be'vis]

alibi	alibi (ett)	['alibi]
innocent (not guilty)	oskyldig	[ʊ:'ʃylʲdig]
injustice	orättfärdighet (en)	['ʊræt‚fæːɖihet]
unjust, unfair (adj)	orättfärdig	['ʊræt‚fæːɖig]

criminal (adj)	kriminell	[krimi'nɛlʲ]
to confiscate (vt)	att konfiskera	[at kɔnfi'skera]
drug (illegal substance)	drog, narkotika (en)	['drʊg], [nar'kotika]
weapon, gun	vapen (ett)	['vapən]
to disarm (vt)	att avväpna	[at 'av‚vɛpna]
to order (command)	att befalla	[at be'falʲa]

to disappear (vi)	**att försvinna**	[at fœ:'ʂvina]
law	**lag (en)**	['lʲag]
legal, lawful (adj)	**laglig**	['lʲaglig]
illegal, illicit (adj)	**olovlig**	[ʊ:'lʲovlig]
responsibility (blame)	**ansvar (ett)**	['anˌsvar]
responsible (adj)	**ansvarig**	['anˌsvarig]

NATURE

The Earth. Part 1

195. Outer space

space	rymden, kosmos (ett)	[rʏmden], ['kosmɔs]
space (as adj)	rymd-	['rʏmd-]
outer space	yttre rymd (en)	['ytrə ˌrʏmd]
world	värld (en)	['væːɖ]
universe	universum (ett)	[uni'vɛːʂum]
galaxy	galax (en)	[ga'lʲaks]
star	stjärna (en)	['ɧæːɳa]
constellation	stjärnbild (en)	['ɧæːnˌbilʲd]
planet	planet (en)	[plʲa'net]
satellite	satellit (en)	[satɛ'liːt]
meteorite	meteorit (en)	[meteʊ'rit]
comet	komet (en)	[kʊ'met]
asteroid	asteroid (en)	[asterʊ'id]
orbit	bana (en)	['bana]
to revolve	att rotera	[at rʊ'tera]
(~ around the Earth)		
atmosphere	atmosfär (en)	[atmʊ'sfæːr]
the Sun	Solen	['sʊlʲən]
solar system	solsystem (ett)	['sʊlʲ ˌsʏ'stem]
solar eclipse	solförmörkelse (en)	['sʊlʲfør'mœːrkəlʲsə]
the Earth	Jorden	['jʊːɖən]
the Moon	Månen	['moːnən]
Mars	Mars	['maːʂ]
Venus	Venus	['veːnus]
Jupiter	Jupiter	['jupitər]
Saturn	Saturnus	[sa'tuːɳus]
Mercury	Merkurius	[mɛr'kʉrius]
Uranus	Uranus	[ʉ'ranus]
Neptune	Neptunus	[nep'tʉnus]
Pluto	Pluto	['plʉtʊ]
Milky Way	Vintergatan	['vintəˌgatan]
Great Bear (Ursa Major)	Stora bjornen	['stʊra 'bjʊːɳən]

North Star	Polstjärnan	['pʊlʲˌɧæːŋan]
Martian	marsian (en)	[maːʂiʼan]
extraterrestrial (n)	utomjording (en)	['ʉtɔmˌjuːdjisk]
alien	rymdväsen (ett)	['rʏmdˌvɛsən]
flying saucer	flygande tefat (ett)	['flʲygandə 'tefat]

spaceship	rymdskepp (ett)	['rʏmdˌɧɛp]
space station	rymdstation (en)	['rʏmd staʼɧʊn]
blast-off	start (en)	['staːt]

engine	motor (en)	['mʊtʊr]
nozzle	dysa (en)	['dysa]
fuel	bränsle (ett)	['brɛnslʲe]

cockpit, flight deck	cockpit, flygdäck (en)	['kɔkpit], ['flʏgˌdɛk]
antenna	antenn (en)	[anʼtɛn]
porthole	fönster (ett)	['fœnstər]
solar panel	solbatteri (ett)	['sʊlʲˌbatɛ'riː]
spacesuit	rymddräkt (en)	['rʏmdˌdrɛkt]

| weightlessness | tyngdlöshet (en) | ['tʏŋdlʲøsˌhet] |
| oxygen | syre, oxygen (ett) | ['syrə], ['oksygən] |

| docking (in space) | dockning (en) | ['dɔkniŋ] |
| to dock (vi, vt) | att docka | [at 'dɔka] |

observatory	observatorium (ett)	[ɔbsɛrva'tʊrium]
telescope	teleskop (ett)	[telʲe'skɔp]
to observe (vt)	att observera	[at ɔbsɛr'vera]
to explore (vt)	att utforska	[at 'ʉtˌfɔːʂka]

196. The Earth

the Earth	Jorden	['jʊːdən]
the globe (the Earth)	jordklot (ett)	['jʊːdˌklʲʊt]
planet	planet (en)	[plʲa'net]

atmosphere	atmosfär (en)	[atmʊ'sfæːr]
geography	geografi (en)	[jeʊgra'fiː]
nature	natur (en)	[na'tʉːr]

globe (table ~)	glob (en)	['glʲʊb]
map	karta (en)	['kaːʈa]
atlas	atlas (en)	['atlʲas]

Europe	Europa	[eu'rʊpa]
Asia	Asien	['asiən]
Africa	Afrika	['afrika]
Australia	Australien	[au'straliən]
America	Amerika	[a'merika]

| North America | Nordamerika | ['nʊːd̪ a'merika] |
| South America | Sydamerika | ['syd a'merika] |

| Antarctica | Antarktis | [an'tarktis] |
| the Arctic | Arktis | ['arktis] |

197. Cardinal directions

north	norr	['nɔr]
to the north	norrut	['nɔrʉt]
in the north	i norr	[i 'nɔr]
northern (adj)	nordlig	['nʊːd̪lig]

south	söder (en)	['søːdər]
to the south	söderut	['søːdərʉt]
in the south	i söder	[i 'søːdər]
southern (adj)	syd-, söder	['syd-], ['søːdər]

west	väster (en)	['vɛstər]
to the west	västerut	['vɛstərʉt]
in the west	i väst	[i vɛst]
western (adj)	västra	['vɛstra]

east	öster (en)	['œstər]
to the east	österut	['œstərʉt]
in the east	i öst	[i 'œst]
eastern (adj)	östra	['œstra]

198. Sea. Ocean

sea	hav (ett)	['hav]
ocean	ocean (en)	[ʊsə'an]
gulf (bay)	bukt (en)	['bukt]
straits	sund (ett)	['sund]

| land (solid ground) | fastland (ett) | ['fastˌlʲand] |
| continent (mainland) | fastland (ett), kontinent (en) | ['fastˌlʲand], [kɔnti'nɛnt] |

island	ö (en)	['øː]
peninsula	halvö (en)	['halʲvˌøː]
archipelago	skärgård, arkipelag (en)	['ɧæːrˌgoːd], [arkipe'lʲag]

bay, cove	bukt (en)	['bukt]
harbor	hamn (en)	['hamn]
lagoon	lagun (en)	[lʲa'gʉːn]
cape	udde (en)	['udə]
atoll	atoll (en)	[a'tɔlʲ]
reef	rev (ett)	['rev]

| coral | korall (en) | [kɔ'ralʲ] |
| coral reef | korallrev (ett) | [kɔ'ralʲˌrev] |

deep (adj)	djup	['jɵːp]
depth (deep water)	djup (ett)	['jɵːp]
abyss	avgrund (en)	['avˌgrʉnd]
trench (e.g., Mariana ~)	djuphavsgrav (en)	['jɵːphavsˌgrav]

| current (Ocean ~) | ström (en) | ['strøːm] |
| to surround (bathe) | att omge | [at 'ɔmje] |

| shore | kust (en) | ['kust] |
| coast | kust (en) | ['kust] |

flow (flood tide)	flod (en)	['flʲʊd]
ebb (ebb tide)	ebb (en)	['ɛb]
shoal	sandbank (en)	['sandˌbaŋk]
bottom (~ of the sea)	botten (en)	['bɔtən]

wave	våg (en)	['voːg]
crest (~ of a wave)	vågkam (en)	['voːgˌkam]
spume (sea foam)	skum (ett)	['skum]

storm (sea storm)	storm (en)	['stɔrm]
hurricane	orkan (en)	[ɔr'kan]
tsunami	tsunami (en)	[tsu'nami]
calm (dead ~)	stiltje (en)	['stilʲtjə]
quiet, calm (adj)	stilla	['stilʲa]

| pole | pol (en) | ['pʊlʲ] |
| polar (adj) | pol-, polar- | ['pʊlʲ-], [pʊ'lʲar-] |

latitude	latitud (en)	[lʲati'tɵːd]
longitude	longitud (en)	[lʲɔnji'tɵːd]
parallel	breddgrad (en)	['brɛdˌgrad]
equator	ekvator (en)	[ɛ'kvatʊr]

sky	himmel (en)	['himəlʲ]
horizon	horisont (en)	[hʊri'sɔnt]
air	luft (en)	['lʉft]

lighthouse	fyr (en)	['fyr]
to dive (vi)	att dyka	[at 'dyka]
to sink (ab. boat)	att sjunka	[at 'ɧuŋka]
treasures	skatter (pl)	['skatər]

199. Seas' and Oceans' names

| Atlantic Ocean | Atlanten | [at'lʲantən] |
| Indian Ocean | Indiska oceanen | ['indiska ʊsə'anən] |

| Pacific Ocean | Stilla havet | ['stil⃰a 'havɛt] |
| Arctic Ocean | Norra ishavet | ['nɔra ͵is'havɛt] |

Black Sea	Svarta havet	['svaːʈa 'havɛt]
Red Sea	Röda havet	['røːda 'havɛt]
Yellow Sea	Gula havet	['gʉːl⃰a 'havɛt]
White Sea	Vita havet	['vita 'havɛt]

Caspian Sea	Kaspiska havet	['kaspiska 'havɛt]
Dead Sea	Döda havet	['døːda 'havɛt]
Mediterranean Sea	Medelhavet	['medəl⃰͵havɛt]

| Aegean Sea | Egeiska havet | [ɛ'gejska 'havɛt] |
| Adriatic Sea | Adriatiska havet | [adri'atiska 'havɛt] |

Arabian Sea	Arabiska havet	[a'rabiska 'havɛt]
Sea of Japan	Japanska havet	[ja'panska 'havɛt]
Bering Sea	Beringshavet	['berings͵havɛt]
South China Sea	Sydkinesiska havet	['sydɕi͵nesiska 'havɛt]

Coral Sea	Korallhavet	[kɔ'ral⃰͵havɛt]
Tasman Sea	Tasmanhavet	[tas'man͵havɛt]
Caribbean Sea	Karibiska havet	[ka'ribiska 'havɛt]

| Barents Sea | Barentshavet | ['barɛnts͵havɛt] |
| Kara Sea | Karahavet | ['kara͵havɛt] |

North Sea	Nordsjön	['nʊːɖ͵ɧøːn]
Baltic Sea	Östersjön	['œstɛː͵ɧøːn]
Norwegian Sea	Norska havet	['nɔːʂka 'havɛt]

200. Mountains

mountain	berg (ett)	['bɛrj]
mountain range	bergskedja (en)	['bɛrj͵ɕedja]
mountain ridge	bergsrygg (en)	['bɛrjs͵rʏg]

summit, top	topp (en)	['tɔp]
peak	tinne (en)	['tinə]
foot (~ of the mountain)	fot (en)	['fʊt]
slope (mountainside)	sluttning (en)	['slʉːtniŋ]

volcano	vulkan (en)	[vʉl⃰'kan]
active volcano	verksam vulkan (en)	['vɛrksam vʉl⃰'kan]
dormant volcano	slocknad vulkan (en)	['sl⃰ɔknad vʉl⃰'kan]

eruption	utbrott (ett)	['ʉt͵brɔt]
crater	krater (en)	['kratər]
magma	magma (en)	['magma]
lava	lava (en)	['l⃰ava]

molten (~ lava)	glödgad	['glⁱœdgad]
canyon	kanjon (en)	['kanjɔn]
gorge	klyfta (en)	['klⁱyfta]
crevice	skreva (en)	['skreva]
abyss (chasm)	avgrund (en)	['av͵grʉnd]

pass, col	pass (ett)	['pas]
plateau	platå (en)	[plⁱa'to:]
cliff	klippa (en)	['klipa]
hill	kulle, backe (en)	['kulⁱə], ['bakə]

glacier	glaciär, jökel (en)	[glⁱas'jæ:r], ['jø:kəlⁱ]
waterfall	vattenfall (ett)	['vatən͵falⁱ]
geyser	gejser (en)	['gɛjsər]
lake	sjö (en)	['ɧø:]

plain	slätt (en)	['slⁱæt]
landscape	landskap (ett)	['lⁱaŋ͵skap]
echo	eko (ett)	['ɛkʊ]

alpinist	alpinist (en)	['alⁱpi͵nist]
rock climber	bergsbestigare (en)	['bɛrjs͵be'stigarə]
to conquer (in climbing)	att erövra	[at ɛ'rœvra]
climb (an easy ~)	bestigning (en)	[be'stigniŋ]

201. Mountains names

The Alps	Alperna	['alⁱpɛ:ŋa]
Mont Blanc	Mont Blanc	[͵mɔn'blⁱaŋ]
The Pyrenees	Pyrenéerna	[pyre'neæ:ŋa]

The Carpathians	Karpaterna	[kar'patɛ:ŋa]
The Ural Mountains	Uralbergen	[ʉ'ralⁱ͵bɛrjən]
The Caucasus Mountains	Kaukasus	['kaukasus]
Mount Elbrus	Elbrus	['ɛlⁱbrʉs]

The Altai Mountains	Altaj	[alⁱ'taj]
The Tian Shan	Tian Shan	[ti'anʃan]
The Pamir Mountains	Pamir	[pa'mir]
The Himalayas	Himalaya	[hi'malⁱaja]
Mount Everest	Everest	[ɛve'rɛst]
The Andes	Anderna	['andɛ:ŋa]
Mount Kilimanjaro	Kilimanjaro	[kiliman'jarʊ]

202. Rivers

| river | älv, flod (en) | ['ɛlⁱv], ['flⁱʊd] |
| spring (natural source) | källa (en) | ['ɕɛlⁱa] |

riverbed (river channel)	**flodbädd (en)**	[ˈfliʊdˌbɛd]
basin (river valley)	**flodbassäng (en)**	[ˈfliʊdˌbaˈsɛŋ]
to flow into …	**att mynna ut …**	[at ˈmʏna ʉt …]
tributary	**biflod (en)**	[ˈbiˌfliʊd]
bank (of river)	**strand (en)**	[ˈstrand]
current (stream)	**ström (en)**	[ˈstrøːm]
downstream (adv)	**nedströms**	[ˈnɛdˌstrœms]
upstream (adv)	**motströms**	[ˈmʊtˌstrœms]
inundation	**översvämning (en)**	[ˈøːvəˌsvɛmniŋ]
flooding	**flöde (ett)**	[ˈfliøːdə]
to overflow (vi)	**att flöda över**	[at ˈfliøːda ˌøːvər]
to flood (vt)	**att översvämma**	[at ˈøːvəˌsvɛma]
shallow (shoal)	**grund (ett)**	[ˈgrʉnd]
rapids	**forsar (pl)**	[foˈʂar]
dam	**damm (en)**	[ˈdam]
canal	**kanal (en)**	[kaˈnalʲ]
reservoir (artificial lake)	**reservoar (ett)**	[resɛrvʊˈaːr]
sluice, lock	**sluss (en)**	[ˈslʉːs]
water body (pond, etc.)	**vattensamling (en)**	[ˈvatənˌsamliŋ]
swamp (marshland)	**myr, mosse (en)**	[ˈmyr], [ˈmʊsə]
bog, marsh	**gungfly (ett)**	[ˈguŋˌfly]
whirlpool	**strömvirvel (en)**	[ˈstrøːmˌvirvəlʲ]
stream (brook)	**bäck (en)**	[ˈbɛk]
drinking (ab. water)	**dricks-**	[ˈdriks-]
fresh (~ water)	**söt-, färsk-**	[ˈsøːt-], [ˈfæːʂk-]
ice	**is (en)**	[ˈis]
to freeze over (ab. river, etc.)	**att frysa till**	[at ˈfrysa tilʲ]

203. Rivers' names

Seine	**Seine**	[ˈsɛːn]
Loire	**Loire**	[lʲʊˈaːr]
Thames	**Themsen**	[ˈtɛmsən]
Rhine	**Rhen**	[ˈren]
Danube	**Donau**	[ˈdɔnaʊ]
Volga	**Volga**	[ˈvɔlʲga]
Don	**Don**	[ˈdɔn]
Lena	**Lena**	[ˈlʲena]
Yellow River	**Hwang-ho**	[huaŋˈhʊ]

Yangtze	Yangtze	['jɑŋtsə]
Mekong	Mekong	[me'kɔŋ]
Ganges	Ganges	['gaŋəs]

Nile River	Nilen	['niḷen]
Congo River	Kongo	['kɔŋgʊ]
Okavango River	Okavango	[ɔka'vangʊ]
Zambezi River	Zambezi	[sam'besi]
Limpopo River	Limpopo	[lim'pɔpɔ]
Mississippi River	Mississippi	[misi'sipi]

204. Forest

| forest, wood | skog (en) | ['skʊg] |
| forest (as adj) | skogs- | ['skʊgs-] |

thick forest	tät skog (en)	['tɛt ˌskʊg]
grove	lund (en)	['lʉnd]
forest clearing	glänta (en)	['gḷɛnta]

| thicket | snår (ett) | ['snoːr] |
| scrubland | buskterräng (en) | ['busk tɛ'rɛŋ] |

| footpath (troddenpath) | stig (en) | ['stig] |
| gully | ravin (en) | [ra'vin] |

tree	träd (ett)	['trɛːd]
leaf	löv (ett)	['ḷøːv]
leaves (foliage)	löv, lövverk (ett)	['ḷøːv], ['ḷøːværk]

fall of leaves	lövfällning (en)	['ḷøːvˌfɛḷniŋ]
to fall (ab. leaves)	att falla	[at 'faḷa]
top (of the tree)	trädtopp (en)	['trɛːˌtɔp]

branch	gren, kvist (en)	['gren], ['kvist]
bough	gren (en)	['gren]
bud (on shrub, tree)	knopp (en)	['knɔp]
needle (of pine tree)	nål (en)	['noːḷ]
pine cone	kotte (en)	['kɔtə]

hollow (in a tree)	trädhål (ett)	['trɛːdˌhoːḷ]
nest	bo (ett)	['bʊ]
burrow (animal hole)	lya, håla (en)	['ḷya], ['hoːḷa]

trunk	stam (en)	['stam]
root	rot (en)	['rʊt]
bark	bark (en)	['bark]
moss	mossa (en)	['mɔsa]
to uproot (remove trees or tree stumps)	att rycka upp med rötterna	[at 'rʏka up me 'rœttɛːˌŋa]

to chop down	att fälla	[at 'fɛlʲa]
to deforest (vt)	att hugga ner	[at 'huga ner]
tree stump	stubbe (en)	['stubə]

campfire	bål (ett)	['boːlʲ]
forest fire	skogsbrand (en)	['skʊgsˌbrand]
to extinguish (vt)	att släcka	[at 'slʲɛka]

forest ranger	skogsvakt (en)	['skʊgsˌvakt]
protection	värn, skydd (ett)	['væːn], [ʃʏd]
to protect (~ nature)	att skydda	[at 'ʃʏda]
poacher	tjuvskytt (en)	['ɕʉːvˌʃʏt]
steel trap	sax (en)	['saks]

| to gather, to pick (vt) | att plocka | [at 'plʲɔka] |
| to lose one's way | att gå vilse | [at 'goː 'vilʲsə] |

205. Natural resources

natural resources	naturresurser (pl)	[naˈtʉːr reˈsurʂər]
minerals	mineraler (pl)	[mineˈralʲər]
deposits	fyndigheter (pl)	['fʏndiˌhetər]
field (e.g., oilfield)	fält (ett)	['fɛlʲt]

to mine (extract)	att utvinna	[at 'ʉtˌvina]
mining (extraction)	utvinning (en)	['ʉtˌviniŋ]
ore	malm (en)	['malʲm]
mine (e.g., for coal)	gruva (en)	['grʉva]
shaft (mine ~)	gruvschakt (ett)	['grʉːvˌʃakt]
miner	gruvarbetare (en)	['grʉːvˌarˈbetarə]

| gas (natural ~) | gas (en) | ['gas] |
| gas pipeline | gasledning (en) | ['gasˌlʲedniŋ] |

oil (petroleum)	olja (en)	['ɔlja]
oil pipeline	oljeledning (en)	['ɔljəˌlʲedniŋ]
oil well	oljekälla (en)	['ɔljəˌɕæla]
derrick (tower)	borrtorn (ett)	['bɔrˌtuːn]
tanker	tankfartyg (ett)	['taŋkˌfaːˈtyg]

sand	sand (en)	['sand]
limestone	kalksten (en)	[kalʲkˌsten]
gravel	grus (ett)	['grʉːs]
peat	torv (en)	['tɔrv]
clay	lera (en)	['lʲera]
coal	kol (ett)	['kɔlʲ]

iron (ore)	järn (ett)	['jæːn]
gold	guld (ett)	['gulʲd]
silver	silver (ett)	['silʲvər]

nickel	**nickel (en)**	['nikəlʲ]
copper	**koppar (en)**	['kopar]
zinc	**zink (en)**	['siŋk]
manganese	**mangan (en)**	[man'gan]
mercury	**kvicksilver (ett)**	['kvik͵silʲvər]
lead	**bly (ett)**	['blʲy]
mineral	**mineral (ett)**	[minə'ralʲ]
crystal	**kristall (en)**	[kri'stalʲ]
marble	**marmor (en)**	['marmʊr]
uranium	**uran (ett)**	[ʉ'ran]

The Earth. Part 2

206. Weather

weather	väder (ett)	['vɛːdər]
weather forecast	väderprognos (en)	['vɛːdər̩prɔg'nɔːs]
temperature	temperatur (en)	[tɛmpəra'tʉːr]
thermometer	termometer (en)	[tɛrmʊ'metər]
barometer	barometer (en)	[barʊ'metər]
humid (adj)	fuktig	['fuːktig]
humidity	fuktighet (en)	['fuːktig̩het]
heat (extreme ~)	hetta (en)	['hɛta]
hot (torrid)	het	['het]
it's hot	det är hett	[dɛ æːr 'hɛt]
it's warm	det är varmt	[dɛ æːr varmt]
warm (moderately hot)	varm	['varm]
it's cold	det är kallt	[dɛ æːr 'kalʲt]
cold (adj)	kall	['kalʲ]
sun	sol (en)	['sʊlʲ]
to shine (vi)	att skina	[at 'ɧina]
sunny (day)	solig	['sʊlig]
to come up (vi)	att gå upp	[at 'goː 'up]
to set (vi)	att gå ner	[at 'goː ˌner]
cloud	moln (ett), sky (en)	['mɔlʲn], ['ɧy]
cloudy (adj)	molnig	['mɔlʲnig]
rain cloud	regnmoln (ett)	['rɛgn̩mɔlʲn]
somber (gloomy)	mörk, mulen	['mœːrk], ['mʉːlʲen]
rain	regn (ett)	['rɛgn]
it's raining	det regnar	[dɛ 'rɛgnar]
rainy (~ day, weather)	regnväders-	['rɛgn̩vɛdəʂ-]
to drizzle (vi)	att duggregna	[at 'dug̩rɛgna]
pouring rain	hällande regn (ett)	['hɛlʲandə 'rɛgn]
downpour	spöregn (ett)	['spøːˌrɛgn]
heavy (e.g., ~ rain)	kraftigt, häftigt	['kraftigt], ['hɛftigt]
puddle	pöl, vattenpuss (en)	['pøːlʲ], ['vatən̩pus]
to get wet (in rain)	att bli våt	[at bli 'voːt]
fog (mist)	dimma (en)	['dima]
foggy	dimmig	['dimig]

| snow | snö (en) | ['snø:] |
| it's snowing | det snöar | [dɛ 'snø:ar] |

207. Severe weather. Natural disasters

thunderstorm	åskväder (ett)	['ɔsk‚vɛdər]
lightning (~ strike)	blixt (en)	['blikst]
to flash (vi)	att blixtra	[at 'blikstra]

thunder	åska (en)	['ɔska]
to thunder (vi)	att åska	[at 'ɔska]
it's thundering	det åskar	[dɛ 'ɔskar]

| hail | hagel (ett) | ['hagəlʲ] |
| it's hailing | det haglar | [dɛ 'haglʲar] |

| to flood (vt) | att översvämma | [at 'ø:və‚svɛma] |
| flood, inundation | översvämning (en) | ['ø:və‚svɛmniŋ] |

earthquake	jordskalv (ett)	['ju:d‚skalv]
tremor, quake	skalv (ett)	['skalʲv]
epicenter	epicentrum (ett)	[ɛpi'sɛntrum]
eruption	utbrott (ett)	['ʉt‚brɔt]
lava	lava (en)	['lʲava]

twister	tromb (en)	['trɔmb]
tornado	tornado (en)	[tʊ'ŋadʊ]
typhoon	tyfon (en)	[ty'fon]

hurricane	orkan (en)	[ɔr'kan]
storm	storm (en)	['stɔrm]
tsunami	tsunami (en)	[tsu'nami]

cyclone	cyklon (en)	[tsɤ'klʲɔn]
bad weather	oväder (ett)	[ʊ'vɛ:dər]
fire (accident)	brand (en)	['brand]
disaster	katastrof (en)	[kata'strɔf]
meteorite	meteorit (en)	[meteʊ'rit]

avalanche	lavin (en)	[lʲa'vin]
snowslide	snöskred, snöras (ett)	['snø:‚skred], ['snø:‚ras]
blizzard	snöstorm (en)	['snø:‚stɔrm]
snowstorm	snöstorm (en)	['snø:‚stɔrm]

208. Noises. Sounds

| silence (quiet) | stillhet (en) | ['stɤlʲ‚het] |
| sound | ljud (ett) | ['jʉ:d] |

noise	stoj (ett)	['stoj]
to make noise	att stoja	[at 'stoja]
noisy (adj)	stojande	['stojandə]

loudly (to speak, etc.)	högt	['hœgt]
loud (voice, etc.)	hög	['høːg]
constant (e.g., ~ noise)	konstant	[kɔn'stant]

cry, shout (n)	skrik (ett)	['skrik]
to cry, to shout (vi)	att skrika	[at 'skrika]
whisper	viskning (en)	['viskniŋ]
to whisper (vi, vt)	att viska	[at 'viska]

barking (dog's ~)	skall (ett)	['skalʲ]
to bark (vi)	att skälla	[at 'ɦɛlʲa]

groan (of pain, etc.)	stön (ett)	['støːn]
to groan (vi)	att stöna	[at 'støːna]
cough	hosta (en)	['hʊsta]
to cough (vi)	att hosta	[at 'hʊsta]

whistle	vissling (en)	['visliŋ]
to whistle (vi)	att vissla	[at 'vislʲa]
knock (at the door)	knackning (en)	['knakniŋ]
to knock (at the door)	att knacka	[at 'knaka]

to crack (vi)	att spricka	[at 'sprika]
crack (cracking sound)	spricka (en)	['sprika]

siren	siren (en)	[si'ren]
whistle (factory ~, etc.)	vissla (en)	['vislʲa]
to whistle (ab. train)	att tuta	[at 'tʉːta]
honk (car horn sound)	tuta (en)	['tʉːta]
to honk (vi)	att tuta	[at 'tʉːta]

209. Winter

winter (n)	vinter (en)	['vintər]
winter (as adj)	vinter-	['vintər-]
in winter	på vintern	[pɔ 'vintərn]

snow	snö (en)	['snøː]
it's snowing	det snöar	[dɛ 'snøːar]
snowfall	snöfall (ett)	['snøːˌfalʲ]
snowdrift	snödriva (en)	['snøːˌdriva]

snowflake	snöflinga (en)	['snøːˌfliŋa]
snowball	snöboll (en)	['snøːˌbɔlʲ]
snowman	snögubbe (en)	['snøːˌgubə]
icicle	istapp (en)	['isˌtap]

213

December	december (en)	[de'sɛmbər]
January	januari (en)	['januˌari]
February	februari (en)	[fɛbru'ari]

| frost (severe ~, freezing cold) | frost (en) | ['frɔst] |
| frosty (weather, air) | frostig | ['frɔstig] |

below zero (adv)	under noll	['undə ˌnɔlʲ]
first frost	lätt frost (en)	[lʲæt frɔst]
hoarfrost	rimfrost (en)	['rimˌfrɔst]

| cold (cold weather) | kyla (en) | ['ɕylʲa] |
| it's cold | det är kallt | [dɛ æ:r 'kalʲt] |

| fur coat | päls (en) | ['pɛlʲs] |
| mittens | vantar (pl) | ['vantar] |

to get sick	att bli sjuk	[at bli 'ɧʉ:k]
cold (illness)	förkylning (en)	[før'ɕylʲniŋ]
to catch a cold	att bli förkyld	[at bli før'ɕylʲd]

ice	is (en)	['is]
black ice	isbeläggning (en)	['isˌbe'lʲɛgniŋ]
to freeze over (ab. river, etc.)	att frysa till	[at 'frysa tilʲ]
ice floe	isflak (ett)	['isˌflʲak]

skis	skidor (pl)	['ɧidʊr]
skier	skidåkare (en)	['ɧidˌo:karə]
to ski (vi)	att åka skidor	[at 'o:ka 'ɧidʊr]
to skate (vi)	att åka skridskor	[at 'o:ka 'skriˌskʊr]

Fauna

210. Mammals. Predators

predator	rovdjur (ett)	['rʊvjʉːr]
tiger	tiger (en)	['tigər]
lion	lejon (ett)	['lʲejɔn]
wolf	ulv (en)	['ulʲv]
fox	räv (en)	['rɛːv]
jaguar	jaguar (en)	[jaguar]
leopard	leopard (en)	[lʲeʊ'paːd]
cheetah	gepard (en)	[je'paːd]
black panther	panter (en)	['pantər]
puma	puma (en)	['pʉːma]
snow leopard	snöleopard (en)	['snø: lʲeʊ'paːd]
lynx	lodjur (ett), lo (en)	['lʲʊjʉːr], ['lʲʊ]
coyote	koyot, prärievarg (en)	[kɔ'jʊt], ['præːrieˌvarj]
jackal	sjakal (en)	[ɧa'kalʲ]
hyena	hyena (en)	[hy'ena]

211. Wild animals

animal	djur (ett)	['jʉːr]
beast (animal)	best (en), djur (ett)	['bɛst], ['jʉːr]
squirrel	ekorre (en)	['ɛkɔrə]
hedgehog	igelkott (en)	['igəlʲˌkɔt]
hare	hare (en)	['harə]
rabbit	kanin (en)	[ka'nin]
badger	grävling (en)	['grɛvliŋ]
raccoon	tvättbjörn (en)	['tvætˌbjøːɳ]
hamster	hamster (en)	['hamstər]
marmot	murmeldjur (ett)	['murməlʲjʉːr]
mole	mullvad (en)	['mulʲˌvad]
mouse	mus (en)	['mʉːs]
rat	råtta (en)	['rɔta]
bat	fladdermus (en)	['flʲadərˌmʉːs]
ermine	hermelin (en)	[hɛrme'lin]
sable	sobel (en)	['sɔbəlʲ]

marten	mård (en)	['moːɖ]
weasel	vessla (en)	['vɛslʲa]
mink	mink (en)	['miŋk]

| beaver | bäver (en) | ['bɛːvər] |
| otter | utter (en) | ['ʉːtər] |

horse	häst (en)	['hɛst]
moose	älg (en)	['ɛlj]
deer	hjort (en)	['jʉːt]
camel	kamel (en)	[ka'melʲ]

bison	bison (en)	['bisɔn]
aurochs	uroxe (en)	['ʉˌroksə]
buffalo	buffel (en)	['bufəlʲ]

zebra	sebra (en)	['sebra]
antelope	antilop (en)	[anti'lʲʊp]
roe deer	rådjur (ett)	['rɔːjʉːr]
fallow deer	dovhjort (en)	['dɔvˌjʉːt]
chamois	gems (en)	['jɛms]
wild boar	vildsvin (ett)	['vilʲdˌsvin]

whale	val (en)	['valʲ]
seal	säl (en)	['sɛːlʲ]
walrus	valross (en)	['valʲˌrɔs]
fur seal	pälssäl (en)	['pɛlʲsˌsɛlʲ]
dolphin	delfin (en)	[dɛlʲ'fin]

bear	björn (en)	['bjøːɳ]
polar bear	isbjörn (en)	['isˌbjøːɳ]
panda	panda (en)	['panda]

monkey	apa (en)	['apa]
chimpanzee	schimpans (en)	[ɧim'pans]
orangutan	orangutang (en)	[ʊ'raŋgʊˌtaŋ]
gorilla	gorilla (en)	[gɔ'rilʲa]
macaque	makak (en)	[ma'kak]
gibbon	gibbon (en)	[gi'bʊn]

elephant	elefant (en)	[ɛlʲe'fant]
rhinoceros	noshörning (en)	['nʊsˌhøːɳiɳ]
giraffe	giraff (en)	[ɧi'raf]
hippopotamus	flodhäst (en)	['flʲʊdˌhɛst]

| kangaroo | känguru (en) | ['ɕɛngurʊ] |
| koala (bear) | koala (en) | [kʊ'alʲa] |

mongoose	mangust, mungo (en)	['mangust], ['muŋgʊ]
chinchilla	chinchilla (en)	[ʃin'ʃilʲa]
skunk	skunk (en)	['skuŋk]
porcupine	piggsvin (ett)	['pigˌsvin]

212. Domestic animals

cat	**katt (en)**	['kat]
tomcat	**hankatt (en)**	['han,kat]
dog	**hund (en)**	['hund]
horse	**häst (en)**	['hɛst]
stallion (male horse)	**hingst (en)**	['hiŋst]
mare	**sto (ett)**	['stʊ:]
cow	**ko (en)**	['kɔ:]
bull	**tjur (en)**	['ɕʉ:r]
ox	**oxe (en)**	['ʊksə]
sheep (ewe)	**får (ett)**	['fo:r]
ram	**bagge (en)**	['bagə]
goat	**get (en)**	['jet]
billy goat, he-goat	**getabock (en)**	['jeta,bok]
donkey	**åsna (en)**	['ɔsna]
mule	**mula (en)**	['mʉlʲa]
pig, hog	**svin (ett)**	['svin]
piglet	**griskulting (en)**	['gris,kulʲtiŋ]
rabbit	**kanin (en)**	[ka'nin]
hen (chicken)	**höna (en)**	['hø:na]
rooster	**tupp (en)**	['tup]
duck	**anka (en)**	['aŋka]
drake	**andrik, andrake (en)**	['andrik], ['andrakə]
goose	**gås (en)**	['go:s]
tom turkey, gobbler	**kalkontupp (en)**	[kalʲ'kʊn,tup]
turkey (hen)	**kalkonhöna (en)**	[kalʲ'kʊn,hø:na]
domestic animals	**husdjur (pl)**	['hʉs,jʉ:r]
tame (e.g., ~ hamster)	**tam**	['tam]
to tame (vt)	**att tämja**	[at 'tɛmja]
to breed (vt)	**att avla, att föda upp**	[at 'avlʲa], [at 'fø:da up]
farm	**farm, lantgård (en)**	[farm], ['lʲant,go:ḍ]
poultry	**fjäderfä (ett)**	['fjɛ:dər,fɛ:]
cattle	**boskap (en)**	['bʊskap]
herd (cattle)	**hjord (en)**	['jʊ:ḍ]
stable	**stall (ett)**	['stalʲ]
pigpen	**svinstia (en)**	['svin,stia]
cowshed	**ladugård (en),**	['lʲadʉ,go:ḍ],
	kostall (ett)	['kostalʲ]
rabbit hutch	**kaninbur (en)**	[ka'nin,bʉ:r]
hen house	**hönshus (ett)**	['hø:ns,hʉs]

213. Dogs. Dog breeds

dog	hund (en)	['hund]
sheepdog	vallhund (en)	['valʲˌhund]
German shepherd	tysk schäferhund (en)	['tʏsk 'ʃɛfərˌhund]
poodle	pudel (en)	['pʉːdəlʲ]
dachshund	tax (en)	['taks]
bulldog	bulldogg (en)	['bulʲˌdɔg]
boxer	boxare (en)	['bʊksarə]
mastiff	mastiff (en)	[mas'tif]
Rottweiler	rottweiler (en)	['rɔtˌvejlʲer]
Doberman	dobermann (en)	['dɔbɛrman]
basset	basset (en)	['basɛt]
bobtail	bobtail (en)	['bʊbtɛjlʲ]
Dalmatian	dalmatiner (en)	[dalʲma'tinər]
cocker spaniel	cocker spaniel (en)	['kɔker ˌspaniəlʲ]
Newfoundland	newfoundland (en)	[nju'faʊndˌlʲend]
Saint Bernard	sankt bernhardshund (en)	['saŋkt 'bɛːɳaːdʂˌhund]
husky	husky (en)	['haski]
Chow Chow	chow chow (en)	['tʃaʊ tʃaʊ]
spitz	spets (en)	['spets]
pug	mops (en)	['mɔps]

214. Sounds made by animals

barking (n)	skall (ett)	['skalʲ]
to bark (vi)	att skälla	[at 'ɧɛlʲa]
to meow (vi)	att jama	[at 'jama]
to purr (vi)	att spinna	[at 'spina]
to moo (vi)	att råma	[at 'roːma]
to bellow (bull)	att ryta	[at 'ryta]
to growl (vi)	att morra	[at 'mɔːra]
howl (n)	yl (ett)	['ylʲ]
to howl (vi)	att yla	[at 'ylʲa]
to whine (vi)	att gnälla	[at 'gnɛlʲa]
to bleat (sheep)	att bräka	[at 'brɛːka]
to oink, to grunt (pig)	att grymta	[at 'grʏmta]
to squeal (vi)	att skrika	[at 'skrika]
to croak (vi)	att kväka	[at 'kvɛːka]
to buzz (insect)	att surra	[at 'sura]

to chirp (crickets, grasshopper)	**att gnissla**	[at 'gnislʲa]

215. Young animals

cub	**unge (en)**	['ʊŋə]
kitten	**kattunge (en)**	['katˌʊŋə]
baby mouse	**musunge (en)**	['mʉːsˌʊŋə]
puppy	**valp (en)**	['valʲp]

leveret	**harunge (en)**	['harˌʊŋə]
baby rabbit	**kaninunge (en)**	[ka'ninˌʊŋə]
wolf cub	**ulvunge (en)**	['ulʲvˌʊŋə]
fox cub	**rävunge (en)**	['rɛːvˌʊŋə]
bear cub	**björnunge (en)**	['bjøːɳˌʊŋə]

lion cub	**lejonunge (en)**	['lʲejɔnˌʊŋə]
tiger cub	**tigerunge (en)**	['tigərˌʊŋə]
elephant calf	**elefantunge (en)**	[ɛlʲe'fantˌʊŋə]

piglet	**griskulting (en)**	['grisˌkulʲtiŋ]
calf (young cow, bull)	**kalv (en)**	['kalʲv]
kid (young goat)	**killing (en)**	['ɕiliŋ]
lamb	**lamm (ett)**	['lʲam]
fawn (young deer)	**hjortkalv (en)**	['jʊːʈˌkalʲv]
young camel	**kamelunge (en)**	[ka'melʲˌʊŋə]

snakelet (baby snake)	**ormunge (en)**	['ʊrmˌʊŋə]
froglet (baby frog)	**grodunge (en)**	['grʊdˌʊŋə]

baby bird	**fågelunge (en)**	['foːɡəlʲˌʊŋə]
chick (of chicken)	**kyckling (en)**	['ɕykliŋ]
duckling	**ankunge (en)**	['aŋkˌʊŋə]

216. Birds

bird	**fågel (en)**	['foːɡəlʲ]
pigeon	**duva (en)**	['dʉːva]
sparrow	**sparv (en)**	['sparv]
tit (great tit)	**talgoxe (en)**	['taljʊksə]
magpie	**skata (en)**	['skata]

raven	**korp (en)**	['kɔrp]
crow	**kråka (en)**	['kroːka]
jackdaw	**kaja (en)**	['kaja]
rook	**råka (en)**	['roːka]
duck	**anka (en)**	['aŋka]
goose	**gås (en)**	['goːs]

pheasant	fasan (en)	[fa'san]
eagle	örn (en)	['ø:ŋ]
hawk	hök (en)	['hø:k]
falcon	falk (en)	['falʲk]
vulture	gam (en)	['gam]
condor (Andean ~)	kondor (en)	['kɔn̩dor]

swan	svan (en)	['svan]
crane	trana (en)	['trana]
stork	stork (en)	['stɔrk]

parrot	papegoja (en)	[pape'gɔja]
hummingbird	kolibri (en)	['kɔlibri]
peacock	påfågel (en)	['po:ˌfo:gəlʲ]

| ostrich | struts (en) | ['struts] |
| heron | häger (en) | ['hɛ:gər] |

| flamingo | flamingo (en) | [flʲa'mingɔ] |
| pelican | pelikan (en) | [peli'kan] |

| nightingale | näktergal (en) | ['nɛktəˌgalʲ] |
| swallow | svala (en) | ['svalʲa] |

thrush	trast (en)	['trast]
song thrush	sångtrast (en)	['sɔŋˌtrast]
blackbird	koltrast (en)	['kɔlʲˌtrast]

swift	tornseglare, tornsvala (en)	['tʊ:ŋˌseglarə], ['tʊ:ŋˌsvalʲa]
lark	lärka (en)	['lʲæ:rka]
quail	vaktel (en)	['vaktəlʲ]

woodpecker	hackspett (en)	['hakˌspet]
cuckoo	gök (en)	['jø:k]
owl	uggla (en)	['uglʲa]
eagle owl	berguv (en)	['bɛrjˌʉ:v]
wood grouse	tjäder (en)	['ɕɛ:dər]

| black grouse | orre (en) | ['ɔrə] |
| partridge | rapphöna (en) | ['rapˌhø:na] |

starling	stare (en)	['starə]
canary	kanariefågel (en)	[ka'nariəˌfo:gəlʲ]
hazel grouse	järpe (en)	['jæ:rpə]

| chaffinch | bofink (en) | ['bʊˌfiŋk] |
| bullfinch | domherre (en) | ['dʊmhɛrə] |

seagull	mås (en)	['mo:s]
albatross	albatross (en)	['alʲbaˌtrɔs]
penguin	pingvin (en)	[piŋ'vin]

217. Birds. Singing and sounds

to sing (vi)	att sjunga	[at 'ɧuːŋa]
to call (animal, bird)	att skrika	[at 'skrika]
to crow (rooster)	att gala	[at 'galʲa]
cock-a-doodle-doo	kuckeliku	[kɵkeliˈkɵː]
to cluck (hen)	att kackla	[at 'kaklʲa]
to caw (vi)	att kraxa	[at 'kraksa]
to quack (duck)	att snattra	[at 'snatra]
to cheep (vi)	att pipa	[at 'pipa]
to chirp, to twitter	att kvittra	[at 'kvitra]

218. Fish. Marine animals

bream	brax (en)	['braks]
carp	karp (en)	['karp]
perch	ábborre (en)	['abɔrə]
catfish	mal (en)	['malʲ]
pike	gädda (en)	['jɛda]
salmon	lax (en)	['lʲaks]
sturgeon	stör (en)	['støːr]
herring	sill (en)	['silʲ]
Atlantic salmon	atlanterhavslax (en)	[atˈlantərhavˌlʲaks]
mackerel	makrill (en)	['makrilʲ]
flatfish	rödspätta (en)	['røːdˌspæta]
zander, pike perch	gös (en)	['jøːs]
cod	torsk (en)	['tɔʂk]
tuna	tonfisk (en)	['tʊnˌfisk]
trout	öring (en)	['øːriŋ]
eel	ål (en)	['oːlʲ]
electric ray	elektrisk rocka (en)	[ɛ'lʲektriskˌrɔka]
moray eel	muräna (en)	[mɵ'rɛna]
piranha	piraya (en)	[pi'raja]
shark	haj (en)	['haj]
dolphin	delfin (en)	[dɛlʲ'fin]
whale	val (en)	['valʲ]
crab	krabba (en)	['kraba]
jellyfish	manet, medusa (en)	[ma'net], [me'dɵsa]
octopus	bläckfisk (en)	['blʲɛkˌfisk]
starfish	sjöstjärna (en)	['ɧøːˌɧæːŋa]
sea urchin	sjöpiggsvin (ett)	['ɧøːˌpigsvin]

seahorse	sjöhäst (en)	['ɧøːˌhɛst]
oyster	ostron (ett)	['ʊstrʊn]
shrimp	räka (en)	['rɛːka]
lobster	hummer (en)	['humər]
spiny lobster	languster (en)	[lʲaŋ'gustər]

219. Amphibians. Reptiles

snake	orm (en)	['ʊrm]
venomous (snake)	giftig	['jiftig]

viper	huggorm (en)	['hɵgˌʊrm]
cobra	kobra (en)	['kɔbra]
python	pytonorm (en)	[py'tɔnˌʊrm]
boa	boaorm (en)	['bʊaˌʊrm]

grass snake	snok (en)	['snʊk]
rattle snake	skallerorm (en)	['skalʲerˌʊrm]
anaconda	anaconda (en)	[ana'kɔnda]

lizard	ödla (en)	['ødlʲa]
iguana	iguana (en)	[igu'ana]
monitor lizard	varan (en)	[va'ran]
salamander	salamander (en)	[salʲa'mandər]
chameleon	kameleont (en)	[kamelʲe'ɔnt]
scorpion	skorpion (en)	[skɔrpi'ʊn]

turtle	sköldpadda (en)	['ɧœlʲdˌpada]
frog	groda (en)	['grʊda]
toad	padda (en)	['pada]
crocodile	krokodil (en)	[krɔkɔ'dilʲ]

220. Insects

insect, bug	insekt (en)	['insɛkt]
butterfly	fjäril (en)	['fʲæːrilʲ]
ant	myra (en)	['myra]
fly	fluga (en)	['flɵːga]
mosquito	mygga (en)	['mɤga]
beetle	skalbagge (en)	['skalʲˌbagə]

wasp	geting (en)	['jɛtiŋ]
bee	bi (ett)	['bi]
bumblebee	humla (en)	['humlʲa]
gadfly (botfly)	styngfluga (en)	['stɤŋˌflɵːga]

spider	spindel (en)	['spindəlʲ]
spiderweb	spindelnät (ett)	['spindəlˌnɛːt]

dragonfly	trollslända (en)	['trolˌslˠɛnda]
grasshopper	gräshoppa (en)	['grɛsˌhɔpa]
moth (night butterfly)	nattfjäril (en)	['natˌfjæːrilˠ]

cockroach	kackerlacka (en)	['kakɛːˌlˠaka]
tick	fästing (en)	['fɛstiŋ]
flea	loppa (en)	['lˠɔpa]
midge	knott (ett)	['knot]

locust	vandringsgräs-hoppa (en)	['vandriŋˌgrɛs 'hɔparə]
snail	snigel (en)	['snigəlˠ]
cricket	syrsa (en)	['syʂa]
lightning bug	lysmask (en)	['lˠysˌmask]
ladybug	nyckelpiga (en)	['nʏkəlˠˌpiga]
cockchafer	ollonborre (en)	['ɔlˠɔnˌbɔrə]

leech	igel (en)	['iːgəlˠ]
caterpillar	fjärilslarv (en)	['fjæːrilˠsˌlˠarv]
earthworm	daggmask (en)	['dagˌmask]
larva	larv (en)	['lˠarv]

221. Animals. Body parts

beak	näbb (ett)	['nɛb]
wings	vingar (pl)	['viŋar]
foot (of bird)	fot (en)	['fʊt]
feathers (plumage)	fjäderdräkt (en)	['fjɛːdəˌdrɛkt]
feather	fjäder (en)	['fjɛːdər]
crest	tofs (en)	['tofs]

gills	gälar (pl)	['jɛːˌlˠar]
spawn	rom (en), ägg (pl)	['rom], ['ɛg]
larva	larv (en)	['lˠarv]
fin	fena (en)	['fena]
scales (of fish, reptile)	fjäll (ett)	['fˠælˠ]

fang (canine)	hörntand (en)	['høːɳˌtand]
paw (e.g., cat's ~)	tass (en)	['tas]
muzzle (snout)	mule (en)	['mʉlˠe]
mouth (of cat, dog)	gap (ett)	['gap]
tail	svans (en)	['svans]
whiskers	morrhår (ett)	['morˌhɔːr]

| hoof | klöv, hov (en) | ['kløːv], ['hɔːv] |
| horn | horn (ett) | ['hʊːɳ] |

carapace	ryggsköld (en)	['rʏgˌɧœlˠd]
shell (of mollusk)	skal (ett)	['skalˠ]
eggshell	äggskal (ett)	['ɛgˌskalˠ]

| animal's hair (pelage) | päls (en) | ['pɛlʲs] |
| pelt (hide) | skinn (ett) | ['ɧin] |

222. Actions of animals

to fly (vi)	att flyga	[at 'flʲyga]
to fly in circles	att kretsa	[at 'krɛtsa]
to fly away	att flyga bort	[at 'flʲyga ˌbɔːt]
to flap (~ the wings)	att flaxa	[at 'flʲaksa]

to peck (vi)	att picka	[at 'pika]
to sit on eggs	att kläcka ägg	[at 'klʲɛka 'ɛg]
to hatch out (vi)	att kläckas	[at 'klʲɛkas]
to build a nest	att bygga boet	[at 'bʏga 'boət]

to slither, to crawl	att krypa	[at 'krypa]
to sting, to bite (insect)	att sticka	[at 'stika]
to bite (ab. animal)	att bita	[at 'bita]

to sniff (vt)	att sniffa	[at 'snifa]
to bark (vi)	att skälla	[at 'ɧɛlʲa]
to hiss (snake)	att väsa	[at 'vɛːsa]
to scare (vt)	att skrämma	[at 'skrɛma]
to attack (vt)	att överfalla	[at 'øːvəˌfalʲa]

to gnaw (bone, etc.)	att gnaga	[at 'gnaga]
to scratch (with claws)	att klösa	[at 'klʲøːsa]
to hide (vi)	att gömma sig	[at 'jœma sɛj]

to play (kittens, etc.)	att leka	[at 'lʲeka]
to hunt (vi, vt)	att jaga	[at 'jaga]
to hibernate (vi)	att gå i dvala	[at 'goː i 'dvala]
to go extinct	att dö ut	[at 'døː ʉt]

223. Animals. Habitats

habitat	habitat	[habi'tat]
migration	migration (en)	[migra'ɧʊn]
mountain	berg (ett)	['bɛrj]
reef	rev (ett)	['rev]
cliff	klippa (en)	['klipa]

forest	skog (en)	['skʊg]
jungle	djungel (en)	['juŋəlʲ]
savanna	savann (en)	[sa'van]
tundra	tundra (en)	['tundra]
steppe	stäpp (en)	['stɛp]
desert	öken (en)	['øːkən]

oasis	oas (en)	[ɔ'as]
sea	hav (ett)	['hav]
lake	sjö (en)	['fjøː]
ocean	ocean (en)	[ʊsə'an]

swamp (marshland)	träsk (ett), myr (en)	['trɛsk], ['myr]
freshwater (adj)	sötvattens-	['søːtˌvatəns-]
pond	damm (en)	['dam]
river	älv, flod (en)	['ɛlʲv], ['flʲʊd]

den (bear's ~)	ide (ett)	['ide]
nest	bo (ett)	['bʊ]
hollow (in a tree)	trädhål (ett)	['trɛːdˌhoːlʲ]
burrow (animal hole)	lya, håla (en)	['lʲya], ['hoːlʲa]
anthill	myrstack (en)	['myrˌstak]

224. Animal care

| zoo | zoo (ett) | ['sʊː] |
| nature preserve | naturreservat (ett) | [na'tʉːr resɛr'vat] |

breeder (cattery, kennel, etc.)	uppfödare (en)	['upˌføːdarə]
open-air cage	voljär (en)	[vɔ'ljær]
cage	bur (en)	['bʉːr]
doghouse (kennel)	hundkoja (en)	['hundˌkɔja]

dovecot	duvslag (ett)	['dʉvˌslʲag]
aquarium (fish tank)	akvarium (ett)	[a'kvarium]
dolphinarium	delfinarium (ett)	[dɛlʲfi'narium]

to breed (animals)	att avla, att föda upp	[at 'avlʲa], [at 'føːda up]
brood, litter	kull (en)	['kulʲ]
to tame (vt)	att tämja	[at 'tɛmja]
feed (fodder, etc.)	foder (ett)	['fʊdər]
to feed (vt)	att utfodra	[at 'ʉtˌfɔːdra]
to train (animals)	att dressera	[at drɛ'sera]

pet store	djuraffär (en)	['jʉːra'fæːr]
muzzle (for dog)	munkorg (ett)	['munˌkɔrj]
collar (e.g., dog ~)	halsband (ett)	['halʲsˌband]
name (of animal)	namn (ett)	['namn]
pedigree (of dog)	stamtavla (en)	['stamˌtavlʲa]

225. Animals. Miscellaneous

| pack (wolves) | flock (en) | ['flʲɔk] |
| flock (birds) | flock (en) | ['flʲɔk] |

shoal, school (fish)	stim (ett)	['stim]
herd (horses)	hjord (en)	['jʊːd]
male (n)	hane (en)	['hanə]
female (n)	hona (en)	['hʊna]
hungry (adj)	hungrig	['huŋrig]
wild (adj)	vild	['vilʲd]
dangerous (adj)	farlig	['faːlʲig]

226. Horses

horse	häst (en)	['hɛst]
breed (race)	ras (en)	['ras]
foal	föl (ett)	['føːlʲ]
mare	sto (ett)	['stʊː]
mustang	mustang (en)	[mʉ'staŋ]
pony	ponny (en)	['pɔni]
draft horse	kallblodshäst (en)	['kalʲblʲʊd‚hɛst]
mane	man (en)	['man]
tail	svans (en)	['svans]
hoof	hov (en)	['hɔːv]
horseshoe	hästsko (en)	['hɛst‚skʊ]
to shoe (vt)	att sko	[at 'skʊː]
blacksmith	smed (en)	['smed]
saddle	sadel (en)	['sadəlʲ]
stirrup	stigbygel (en)	['stig‚bygəlʲ]
bridle	betsel (ett)	['bɛtsəlʲ]
reins	tömmar (pl)	['tœmar]
whip (for riding)	piska (en)	['piska]
rider	ryttare (en)	['rʏtarə]
to saddle up (vt)	att sadla	[at 'sadlʲa]
to mount a horse	att stiga till häst	[at 'stiga tilʲ 'hɛst]
gallop	galopp (en)	[ga'lʲɔp]
to gallop (vi)	att galoppera	[at galʲɔ'pera]
trot (n)	trav (ett)	['trav]
at a trot (adv)	i trav	[i 'trav]
to go at a trot	att trava	[at 'trava]
racehorse	kapplöpningshäst (en)	['kap‚lœpniŋs 'hɛst]
horse racing	hästkapplöpning (en)	['hɛst‚kap'lʲœpniŋ]
stable	stall (ett)	['stalʲ]
to feed (vt)	att utfodra	[at 'ʉt‚fɔːdra]

hay	hö (ett)	['hø:]
to water (animals)	att vattna	[at 'vatna]
to wash (horse)	att borsta	[at 'bɔːʂta]
horse-drawn cart	kärra (en)	['ɕæːra]
to graze (vi)	att beta	[at 'beta]
to neigh (vi)	att gnägga	[at 'gnɛga]
to kick (about horse)	att sparka bakut	[at 'sparka ˌbakʉt]

Flora

227. Trees

tree	**träd (ett)**	['trɛ:d]
deciduous (adj)	**löv-**	['lʲø:v-]
coniferous (adj)	**barr-**	['bar-]
evergreen (adj)	**eviggrönt**	['ɛvi̩grœnt]
apple tree	**äppelträd (ett)**	['ɛpelʲˌtrɛd]
pear tree	**päronträd (ett)**	['pæːrɔnˌtrɛd]
sweet cherry tree	**fågelbärsträd (ett)**	['fo:gəlʲbæ:ʂˌtrɛd]
sour cherry tree	**körsbärsträd (ett)**	['ɕø:ʂbæ:ʂˌtrɛd]
plum tree	**plommonträd (ett)**	['plʲʊmɔnˌtrɛd]
birch	**björk (en)**	['bjœrk]
oak	**ek (en)**	['ɛk]
linden tree	**lind (en)**	['lind]
aspen	**asp (en)**	['asp]
maple	**lönn (en)**	['lʲøn]
spruce	**gran (en)**	['gran]
pine	**tall (en)**	['talʲ]
larch	**lärk (en)**	['lʲæ:rk]
fir tree	**silvergran (en)**	['silʲvərˌgran]
cedar	**ceder (en)**	['sedər]
poplar	**poppel (en)**	['pɔpəlʲ]
rowan	**rönn (en)**	['rœn]
willow	**pil (en)**	['pilʲ]
alder	**al (en)**	['alʲ]
beech	**bok (en)**	['bʊk]
elm	**alm (en)**	['alʲm]
ash (tree)	**ask (en)**	['ask]
chestnut	**kastanjeträd (ett)**	[ka'stanjəˌtrɛd]
magnolia	**magnolia (en)**	[maŋ'nʊlia]
palm tree	**palm (en)**	['palʲm]
cypress	**cypress (en)**	[sɤ'prɛs]
mangrove	**mangroveträd (ett)**	[maŋ'rɔvəˌtrɛd]
baobab	**apbrödsträd (ett)**	['apbrødsˌtrɛd]
eucalyptus	**eukalyptus (en)**	[euka'lʲyptʉs]
sequoia	**sequoia (en)**	[sek'vɔja]

228. Shrubs

bush	buske (en)	['buskə]
shrub	buske (en)	['buskə]
grapevine	vinranka (en)	['vin,raŋka]
vineyard	vingård (en)	['vin,go:d]
raspberry bush	hallonsnår (ett)	['halʲon,sno:r]
blackcurrant bush	svarta vinbär (ett)	['sva:ʈa 'vinbæ:r]
redcurrant bush	röd vinbärsbuske (en)	['rø:d 'vinbæ:ʂ,buskə]
gooseberry bush	krusbärsbuske (en)	['krʉ:sbæ:ʂ,buskə]
acacia	akacia (en)	[a'kasia]
barberry	berberis (en)	['bɛrberis]
jasmine	jasmin (en)	[has'min]
juniper	en (en)	['en]
rosebush	rosenbuske (en)	['rʊsən,buskə]
dog rose	stenros, hundros (en)	['stenrʊs], ['hundrʊs]

229. Mushrooms

mushroom	svamp (en)	['svamp]
edible mushroom	matsvamp (en)	['mat,svamp]
poisonous mushroom	giftig svamp (en)	['jiftig ,svamp]
cap (of mushroom)	hatt (en)	['hat]
stipe (of mushroom)	fot (en)	['fʊt]
cep (Boletus edulis)	stensopp (en)	['sten,sɔp]
orange-cap boletus	aspsopp (en)	['asp,sɔp]
birch bolete	björksopp (en)	['bjœrk,sɔp]
chanterelle	kantarell (en)	[kanta'rɛlʲ]
russula	kremla (en)	['krɛmlʲa]
morel	murkla (en)	['mʉ:rklʲa]
fly agaric	flugsvamp (en)	['flʉ:g,svamp]
death cap	lömsk flugsvamp (en)	['lʲømsk 'flʉ:g,svamp]

230. Fruits. Berries

fruit	frukt (en)	['frʉkt]
fruits	frukter (pl)	['frʉktər]
apple	äpple (ett)	['ɛplʲe]
pear	päron (ett)	['pæ:rɔn]
plum	plommon (ett)	['plʲʊmɔn]
strawberry (garden ~)	jordgubbe (en)	['jʊ:d,gubə]

sour cherry	körsbär (ett)	['ɕøːʂˌbæːr]
sweet cherry	fågelbär (ett)	['foːgəlʲˌbæːr]
grape	druva (en)	['druːva]

raspberry	hallon (ett)	['halʲɔn]
blackcurrant	svarta vinbär (ett)	['svaːʈa 'vinbæːr]
redcurrant	röda vinbär (ett)	['røːda 'vinbæːr]
gooseberry	krusbär (ett)	['kruːsˌbæːr]
cranberry	tranbär (ett)	['tranˌbæːr]

orange	apelsin (en)	[apɛlʲ'sin]
mandarin	mandarin (en)	[manda'rin]
pineapple	ananas (en)	['ananas]
banana	banan (en)	['banan]
date	dadel (en)	['dadəlʲ]

lemon	citron (en)	[si'trʊn]
apricot	aprikos (en)	[apri'kʊs]
peach	persika (en)	['pɛʂika]
kiwi	kiwi (en)	['kivi]
grapefruit	grapefrukt (en)	['grɛjpˌfrʉkt]

berry	bär (ett)	['bæːr]
berries	bär (pl)	['bæːr]
cowberry	lingon (ett)	['liŋɔn]
wild strawberry	skogssmultron (ett)	['skʊgsˌsmulʲtrɔːn]
bilberry	blåbär (ett)	['blʲoːˌbæːr]

231. Flowers. Plants

| flower | blomma (en) | ['blʲʊma] |
| bouquet (of flowers) | bukett (en) | [bʉ'kɛt] |

rose (flower)	ros (en)	['rʊs]
tulip	tulpan (en)	[tulʲ'pan]
carnation	nejlika (en)	['nɛjlika]
gladiolus	gladiolus (en)	[glʲadi'ɔlʉːs]

cornflower	blåklint (en)	['blʲoːˌklint]
harebell	blåklocka (en)	['blʲoːˌklʲɔka]
dandelion	maskros (en)	['maskrʊs]
camomile	kamomill (en)	[kamɔ'milʲ]

aloe	aloe (en)	['alʲʊe]
cactus	kaktus (en)	['kaktus]
rubber plant, ficus	fikus (en)	['fikus]

lily	lilja (en)	['lilʲja]
geranium	geranium (en)	[je'ranium]
hyacinth	hyacint (en)	[hya'sint]

mimosa	mimosa (en)	[mi'mɔːsa]
narcissus	narciss (en)	[nar'sis]
nasturtium	blomsterkrasse (en)	['blɔmstər‚krasə]

orchid	orkidé (en)	[ɔrki'deː]
peony	pion (en)	[pi'ʊn]
violet	viol (en)	[vi'ʊlʲ]

pansy	styvmorsviol (en)	['styvmʊrs vi'ʊlʲ]
forget-me-not	förgätmigej (en)	[fø‚rʲæt mi 'gej]
daisy	tusensköna (en)	['tʉːsən‚ɧøːna]

poppy	vallmo (en)	['valʲmʊ]
hemp	hampa (en)	['hampa]
mint	mynta (en)	['mʏnta]
lily of the valley	liljekonvalje (en)	['lilje kʊn 'valjə]
snowdrop	snödropp (en)	['snøː‚drop]

nettle	nässla (en)	['nɛslʲa]
sorrel	syra (en)	['syra]
water lily	näckros (en)	['nɛkrʊs]
fern	ormbunke (en)	['ʊrm‚bʊŋkə]
lichen	lav (en)	['lʲav]

greenhouse (tropical ~)	drivhus (ett)	['driv‚hʉs]
lawn	gräsplan, gräsmatta (en)	['grɛs‚plan], ['grɛs‚mata]
flowerbed	blomsterrabatt (en)	['blʲomstər‚rabat]

plant	växt (en)	['vɛkst]
grass	gräs (ett)	['grɛːs]
blade of grass	grässtrå (ett)	['grɛːs‚stroː]

leaf	löv (ett)	['lʲøːv]
petal	kronblad (ett)	['krɔn‚blʲad]
stem	stjälk (en)	['ɧɛlʲk]
tuber	rotknöl (en)	['rʊt‚knøːlʲ]

| young plant (shoot) | ung planta (en) | ['ʊŋ 'planta] |
| thorn | törne (ett) | ['tøːɳə] |

to blossom (vi)	att blomma	[at 'blʲʊma]
to fade, to wither	att vissna	[at 'visna]
smell (odor)	lukt (en)	['lʉkt]
to cut (flowers)	att skära av	[at 'ɧæːra av]
to pick (a flower)	att plocka	[at 'plʲɔka]

232. Cereals, grains

| grain | korn, spannmål (ett) | ['kʊːn], ['span‚moːlʲ] |
| cereal crops | spannmål (ett) | ['span‚moːlʲ] |

ear (of barley, etc.)	ax (ett)	['aks]
wheat	vete (ett)	['vetə]
rye	råg (en)	['roːg]
oats	havre (en)	['havrə]
millet	hirs (en)	['hyʂ]
barley	korn (ett)	['kʊːɳ]
corn	majs (en)	['majs]
rice	ris (ett)	['ris]
buckwheat	bovete (ett)	['bʊˌvetə]
pea plant	ärt (en)	['æːt]
kidney bean	böna (en)	['bøna]
soy	soja (en)	['sɔja]
lentil	lins (en)	['lins]
beans (pulse crops)	bönor (pl)	['bønʊr]

233. Vegetables. Greens

vegetables	grönsaker (pl)	['grøːnˌsakər]
greens	grönsaker (pl)	['grøːnˌsakər]
tomato	tomat (en)	[tʊ'mat]
cucumber	gurka (en)	['gurka]
carrot	morot (en)	['mʊˌrʊt]
potato	potatis (en)	[pʊ'tatis]
onion	lök (en)	['lʲøːk]
garlic	vitlök (en)	['vitˌlʲøːk]
cabbage	kål (en)	['koːlʲ]
cauliflower	blomkål (en)	['blʲʊmˌkoːlʲ]
Brussels sprouts	brysselkål (en)	['brʏsɛlʲˌkoːlʲ]
broccoli	broccoli (en)	['brɔkɔli]
beetroot	rödbeta (en)	['røːdˌbeta]
eggplant	aubergine (en)	[ɔbɛr'ʒin]
zucchini	squash, zucchini (en)	['skvɔːɕ], [su'kini]
pumpkin	pumpa (en)	['pumpa]
turnip	rova (en)	['rʊva]
parsley	persilja (en)	[pɛ'ʂilja]
dill	dill (en)	['dilʲ]
lettuce	sallad (en)	['salʲad]
celery	selleri (en)	['sɛlʲeri]
asparagus	sparris (en)	['sparis]
spinach	spenat (en)	[spe'nat]
pea	ärter (pl)	['æːtər]
beans	bönor (pl)	['bønʊr]
corn (maize)	majs (en)	['majs]

kidney bean	böna (en)	['bøna]
pepper	peppar (en)	['pɛpar]
radish	rädisa (en)	['rɛːdisa]
artichoke	kronärtskocka (en)	['krʊnæːˌskɔka]

REGIONAL GEOGRAPHY

Countries. Nationalities

234. Western Europe

Europe	Europa	[euˈrʉpa]
European Union	Europeiska unionen	[eurʉˈpeiska unˈjʉnən]
European (n)	europé (en)	[eurʉˈpe:]
European (adj)	europeisk	[eurʉˈpeisk]

Austria	Österrike	[ˈœstɛˌrikə]
Austrian (masc.)	österrikare (en)	[ˈœstɛˌriːkarə]
Austrian (fem.)	österrikiska (en)	[ˈœstɛˌriːkiska]
Austrian (adj)	österrikisk	[ˈœstɛˌriːkisk]

Great Britain	Storbritannien	[ˈstʉrˌbriˈtaniən]
England	England	[ˈɛŋlʲand]
British (masc.)	britt (en)	[ˈbrit]
British (fem.)	britt (en)	[ˈbrit]
English, British (adj)	engelsk, britisk	[ˈɛŋɛlʲsk], [ˈbritisk]

Belgium	Belgien	[ˈbɛlʲgiən]
Belgian (masc.)	belgare (en)	[ˈbɛlʲgarə]
Belgian (fem.)	belgiska (en)	[ˈbɛlʲgiska]
Belgian (adj)	belgisk	[ˈbɛlʲgisk]

Germany	Tyskland	[ˈtʏsklʲand]
German (masc.)	tysk (en)	[ˈtʏsk]
German (fem.)	tyska (en)	[ˈtʏska]
German (adj)	tysk	[ˈtʏsk]

Netherlands	Nederländerna	[ˈnedɛːˌlʲɛndɛːɳa]
Holland	Holland	[ˈhɔlʲand]
Dutch (masc.)	holländare (en)	[ˈhɔˌlʲɛndarə]
Dutch (fem.)	holländska (en)	[ˈhɔˌlʲɛnska]
Dutch (adj)	holländsk	[ˈhɔˌlʲɛnsk]

Greece	Grekland	[ˈgreklʲand]
Greek (masc.)	grek (en)	[ˈgrek]
Greek (fem.)	grekiska (en)	[ˈgrekiska]
Greek (adj)	grekisk	[ˈgrekisk]

Denmark	Danmark	[ˈdaŋmark]
Dane (masc.)	dansk (en)	[ˈdaŋsk]

| Dane (fem.) | danska (en) | ['daŋska] |
| Danish (adj) | dansk | ['daŋsk] |

Ireland	Irland	['iɭand]
Irish (masc.)	irer (en)	['irər]
Irish (fem.)	iriska (en)	['iriska]
Irish (adj)	irisk	['irisk]

Iceland	Island	['isɭand]
Icelander (masc.)	islänning (en)	['is͵ɭɛniŋ]
Icelander (fem.)	isländska (en)	['is͵ɭɛŋska]
Icelandic (adj)	isländsk	['is͵ɭɛŋsk]

Spain	Spanien	['spaniən]
Spaniard (masc.)	spanjor (en)	['span͵jʊːr]
Spaniard (fem.)	spanjorska (en)	['span͵jʊːʂka]
Spanish (adj)	spansk	['spansk]

Italy	Italien	[i'taliən]
Italian (masc.)	italienare (en)	[ita'ljɛnarə]
Italian (fem.)	italienska (en)	[ita'ljɛnska]
Italian (adj)	italiensk	[ita'ljɛnsk]

Cyprus	Cypern	['sypɛːɳ]
Cypriot (masc.)	cypriot (en)	[sʏpri'ʊt]
Cypriot (fem.)	cypriotiska (en)	[sʏpri'ʊtiska]
Cypriot (adj)	cypriotisk	[sʏpri'ʊtisk]

Malta	Malta	['malɭta]
Maltese (masc.)	maltesare (en)	[malɭ'tesarə]
Maltese (fem.)	maltesiska (en)	[malɭ'tesiska]
Maltese (adj)	maltesisk	[malɭ'tesisk]

Norway	Norge	['nɔrjə]
Norwegian (masc.)	norrman (en)	['nɔrman]
Norwegian (fem.)	norska (en)	['nɔːʂka]
Norwegian (adj)	norsk	['nɔːʂk]

Portugal	Portugal	['pɔːʈugalɉ]
Portuguese (masc.)	portugis (en)	[pɔːʈu'giːs]
Portuguese (fem.)	portugisiska (en)	[pɔːʈu'giːsiska]
Portuguese (adj)	portugisisk	[pɔːʈu'giːsisk]

Finland	Finland	['finɭand]
Finn (masc.)	finne (en)	['finə]
Finn (fem.)	finska (en)	['finska]
Finnish (adj)	finsk	['finsk]

France	Frankrike	['fraŋkrikə]
French (masc.)	fransman (en)	['frans͵man]
French (fem.)	fransyska (en)	['fransʏska]
French (adj)	fransk	['fransk]

Sweden	**Sverige**	['svɛrijə]
Swede (masc.)	**svensk (en)**	['svɛnsk]
Swede (fem.)	**svenska (en)**	['svɛnska]
Swedish (adj)	**svensk**	['svɛnsk]

Switzerland	**Schweiz**	['ʃvɛjts]
Swiss (masc.)	**schweizare (en)**	['ʃvɛjtsarə]
Swiss (fem.)	**schweiziska (en)**	['ʃvɛjtsiska]
Swiss (adj)	**schweizisk**	['ʃvɛjtsisk]

Scotland	**Skottland**	['skɔtlʲand]
Scottish (masc.)	**skotte (en)**	['skɔtə]
Scottish (fem.)	**skotska (en)**	['skɔtska]
Scottish (adj)	**skotsk**	['skɔtsk]

Vatican	**Vatikanstaten**	[vati'kanˌstatən]
Liechtenstein	**Liechtenstein**	['lihtənstajn]
Luxembourg	**Luxemburg**	['lɤksəmˌburj]
Monaco	**Monaco**	['mɔnakɔ]

235. Central and Eastern Europe

Albania	**Albanien**	[alʲ'baniən]
Albanian (masc.)	**alban (en)**	[alʲ'ban]
Albanian (fem.)	**albanska (en)**	[alʲ'banska]
Albanian (adj)	**albansk**	[alʲ'bansk]

Bulgaria	**Bulgarien**	[bɤlʲ'gariən]
Bulgarian (masc.)	**bulgar (en)**	[bɤlʲ'gar]
Bulgarian (fem.)	**bulgariska (en)**	[bɤlʲ'gariska]
Bulgarian (adj)	**bulgarisk**	[bɤlʲ'garisk]

Hungary	**Ungern**	['uɲɛ:ɳ]
Hungarian (masc.)	**ungrare (en)**	['uɲrarə]
Hungarian (fem.)	**ungerska (en)**	['uɲɛʂka]
Hungarian (adj)	**ungersk**	['uɲɛʂk]

Latvia	**Lettland**	['lʲetlʲand]
Latvian (masc.)	**lett (en)**	['lʲet]
Latvian (fem.)	**lettiska (en)**	['lʲetiska]
Latvian (adj)	**lettisk**	['lʲetisk]

Lithuania	**Litauen**	[li'tauən]
Lithuanian (masc.)	**litauer (en)**	[li'tauər]
Lithuanian (fem.)	**litauiska (en)**	[li'tauiska]
Lithuanian (adj)	**litauisk**	[li'tauisk]

Poland	**Polen**	['pɔlʲen]
Pole (masc.)	**polack (en)**	[pɔ'lʲak]
Pole (fem.)	**polska (en)**	['pɔlʲska]

Polish (adj)	polsk	['pɔlˡsk]
Romania	Rumänien	[rʉ'mɛ:niǝn]
Romanian (masc.)	rumän (en)	[rʉ'mɛ:n]
Romanian (fem.)	rumänska (en)	[rʉ'mɛ:nska]
Romanian (adj)	rumänsk	[rʉ'mɛ:nsk]

Serbia	Serbien	['sɛrbiǝn]
Serbian (masc.)	serb (en)	['sɛrb]
Serbian (fem.)	serbiska (en)	['sɛrbiska]
Serbian (adj)	serbisk	['sɛrbisk]

Slovakia	Slovakien	[slˡɔ'vakiǝn]
Slovak (masc.)	slovak (en)	[slˡɔ'vak]
Slovak (fem.)	slovakiska (en)	[slˡɔ'vakiska]
Slovak (adj)	slovakisk	[slˡɔ'vakisk]

Croatia	Kroatien	[krʊ'atiǝn]
Croatian (masc.)	kroat (en)	[krʊ'at]
Croatian (fem.)	kroatiska (en)	[krʊ'atiska]
Croatian (adj)	kroatisk	[krʊ'atisk]

Czech Republic	Tjeckien	['ɕɛkiǝn]
Czech (masc.)	tjeck (en)	['ɕɛk]
Czech (fem.)	tjeckiska (en)	['ɕɛkiska]
Czech (adj)	tjeckisk	['ɕɛkisk]

Estonia	Estland	['ɛstlˡand]
Estonian (masc.)	estländare (en)	['ɛstˌlˡɛndarǝ]
Estonian (fem.)	estländska (en)	['ɛstˌlˡɛŋska]
Estonian (adj)	estnisk	['ɛstnisk]

Bosnia and Herzegovina	Bosnien-Hercegovina	['bɔsniǝn hɛrsǝgɔ'vina]
Macedonia (Republic of ~)	Makedonien	[make'dʊniǝn]
Slovenia	Slovenien	[slˡɔ'veniǝn]
Montenegro	Montenegro	['mɔntǝˌnɛgrʊ]

236. Former USSR countries

Azerbaijan	Azerbajdzjan	[asɛrbaj'ʤˡan]
Azerbaijani (masc.)	azerbajdzjan (en)	[asɛrbaj'ʤan]
Azerbaijani (fem.)	azerbajdzjanska (en)	[asɛrbaj'ʤanska]
Azerbaijani, Azeri (adj)	azerbajdzjansk	[asɛrbaj'ʤˡansk]

Armenia	Armenien	[ar'meniǝn]
Armenian (masc.)	armenier (en)	[ar'meniɛr]
Armenian (fem.)	armeniska (en)	[ar'meniska]
Armenian (adj)	armenisk	[ar'menisk]

| Belarus | Vitryssland | ['vitˌrʏslˡand] |
| Belarusian (masc.) | vitryss (en) | ['vitˌrʏs] |

Belarusian (fem.)	**vitryska (en)**	['vit,rʏska]
Belarusian (adj)	**vitrysk**	['vit,rʏsk]

Georgia	**Georgien**	[je'ɔrgiən]
Georgian (masc.)	**georgier (en)**	[je'ɔrgiər]
Georgian (fem.)	**georgiska (en)**	[je'ɔrgiska]
Georgian (adj)	**georgisk**	[je'ɔrgisk]
Kazakhstan	**Kazakstan**	[ka'sak,stan]
Kazakh (masc.)	**kazakstanier (en)**	[kasak'staniər]
Kazakh (fem.)	**kazakiska (en)**	[ka'sakiska]
Kazakh (adj)	**kazakisk**	[ka'sakisk]

Kirghizia	**Kirgizistan**	[kir'gisi,stan]
Kirghiz (masc.)	**kirgiz (en)**	[kir'gis]
Kirghiz (fem.)	**kirgiziska (en)**	[kir'gisiska]
Kirghiz (adj)	**kirgizisk**	[kir'gisisk]

Moldova, Moldavia	**Moldavien**	[mʊlʲ'daviən]
Moldavian (masc.)	**moldav (en)**	[mʊlʲ'dav]
Moldavian (fem.)	**moldaviska (en)**	[mʊlʲ'daviska]
Moldavian (adj)	**moldavisk**	[mʊlʲ'davisk]
Russia	**Ryssland**	['rʏslʲand]
Russian (masc.)	**ryss (en)**	['rʏs]
Russian (fem.)	**ryska (en)**	['rʏska]
Russian (adj)	**rysk**	['rʏsk]

Tajikistan	**Tadzjikistan**	[ta'dʒiki,stan]
Tajik (masc.)	**tadzjik (en)**	[ta'dʒik]
Tajik (fem.)	**tadzjikiska (en)**	[ta'dʒikiska]
Tajik (adj)	**tadzjikisk**	[ta'dʒikisk]

Turkmenistan	**Turkmenistan**	[turk'meni,stan]
Turkmen (masc.)	**turkmen (en)**	[turk'mən]
Turkmen (fem.)	**turkmenska (en)**	[turk'mɛnska]
Turkmenian (adj)	**turkmensk**	[turk'mɛnsk]

Uzbekistan	**Uzbekistan**	[us'beki,stan]
Uzbek (masc.)	**uzbek (en)**	[us'bek]
Uzbek (fem.)	**uzbekiska (en)**	[us'bekiska]
Uzbek (adj)	**uzbekisk**	[us'bekisk]

Ukraine	**Ukraina**	[u'krajna]
Ukrainian (masc.)	**ukrainare (en)**	[u'krajnarə]
Ukrainian (fem.)	**ukrainska (en)**	[u'krajnska]
Ukrainian (adj)	**ukrainsk**	[u'krajnsk]

237. Asia

Asia	**Asien**	['asiən]
Asian (adj)	**asiatisk**	[asi'atisk]

Vietnam	**Vietnam**	['vjɛtnam]
Vietnamese (masc.)	**vietnames (en)**	[vjɛtna'mes]
Vietnamese (fem.)	**vietnamesiska (en)**	[vjɛtna'mesiska]
Vietnamese (adj)	**vietnamesisk**	[vjɛtna'mesisk]
India	**Indien**	['indiən]
Indian (masc.)	**indier (en)**	['indiər]
Indian (fem.)	**indiska (en)**	['indiska]
Indian (adj)	**indisk**	['indisk]
Israel	**Israel**	['israəlʲ]
Israeli (masc.)	**israel (en)**	[isra'elʲ]
Israeli (fem.)	**israeliska (en)**	[isra'eliska]
Israeli (adj)	**israelisk**	[isra'elisk]
Jew (n)	**jude (en)**	['jʉdə]
Jewess (n)	**judinna (en)**	[jʉ'dina]
Jewish (adj)	**judisk**	['jʉdisk]
China	**Kina**	['ɕina]
Chinese (masc.)	**kines (en)**	[ɕi'nes]
Chinese (fem.)	**kinesiska (en)**	[ɕi'nesiska]
Chinese (adj)	**kinesisk**	[ɕi'nesisk]
Korean (masc.)	**korean (en)**	[kʊre'an]
Korean (fem.)	**koreanska (en)**	[kʊre'anska]
Korean (adj)	**koreansk**	[kʊre'ansk]
Lebanon	**Libanon**	['libanɔn]
Lebanese (masc.)	**libanes (en)**	[liba'nes]
Lebanese (fem.)	**libanesiska (en)**	[liba'nesiska]
Lebanese (adj)	**libanesisk**	[liba'nesisk]
Mongolia	**Mongoliet**	[mʊngʊ'liet]
Mongolian (masc.)	**mongol (en)**	[mʊn'gʊlʲ]
Mongolian (fem.)	**mongoliska (en)**	[mʊn'gʊliska]
Mongolian (adj)	**mongolisk**	[mʊn'gʊlisk]
Malaysia	**Malaysia**	[ma'lʲajsia]
Malaysian (masc.)	**malaysier (en)**	[ma'lʲajsiər]
Malaysian (fem.)	**malajiska (en)**	[ma'lʲajiska]
Malaysian (adj)	**malaysisk**	[ma'lʲajsisk]
Pakistan	**Pakistan**	['paki͵stan]
Pakistani (masc.)	**pakistanier (en)**	[paki'staniər]
Pakistani (fem.)	**pakistanska (en)**	[paki'stanska]
Pakistani (adj)	**pakistansk**	[paki'stansk]
Saudi Arabia	**Saudiarabien**	['saudi a'rabiən]
Arab (masc.)	**arab (en)**	[a'rab]
Arab (fem.)	**arabiska (en)**	[a'rabiska]
Arab, Arabic (adj)	**arabisk**	[a'rabisk]

Thailand	**Thailand**	['tajlˈand]
Thai (masc.)	**thailändare (en)**	[tajˈlˈɛndarə]
Thai (fem.)	**thailändska (en)**	['tajˌlˈɛndska]
Thai (adj)	**thailändsk**	[tajˈlˈɛŋsk]
Taiwan	**Taiwan**	[tajˈvan]
Taiwanese (masc.)	**taiwanes (en)**	[tajvaˈnes]
Taiwanese (fem.)	**taiwanesiska (en)**	[tajvaˈnesiska]
Taiwanese (adj)	**taiwanesisk**	[tajvaˈnesisk]
Turkey	**Turkiet**	[turkiet]
Turk (masc.)	**turk (en)**	['turk]
Turk (fem.)	**turkiska (en)**	['turkiska]
Turkish (adj)	**turkisk**	['turkisk]
Japan	**Japan**	[ˈjapan]
Japanese (masc.)	**japan (en)**	[jaˈpan]
Japanese (fem.)	**japanska (en)**	[jaˈpanska]
Japanese (adj)	**japansk**	[jaˈpansk]
Afghanistan	**Afghanistan**	[afˈganiˌstan]
Bangladesh	**Bangladesh**	[banglˈaˈdɛʃ]
Indonesia	**Indonesien**	[indʊˈnesiən]
Jordan	**Jordanien**	[jʊːˈdanien]
Iraq	**Irak**	[iˈrak]
Iran	**Iran**	[iˈran]
Cambodia	**Kambodja**	[kamˈbɔdja]
Kuwait	**Kuwait**	[kʉˈvajt]
Laos	**Laos**	['lˈaɔs]
Myanmar	**Myanmar**	['mjanmar]
Nepal	**Nepal**	[neˈpalˈ]
United Arab Emirates	**Förenade arabrepubliken**	[føˈrenadə aˈrab repubˈlikən]
Syria	**Syrien**	['syriən]
Palestine	**Palestina**	[palˈeˈstina]
South Korea	**Sydkorea**	['sydˌkʊˈrea]
North Korea	**Nordkorea**	['nʊːɖ kʊˈrea]

238. North America

United States of America	**Amerikas Förenta Stater**	[aˈmɛrikas føˈrɛnta ˈstatər]
American (masc.)	**amerikan (en)**	[ameriˈkan]
American (fem.)	**amerikanska (en)**	[ameriˈkanska]
American (adj)	**amerikansk**	[ameriˈkansk]
Canada	**Kanada**	['kanada]
Canadian (masc.)	**kanadensare (en)**	[kanaˈdɛnsarə]

| Canadian (fem.) | kanadensiska (en) | [kana'dɛnsiska] |
| Canadian (adj) | kanadensisk | [kana'dɛnsisk] |

Mexico	Mexiko	['mɛksikɔ]
Mexican (masc.)	mexikan (en)	[mɛksi'kan]
Mexican (fem.)	mexikanska (en)	[mɛksi'kanska]
Mexican (adj)	mexikansk	[mɛksi'kansk]

239. Central and South America

Argentina	Argentina	[argɛn'tina]
Argentinian (masc.)	argentinare (en)	[argɛn'tinarə]
Argentinian (fem.)	argentinska (en)	[argɛn'tinska]
Argentinian (adj)	argentinsk	[argɛn'tinsk]

Brazil	Brasilien	[bra'siliən]
Brazilian (masc.)	brasilianare (en)	[brasili'anarə]
Brazilian (fem.)	brasilianska (en)	[brasili'anska]
Brazilian (adj)	brasiliansk	[brasili'ansk]

Colombia	Colombia	[kɔ'lʲʊmbia]
Colombian (masc.)	colombian (en)	[kɔlʲʊmbi'an]
Colombian (fem.)	colombianska (en)	[kɔlʲʊmbi'anska]
Colombian (adj)	colombiansk	[kɔlʲʊmbi'ansk]

Cuba	Kuba	['kʉːba]
Cuban (masc.)	kuban (en)	[kʉ'ban]
Cuban (fem.)	kubanska (en)	[kʉ'banska]
Cuban (adj)	kubansk	[kʉ'bansk]

Chile	Chile	['ɕiːlʲe]
Chilean (masc.)	chilenare (en)	[ɕi'lʲenarə]
Chilean (fem.)	chilenska (en)	[ɕi'lʲenska]
Chilean (adj)	chilensk	[ɕi'lʲensk]

Bolivia	Bolivia	[bʊ'livia]
Venezuela	Venezuela	[venesu'ɛlʲa]
Paraguay	Paraguay	[parag'waj]
Peru	Peru	[pɛ'rʉ]

Suriname	Surinam	['sʉriˌnam]
Uruguay	Uruguay	[ʉrug'waj]
Ecuador	Ecuador	[ɛkva'dʊr]

The Bahamas	Bahamas	[ba'hamas]
Haiti	Haiti	[ha'iti]
Dominican Republic	Dominikanska republiken	[dɔmini'kanska repu'blikən]

| Panama | Panama | ['panama] |
| Jamaica | Jamaica | [ja'majka] |

240. Africa

Egypt	**Egypten**	[e'jyptən]
Egyptian (masc.)	**egyptier (en)**	[e'jyptiər]
Egyptian (fem.)	**egyptiska (en)**	[e'jyptiska]
Egyptian (adj)	**egyptisk**	[e'jyptisk]

Morocco	**Marocko**	[ma'rɔkʊ]
Moroccan (masc.)	**marockan (en)**	[marʊ'kan]
Moroccan (fem.)	**marockanska (en)**	[marʊ'kanska]
Moroccan (adj)	**marockansk**	[marʊ'kansk]

Tunisia	**Tunisien**	[tʉ'nisiən]
Tunisian (masc.)	**tunisier (en)**	[tʉ'nisiər]
Tunisian (fem.)	**tunisiska (en)**	[tʉ'nisiska]
Tunisian (adj)	**tunisisk**	[tʉ'nisisk]

Ghana	**Ghana**	['gana]
Zanzibar	**Zanzibar**	['sansibar]
Kenya	**Kenya**	['kenja]

| Libya | **Libyen** | ['libiən] |
| Madagascar | **Madagaskar** | [mada'gaskar] |

Namibia	**Namibia**	[na'mibia]
Senegal	**Senegal**	[sene'galʲ]
Tanzania	**Tanzania**	[tansa'nija]
South Africa	**Republiken Sydafrika**	[repu'bliken 'syd,afrika]

African (masc.)	**afrikan (en)**	[afri'kan]
African (fem.)	**afrikanska (en)**	[afri'kanska]
African (adj)	**afrikansk**	[afri'kansk]

241. Australia. Oceania

| Australia | **Australien** | [au'straliən] |
| Australian (masc.) | **australier (en)** | [au'straliər] |

| Australian (fem.) | **australiska (en)** | [au'straliska] |
| Australian (adj) | **australisk** | [au'stralisk] |

| New Zealand | **Nya Zeeland** | ['nya 'se:lʲand] |
| New Zealander (masc.) | **nyzeeländare (en)** | [ny'se:lʲɛndarə] |

| New Zealander (fem.) | **nyzeeländska (en)** | [ny'se:lʲɛŋska] |
| New Zealand (as adj) | **nyzeeländsk** | [ny'se:lʲɛŋsk] |

| Tasmania | **Tasmanien** | [tas'maniən] |
| French Polynesia | **Franska Polynesien** | ['franska polʲy'nesiən] |

242. Cities

Amsterdam	Amsterdam	['amstə‚dam]
Ankara	Ankara	['aŋkara]
Athens	Aten	[a'ten]
Baghdad	Bagdad	['bagdad]
Bangkok	Bangkok	['baŋkɔk]
Barcelona	Barcelona	[barsə'lʲona]

Beijing	Peking	['pekiŋ]
Beirut	Beirut	['bejrut]
Berlin	Berlin	[bɛr'lin]
Mumbai (Bombay)	Bombay	[bɔm'bɛj]
Bonn	Bonn	['bɔn]

Bordeaux	Bordeaux	[bɔ'dɔ:]
Bratislava	Bratislava	[brati'slʲava]
Brussels	Bryssel	['brysəlʲ]
Bucharest	Bukarest	['bʉkarɛst]
Budapest	Budapest	['bʉdapɛst]

Cairo	Kairo	['kajrʉ]
Kolkata (Calcutta)	Kalkutta	[kalʲ'kʉta]
Chicago	Chicago	[ɕi'kagʉ]
Copenhagen	Köpenhamn	['ɕø:pɛn‚hamn]

Dar-es-Salaam	Dar es-Salaam	[dar ɛs sa'lʲam]
Delhi	New Delhi	[nju 'dɛlʲi]
Dubai	Dubai	[dʉ'baj]
Dublin	Dublin	['dablin]
Düsseldorf	Düsseldorf	['dʉsəlʲ‚dɔrf]

Florence	Florens	['flʲørɛns]
Frankfurt	Frankfurt	['fraŋkfʉ:t]
Geneva	Genève	[ʒe'nɛv]

The Hague	Haag	['ha:g]
Hamburg	Hamburg	['hambʉrj]
Hanoi	Hanoi	[ha'nɔj]
Havana	Havanna	[ha'vana]
Helsinki	Helsingfors	['hɛlʲsiŋ‚fɔ:ʂ]
Hiroshima	Hiroshima	[hirɔ'ʃima]
Hong Kong	Hongkong	['hɔŋ‚kɔn]

Istanbul	Istanbul	['istambʉlʲ]
Jerusalem	Jerusalem	[je'rʉsalʲem]
Kyiv	Kiev	['kiev]
Kuala Lumpur	Kuala Lumpur	[ku'alʲa 'lʉmpʉ:r]
Lisbon	Lissabon	['lisabɔn]
London	London	['lʲɔndɔn]
Los Angeles	Los Angeles	[lʲɔs 'anəlʲes]

Lyons	**Lion**	[li'ɔn]
Madrid	**Madrid**	[ma'drid]
Marseille	**Marseille**	[ma'sɛj]
Mexico City	**Mexico City**	['mɛksikɔ 'siti]

Miami	**Miami**	[ma'jami]
Montreal	**Montreal**	[mɔntre'ɔlʲ]
Moscow	**Moskva**	[mɔ'skva]
Munich	**München**	['mʉnɧən]

Nairobi	**Nairobi**	[naj'rɔːbi]
Naples	**Neapel**	[ne'apəlʲ]
New York	**New York**	[nju 'jork]
Nice	**Nice**	['nis]
Oslo	**Oslo**	['ʊslʉ]
Ottawa	**Ottawa**	['ɔtava]

Paris	**Paris**	[pa'ris]
Prague	**Prag**	['prag]
Rio de Janeiro	**Rio de Janeiro**	['riʉ de ʃa'nɛjrʉ]
Rome	**Rom**	['rɔm]

Saint Petersburg	**Sankt Petersburg**	['saŋkt 'peteˌşburj]
Seoul	**Söul**	[sœulʲ]
Shanghai	**Shanghai**	[ʃan'haj]
Singapore	**Singapore**	['siŋapʊr]
Stockholm	**Stockholm**	['stɔkɔlʲm]
Sydney	**Sydney**	['sidni]

Taipei	**Taipei**	[taj'pɛj]
Tokyo	**Tokyo**	['tɔkiʉ]
Toronto	**Toronto**	[tɔ'rɔntʉ]

Venice	**Venedig**	[ve'nedig]
Vienna	**Wien**	['veːn]
Warsaw	**Warszawa**	[vaː'şava]
Washington	**Washington**	['wɔʃiŋtɔn]

243. Politics. Government. Part 1

politics	**politik (en)**	[pʊli'tik]
political (adj)	**politisk**	[pʊ'litisk]
politician	**politiker (en)**	[pʊ'litikər]

state (country)	**stat (en)**	['stat]
citizen	**medborgare (en)**	['mɛdˌbɔrjarə]
citizenship	**medborgarskap (ett)**	[mɛd'bɔrjaˌşkap]

| national emblem | **riksvapen (ett)** | ['riksˌvapən] |
| national anthem | **nationalhymn (en)** | [natɧʊ'nalʲˌhymn] |

government	regering (en)	[re'jeriŋ]
head of state	statschef (en)	['stats,ʃef]
parliament	parlament (ett)	[parla'mɛnt]
party	parti (ett)	[pa:'ʈi:]
capitalism	kapitalism (en)	[kapita'lism]
capitalist (adj)	kapitalistisk	[kapita'listisk]
socialism	socialism (en)	[sɔsia'lism]
socialist (adj)	socialistisk	[sɔsia'listisk]
communism	kommunism (en)	[kɔmu'nism]
communist (adj)	kommunistisk	[kɔmu'nistisk]
communist (n)	kommunist (en)	[kɔmu'nist]
democracy	demokrati (en)	[demʊkra'ti:]
democrat	demokrat (en)	[demʊ'krat]
democratic (adj)	demokratisk	[demʊ'kratisk]
Democratic party	Demokratiska partiet	[demɔ'kratiska pa:'ʈi:et]
liberal (n)	liberal (en)	[libə'ralʲ]
liberal (adj)	liberal-	[libə'ralʲ-]
conservative (n)	konservativ (en)	[kɔn'sɛrva,tiv]
conservative (adj)	konservativ	[kɔn'sɛrva,tiv]
republic (n)	republik (en)	[repu'blik]
republican (n)	republikan (en)	[republi'kan]
Republican party	republikanskt parti (ett)	[republi'kansk pa:'ʈi:]
elections	val (ett)	['valʲ]
to elect (vt)	att välja	[at 'vɛlja]
elector, voter	väljare (en)	['vɛljarə]
election campaign	valkampanj (en)	['valʲkam,panʲ]
voting (n)	omröstning (en)	['ɔm,rœstniŋ]
to vote (vi)	att rösta	[at 'rœsta]
suffrage, right to vote	rösträtt (en)	['rœst,ræt]
candidate	kandidat (en)	[kandi'dat]
to be a candidate	att kandidera	[at kandi'dera]
campaign	kampanj (en)	[kam'panʲ]
opposition (as adj)	oppositions-	[ɔpɔsi'ɧʊns-]
opposition (n)	opposition (en)	[ɔpɔsi'ɧʊn]
visit	besök (ett)	[be'sø:k]
official visit	officiellt besök (ett)	[ɔfi'sjɛlʲt be'sø:k]
international (adj)	internationell	['intɛ:ɳatʃʊ,nɛlʲ]
negotiations	förhandlingar (pl)	[før'handliŋar]
to negotiate (vi)	att förhandla	[at før'handlʲa]

244. Politics. Government. Part 2

society	samhälle (ett)	['sam‚hɛlʲe]
constitution	konstitution (en)	[kɔnstitu'fʲʊn]
power (political control)	makt (en)	['makt]
corruption	korruption (en)	[kɔrup'fʲʊn]

law (justice)	lag (en)	['lʲag]
legal (legitimate)	laglig	['lʲaglig]

justice (fairness)	rättvisa (en)	['ræt‚visa]
just (fair)	rättvis, rättfärdig	['rætvis], ['ræt‚fæ:dɪg]

committee	kommitté (en)	[kɔmi'te:]
bill (draft law)	lagförslag (ett)	['lʲag‚fœ:'ʂlag]
budget	budget (en)	['budjet]
policy	policy (en)	['pɔlisi]
reform	reform (en)	[re'fɔrm]
radical (adj)	radikal	[radi'kalʲ]

power (strength, force)	kraft (en)	['kraft]
powerful (adj)	mäktig, kraftfull	['mɛktig], ['kraft‚fulʲ]
supporter	anhängare (en)	['an‚hɛːŋarə]
influence	inflytande (ett)	['in‚flʲytandə]

regime (e.g., military ~)	regim (en)	[re'ʃim]
conflict	konflikt (en)	[kɔn'flikt]
conspiracy (plot)	sammansvärning (en)	['samans‚væːɳiŋ]
provocation	provokation (en)	[prɔvʊka'fʲʊn]

to overthrow (regime, etc.)	att störta	[at 'stø:ʈa]
overthrow (of government)	störtande (ett)	['stø:ʈandə]
revolution	revolution (en)	[revʊlʉ'fʲʊn]

coup d'état	statskupp (en)	['stats‚kup]
military coup	militärkupp (en)	[mili'tæ:r‚kup]

crisis	kris (en)	['kris]
economic recession	ekonomisk nedgång (en)	[ɛkʊ'nɔmisk 'ned‚gɔŋ]
demonstrator (protester)	demonstrant (en)	[demɔn'strant]
demonstration	demonstration (en)	[demɔnstra'fʲʊn]
martial law	krigstillstånd (ett)	['krigs‚tilʲ'stɔnd]
military base	militärbas (en)	[mili'tæ:r‚bas]

stability	stabilitet (en)	[stabili'tet]
stable (adj)	stabil	[sta'bilʲ]

exploitation	utsugning (en)	['ʉt‚sʉgniŋ]
to exploit (workers)	att utnyttja	[at 'ʉt‚nʏtja]
racism	rasism (en)	[ra'sism]
racist	rasist (en)	[ra'sist]

| fascism | fascism (en) | [fa'çism] |
| fascist | fascist (en) | [fa'çist] |

245. Countries. Miscellaneous

foreigner	utlänning (en)	['ʉt̪ˌlʲɛniŋ]
foreign (adj)	utländsk	['ʉt̪ˌlʲɛŋsk]
abroad	utomlands	['ʉtɔmˌlʲands]
(in a foreign country)		

emigrant	emigrant (en)	[ɛmi'grant]
emigration	emigration (en)	[ɛmigra'ɧʊn]
to emigrate (vi)	att emigrera	[at ɛmi'grera]

the West	Västen	['vɛstən]
the East	Östen	['œstən]
the Far East	Fjärran Östern	['fʲæːran 'œstɛːɳ]

civilization	civilisation (en)	[sivilisa'ɧʊn]
humanity (mankind)	mänsklighet (en)	['mɛnskligˌhet]
the world (earth)	värld (en)	['væːɖ]
peace	fred (en)	['fred]
worldwide (adj)	världs-	['væːɖs-]

homeland	hemland (ett)	['hɛmˌlʲand]
people (population)	folk (ett)	['fɔlʲk]
population	befolkning (en)	[be'fɔlʲkniŋ]

people (a lot of ~)	folk (ett)	['fɔlʲk]
nation (people)	nation (en)	[nat'ɧʊn]
generation	generation (en)	[jenera'ɧʊn]

territory (area)	territorium (ett)	[tɛri'tʊrium]
region	region (en)	[regi'ʊn]
state (part of a country)	delstat (en)	['dɛlʲˌstat]

tradition	tradition (en)	[tradi'ɧʊn]
custom (tradition)	sedvänja (en)	['sedˌvɛnja]
ecology	ekologi (en)	[ɛkʊlʲʊ'giː]

Indian (Native American)	indian (en)	[indi'an]
Gypsy (masc.)	zigenare (en)	[si'jenərə]
Gypsy (fem.)	zigenska (en)	[si'jenska]
Gypsy (adj)	zigensk	[si'jensk]

empire	kejsardöme, rike (ett)	['çɛjsardømə], ['rikə]
colony	koloni (en)	[kʊlʲʊ'niː]
slavery	slaveri (ett)	[slʲave'riː]
invasion	invasion (en)	[inva'ɧʊn]
famine	hungersnöd (en)	['huŋɛsˌnøːd]

246. Major religious groups. Confessions

religion	**religion (en)**	[reli'jʊn]
religious (adj)	**religiös**	[reli'fŋøːs]
faith, belief	**tro (en)**	['trʊ]
to believe (in God)	**att tro**	[at 'trʊ]
believer	**troende (en)**	['trʊəndə]
atheism	**ateism (en)**	[ate'ism]
atheist	**ateist (en)**	[ate'ist]
Christianity	**kristendom (en)**	['kristən‚dʊm]
Christian (n)	**kristen (en)**	['kristən]
Christian (adj)	**kristen**	['kristən]
Catholicism	**katolicism (en)**	[katʊli'sism]
Catholic (n)	**katolik (en)**	[katʊ'lik]
Catholic (adj)	**katolsk**	[ka'tʊlˈsk]
Protestantism	**protestantism (en)**	[prʊtɛstan'tism]
Protestant Church	**den protestantiska kyrkan**	[dɛn prʊtɛ'stantiska 'çyrkan]
Protestant (n)	**protestant (en)**	[prʊtɛ'stant]
Orthodoxy	**ortodoxi (en)**	[ɔːtɔdɔ'ksiː]
Orthodox Church	**den ortodoxa kyrkan**	[dɛn ɔːtɔ'dɔːksa 'çyrkan]
Orthodox (n)	**ortodox (en)**	[ɔːtɔ'dɔːks]
Presbyterianism	**presbyterianism (en)**	[prɛsbyteria'nism]
Presbyterian Church	**den presbyterianska kyrkan**	[dɛn prɛsbyteri'anska 'çyrkan]
Presbyterian (n)	**presbyter (en)**	[prɛ'sbytər]
Lutheranism	**lutherdom (en)**	['lʉtərdʊm]
Lutheran (n)	**lutheran (en)**	[lʉte'ran]
Baptist Church	**baptism (en)**	[bap'tism]
Baptist (n)	**baptist (en)**	[bap'tist]
Anglican Church	**den anglikanska kyrkan**	[dɛn aŋli'kanska 'çyrkan]
Anglican (n)	**anglikan (en)**	['aŋli‚kan]
Mormonism	**mormonism (en)**	[mɔrmʊ'nism]
Mormon (n)	**mormon (en)**	[mɔr'mʊn]
Judaism	**judendom (en)**	['jʉdən‚dʊm]
Jew (n)	**jude (en)**	['jʉdə]
Buddhism	**Buddism (en)**	[bu'dism]
Buddhist (n)	**buddist (en)**	[bu'dist]
Hinduism	**hinduism (en)**	[hindʉ'iːsm]

Hindu (n)	**hindu (en)**	[hin'dɵ:]
Islam	**islam (en)**	[isˈlʲam]
Muslim (n)	**muselman (en)**	[mɵsɛlʲˈman]
Muslim (adj)	**muselmansk**	[mɵsɛlʲˈmansk]

Shiah Islam	**shiism (en)**	[ʃiˈism]
Shiite (n)	**shiit (en)**	[ʃiˈit]
Sunni Islam	**sunnism (en)**	[suˈni:sm]
Sunnite (n)	**sunnit (en)**	[suˈnit]

247. Religions. Priests

| priest | **präst (en)** | [ˈprɛst] |
| the Pope | **Påven** | [ˈpo:vən] |

monk, friar	**munk (en)**	[ˈmuŋk]
nun	**nunna (en)**	[ˈnuna]
pastor	**pastor (en)**	[ˈpastʊr]

abbot	**abbé (en)**	[aˈbe:]
vicar (parish priest)	**kyrkoherde (en)**	[ˈɕyrkʊˌhɛ:ɖə]
bishop	**biskop (en)**	[ˈbiskɔp]
cardinal	**kardinal (en)**	[ka:ɖiˈnalʲ]

preacher	**predikant (en)**	[prediˈkant]
preaching	**predikan (en)**	[preˈdikan]
parishioners	**sockenbor (pl)**	[ˈsɔkənˌbʊr]

| believer | **troende (en)** | [ˈtrʊəndə] |
| atheist | **ateist (en)** | [ateˈist] |

248. Faith. Christianity. Islam

| Adam | **Adam** | [ˈadam] |
| Eve | **Eva** | [ˈɛva] |

God	**Gud**	[ˈgɵ:d]
the Lord	**Herren**	[ˈhɛrən]
the Almighty	**Den Allsmäktige**	[dɛn ˈalʲsmɛktigə]

sin	**synd (en)**	[ˈsʏnd]
to sin (vi)	**att synda**	[at ˈsʏnda]
sinner (masc.)	**syndare (en)**	[ˈsʏndarə]
sinner (fem.)	**synderska (en)**	[ˈsʏndɛʂka]

hell	**helvete (ett)**	[ˈhɛlʲvetə]
paradise	**paradis (ett)**	[ˈparaˌdis]
Jesus	**Jesus**	[ˈjesus]

Jesus Christ	**Jesus Kristus**	['jesus ˌkristus]
the Holy Spirit	**Den Helige Ande**	[dɛn 'heligə ˌandə]
the Savior	**Frälsaren**	['frɛlʲsarən]
the Virgin Mary	**Jungfru Maria**	['juɲfru ma'ria]
the Devil	**Djävul (en)**	['jɛ:vulʲ]
devil's (adj)	**djävulsk**	['jɛ:vulʲsk]
Satan	**Satan**	['satan]
satanic (adj)	**satanisk**	[sa'tanisk]
angel	**ängel (en)**	['ɛŋəlʲ]
guardian angel	**skyddsängel (en)**	['ɧyds,ɛŋəlʲ]
angelic (adj)	**änglalik**	['ɛŋlʲalik]
apostle	**apostel (en)**	[a'postəlʲ]
archangel	**ärkeängel (en)**	['æ:rkə,ɛŋəlʲ]
the Antichrist	**Antikrist (en)**	['antiˌkrist]
Church	**Kyrkan**	['ɕyrkan]
Bible	**bibel (en)**	['bibəlʲ]
biblical (adj)	**biblisk**	['biblisk]
Old Testament	**Gamla Testamentet**	['gamlʲa tɛsta'mɛntət]
New Testament	**Nya Testamentet**	['nya tɛsta'mɛntət]
Gospel	**evangelium (ett)**	[ɛva'ŋe:lium]
Holy Scripture	**Den Heliga Skrift**	[dɛn 'heliga ˌskrift]
Heaven	**Himmelen, Guds rike**	['himelʲən], ['guds 'rikə]
Commandment	**bud (ett)**	['bu:d]
prophet	**profet (en)**	[pru'fet]
prophecy	**profetia (en)**	[prufe'tsia]
Allah	**Allah**	['alʲa]
Mohammed	**Muhammed**	[mu'hamed]
the Koran	**Koranen**	[ku'ranən]
mosque	**moské (en)**	[mus'ke:]
mullah	**mullah (en)**	[mu'lʲa:]
prayer	**bön (en)**	['bø:n]
to pray (vi, vt)	**att be**	[at 'be:]
pilgrimage	**pilgrimsresa (en)**	['pilʲrimˌresa]
pilgrim	**pilgrim (en)**	['pilʲrim]
Mecca	**Mecka**	['meka]
church	**kyrka (en)**	['ɕyrka]
temple	**tempel (ett)**	['tɛmpəlʲ]
cathedral	**katedral (en)**	[katɛ'dralʲ]
Gothic (adj)	**gotisk**	['gutisk]
synagogue	**synagoga (en)**	['synaˌgɔga]
mosque	**moské (en)**	[mus'ke:]
chapel	**kapell (ett)**	[ka'pɛlʲ]

abbey	abbedi (ett)	['abədi:]
convent	kloster (ett)	['klɔstər]
monastery	kloster (ett)	['klɔstər]

bell (church ~s)	klocka (en)	['klɔka]
bell tower	klocktorn (ett)	['klɔkˌtuːn]
to ring (ab. bells)	att ringa	[at 'riŋa]

cross	kors (ett)	['kɔːʂ]
cupola (roof)	kupol (en)	[kʉ'pɔːlʲ]
icon	ikon (en)	[i'kon]

soul	själ (en)	['ɧɛːlʲ]
fate (destiny)	öde (ett)	['øːdə]
evil (n)	ondska (en)	['ʊŋˌska]
good (n)	godhet (en)	['gʊdˌhet]

vampire	vampyr (en)	[vam'pyr]
witch (evil ~)	häxa (en)	['hɛːksa]
demon	demon (en)	[de'mɔn]
spirit	ande (en)	['andə]

| redemption (giving us ~) | förlossning (en) | [fœː'lʲɔsniŋ] |
| to redeem (vt) | att sona | [at 'sʊna] |

church service, mass	gudstjänst (en)	['guːdˌɕɛnst]
to say mass	att hålla gudstjänst	[at 'hɔːlʲa 'guːdˌɕɛnst]
confession	bikt, bekännelse (en)	[bikt], [be'ɕɛːŋəlʲsə]
to confess (vi)	att skrifta	[at 'skrifta]

saint (n)	helgon (ett)	['hɛlʲgɔn]
sacred (holy)	helig	['hɛlig]
holy water	vigvatten (ett)	['vigˌvatən]

ritual (n)	ritual (en)	[ritu'alʲ]
ritual (adj)	rituell	[ritu'ɛlʲ]
sacrifice	blot (ett)	['blʲʊt]

superstition	vidskepelse (en)	['vidˌɧɛpəlʲsə]
superstitious (adj)	vidskeplig	['vidˌɧɛplig]
afterlife	livet efter detta	['livet ˌɛftə 'deta]
eternal life	det eviga livet	[dɛ 'eviga ˌlivet]

MISCELLANEOUS

249. Various useful words

background (green ~)	**bakgrund (en)**	['bak‚grʉnd]
balance (of situation)	**balans (en)**	[ba'lʲans]
barrier (obstacle)	**hinder (ett)**	['hindər]
base (basis)	**bas (en)**	['bas]
beginning	**början (en)**	['bœrjan]
category	**kategori (en)**	[kategɔ'ri:]
cause (reason)	**orsak (en)**	['ʊ:ʂak]
choice	**val (ett)**	['valʲ]
coincidence	**sammanfall (ett)**	['sam‚anfalʲ]
comfortable (~ chair)	**bekväm**	[bɛk'vɛ:m]
comparison	**jämförelse (en)**	['jɛm‚førəlʲsə]
compensation	**kompensation (en)**	[kɔmpɛnsa'ɧʊn]
degree (extent, amount)	**grad (en)**	['grad]
development	**utveckling (en)**	['ʉt‚vɛkliŋ]
difference	**skillnad (en)**	['ɧilʲnad]
effect (e.g., of drugs)	**effekt (en)**	[ɛ'fɛkt]
effort (exertion)	**ansträngning (en)**	['an‚strɛŋniŋ]
element	**element (ett)**	[ɛlʲe'mɛnt]
end (finish)	**slut (ett)**	['slʉ:t]
example (illustration)	**exempel (ett)**	[ɛk'sɛmpəlʲ]
fact	**faktum (ett)**	['faktum]
frequent (adj)	**frekvent**	[frɛ'kvɛnt]
growth (development)	**växt (en)**	['vɛkst]
help	**hjälp (en)**	['jɛlʲp]
ideal	**ideal (ett)**	[ide'alʲ]
kind (sort, type)	**slag (ett), sort (en)**	['slʲag], ['sɔ:t]
labyrinth	**labyrint (en)**	[lʲaby'rint]
mistake, error	**fel (ett)**	['felʲ]
moment	**moment (ett)**	[mʊ'mɛnt]
object (thing)	**objekt, ting (ett)**	[ɔb'jɛkt], ['tiŋ]
obstacle	**hinder (ett)**	['hindər]
original (original copy)	**original (ett)**	[ɔrigi'nalʲ]
part (~ of sth)	**del (en)**	['delʲ]
particle, small part	**partikel (en)**	[pa:'ʈi:kəlʲ]
pause (break)	**paus (en)**	['paus]

position	position (en)	[pʊsi'ʃʊn]
principle	princip (en)	[prin'sip]
problem	problem (ett)	[prɔ'bⁱlᵉem]

process	process (en)	[prʊ'sɛs]
progress	framsteg (ett)	['fram‚steg]
property (quality)	egenskap (en)	['ɛgɛn‚skap]
reaction	reaktion (en)	[reak'ʃʊn]
risk	risk (en)	['risk]

secret	hemlighet (en)	['hɛmlig‚het]
series	serie (en)	['seriə]
shape (outer form)	form (en)	['fɔrm]
situation	situation (en)	[sitɐa'ʃʊn]
solution	lösning (en)	['lⁱœsniŋ]

standard (adj)	standard-	['standa:ḍ-]
standard (level of quality)	standard (en)	['standa:ḍ]
stop (pause)	uppehåll (ett), vila (en)	['upə'ho:lⁱ], ['vilⁱa]
style	stil (en)	['stilⁱ]

system	system (ett)	[sʏ'stem]
table (chart)	tabell (en)	[ta'bɛlⁱ]
tempo, rate	tempo (ett)	['tɛmpʊ]
term (word, expression)	term (en)	['tɛrm]

thing (object, item)	sak (en), ting (ett)	['sak], ['tiŋ]
truth (e.g., moment of ~)	sanning (en)	['saniŋ]
turn (please wait your ~)	tur (en)	['tɐ:r]
type (sort, kind)	typ (en)	['typ]
urgent (adj)	brådskande	['brɔ‚skandə]

urgently (adv)	brådskande	['brɔ‚skandə]
utility (usefulness)	nytta (en)	['nʏta]
variant (alternative)	variant (en)	[vari'ant]
way (means, method)	sätt (ett)	['sæt]
zone	zon (en)	['sʊn]

250. Modifiers. Adjectives. Part 1

additional (adj)	ytterligare	['ytə‚ligarə]
ancient (~ civilization)	forntida, antikens	['fʊ:n‚tida], [an'tikəns]
artificial (adj)	konstgjord	['kɔnstjʊ:ḍ]
back, rear (adj)	bak-, bakre	[bak-], ['bakrə]
bad (adj)	dålig	['do:lig]

beautiful (~ palace)	vacker	['vakər]
beautiful (person)	vacker	['vakər]
big (in size)	stor	['stʊr]

bitter (taste)	**bitter**	['bitər]
blind (sightless)	**blind**	['blind]
calm, quiet (adj)	**lugn**	['lʉgn]
careless (negligent)	**slarvig**	['slʲarvig]
caring (~ father)	**omtänksam**	['ɔmˌtɛŋksam]
central (adj)	**central**	[sɛn'tralʲ]
cheap (low-priced)	**billig**	['bilig]
cheerful (adj)	**glad, munter**	['glʲad], ['muntər]
children's (adj)	**barnslig**	['baːnʃlig]
civil (~ law)	**civil**	[si'vilʲ]
clandestine (secret)	**hemlig**	['hɛmlig]
clean (free from dirt)	**ren**	['ren]
clear (explanation, etc.)	**klar**	['klʲar]
clever (smart)	**klok**	['klʲʊk]
close (near in space)	**nära**	['næːra]
closed (adj)	**stängd**	['stɛŋd]
cloudless (sky)	**molnfri**	['mɔlʲnˌfriː]
cold (drink, weather)	**kall**	['kalʲ]
compatible (adj)	**förenlig**	[fø'rɛnlig]
contented (satisfied)	**nöjd, tillfreds**	['nœjd], ['tilʲfrɛds]
continuous (uninterrupted)	**oavbruten**	[ʊ:'avˌbrʉːtən]
cool (weather)	**kylig**	['ɕylig]
dangerous (adj)	**farlig**	['faːlʲig]
dark (room)	**mörk**	['mœːrk]
dead (not alive)	**död**	['døːd]
dense (fog, smoke)	**tät**	['tɛt]
destitute (extremely poor)	**utfattig**	['ʉtˌfatig]
different (not the same)	**olik**	[ʊ:'lik]
difficult (decision)	**svår**	['svoːr]
difficult (problem, task)	**komplicerad**	[kɔmpli'serad]
dim, faint (light)	**svag**	['svag]
dirty (not clean)	**smutsig**	['smʉtsig]
distant (in space)	**fjärran**	['fʲæːran]
dry (clothes, etc.)	**torr**	['tɔr]
easy (not difficult)	**lätt, enkel**	['lʲæt], ['ɛŋkəlʲ]
empty (glass, room)	**tom**	['tɔm]
even (e.g., ~ surface)	**jämn**	['jɛmn]
exact (amount)	**precis, exakt**	[prɛ'sis], [ɛk'sakt]
excellent (adj)	**utmärkt**	['ʉtˌmæːrkt]
excessive (adj)	**överdriven**	['øːvəˌdrivən]
expensive (adj)	**dyr**	['dyr]
exterior (adj)	**yttre**	['ytrə]
far (the ~ East)	**fjärran**	['fʲæːran]

fast (quick)	**snabb**	['snab]
fatty (food)	**fet**	['fet]
fertile (land, soil)	**fruktbar**	['frʉkt‚bar]
flat (~ panel display)	**flat**	['flʲat]
foreign (adj)	**utländsk**	['ʉt‚lʲɛŋsk]
fragile (china, glass)	**skör, bräcklig**	['ʃøːr], ['brɛklig]
free (at no cost)	**gratis**	['gratis]
free (unrestricted)	**fri**	['friː]
fresh (~ water)	**söt-, färsk-**	['søːt-], ['fæːʂk-]
fresh (e.g., ~ bread)	**färsk**	['fæːʂk]
frozen (food)	**fryst**	['frʏst]
full (completely filled)	**full**	['fulʲ]
gloomy (house, forecast)	**mörk**	['mœːrk]
good (book, etc.)	**bra**	['brɔː]
good, kind (kindhearted)	**god**	['gʊd]
grateful (adj)	**tacksam, tacknämlig**	['taksam], ['tak'nɛmlig]
happy (adj)	**lycklig**	['lʲyklig]
hard (not soft)	**hård**	['hoːɖ]
heavy (in weight)	**tung**	['tuŋ]
hostile (adj)	**fientlig**	['fjɛntlig]
hot (adj)	**het, varm**	['het], ['varm]
huge (adj)	**enorm**	[ɛ'nɔrm]
humid (adj)	**fuktig**	['fuːktig]
hungry (adj)	**hungrig**	['huŋrig]
ill (sick, unwell)	**sjuk**	['ɧʉːk]
immobile (adj)	**orörlig**	[ʊ'røːlʲig]
important (adj)	**viktig**	['viktig]
impossible (adj)	**omöjlig**	[ʊ'mœjlig]
incomprehensible	**obegriplig**	['ʊbe‚gripling]
indispensable (adj)	**nödvändig**	['nøːd‚vɛndig]
inexperienced (adj)	**oerfaren**	['ʊer‚farən]
insignificant (adj)	**obetydlig**	['ʊbe‚tʏdlig]
interior (adj)	**inre**	['inrə]
joint (~ decision)	**gemensam**	[je'mɛnsam]
last (e.g., ~ week)	**förra**	['fœːra]
last (final)	**sista**	['sista]
left (e.g., ~ side)	**vänster**	['vɛnstər]
legal (legitimate)	**laglig**	['lʲaglig]
light (in weight)	**lätt**	['lʲæt]
light (pale color)	**ljus**	['jʉːs]
limited (adj)	**begränsad**	[be'grɛnsad]
liquid (fluid)	**flytande**	['flʲytandə]
long (e.g., ~ hair)	**lång**	['lʲɔŋ]

| loud (voice, etc.) | hög | ['hø:g] |
| low (voice) | låg, lågmäld | ['lˈo:g], ['lˈo:gmɛlˈd] |

251. Modifiers. Adjectives. Part 2

main (principal)	huvud-	['hʉ:vʉd-]
matt, matte	matt	['mat]
meticulous (job)	noggrann	['nʊgran]
mysterious (adj)	mystisk	['mystisk]
narrow (street, etc.)	smal	['smalˈ]

native (~ country)	hem-, födelse-	['hɛm-], ['fødəlˈsə-]
nearby (adj)	nära	['næ:ra]
nearsighted (adj)	närsynt	['næ:ˌsʏnt]
needed (necessary)	nödvändig	['nø:dˌvɛndig]
negative (~ response)	negativ	['negaˌtiv]

neighboring (adj)	grann-	['gran-]
nervous (adj)	nervös	[nɛr'vø:s]
new (adj)	ny	['ny]
next (e.g., ~ week)	nästa	['nɛsta]

nice (kind)	snäll	['snɛlˈ]
nice (voice)	trevlig	['trɛvlig]
normal (adj)	normal	[nɔr'malˈ]
not big (adj)	liten, inte stor	['litən], [ˌintə 'stʊr]
not difficult (adj)	lätt	['lˈæt]

obligatory (adj)	obligatorisk	[ɔbliga'tʊrisk]
old (house)	gammal	['gamalˈ]
open (adj)	öppen	['øpən]
opposite (adj)	motsatt	['mʊtˌsat]

ordinary (usual)	vanlig	['vanlig]
original (unusual)	original	[ɔrigi'nalˈ]
past (recent)	förra	['fœ:ra]
permanent (adj)	fast, permanent	['fast], [pɛrma'nɛnt]
personal (adj)	personlig	[pɛ'ʂʊnlig]

polite (adj)	hövlig, artig	['hœvlig], ['a:ţig]
poor (not rich)	fattig	['fatig]
possible (adj)	möjlig	['mœjlig]
present (current)	nuvarande	['nʉ:ˌvarandə]
previous (adj)	föregående	['førəˌgo:əndə]

principal (main)	huvud-	['hʉ:vʉd-]
private (~ jet)	privat	[pri'vat]
probable (adj)	sannolik	[sanʊ'lik]
prolonged (e.g., ~ applause)	långvarig	['lˈɔŋˌvarig]

public (open to all)	offentlig	[ɔ'fɛntlig]
punctual (person)	punktlig	['puŋktlig]
quiet (tranquil)	lugn	['lʉgn]
rare (adj)	sällsynt	['sɛlʲsʏnt]
raw (uncooked)	rå	['rɔ:]
right (not left)	höger	['hø:gər]

right, correct (adj)	riktig	['riktig]
ripe (fruit)	mogen	['mʊgən]
risky (adj)	riskabel	[ris'kabəlʲ]
sad (~ look)	trist	['trist]

sad (depressing)	sorgmodig	['sɔrj,mʊdig]
safe (not dangerous)	säker	['sɛ:kər]
salty (food)	salt	['salʲt]
satisfied (customer)	belåten	[be'lʲo:tən]

second hand (adj)	begagnad, secondhand	['be,gagnad], ['sekond,hɛnd]
shallow (water)	grund	['grʉnd]
sharp (blade, etc.)	skarp	['skarp]
short (in length)	kort	['kɔ:t]

short, short-lived (adj)	kortvarig	['kɔ:t,varig]
significant (notable)	betydande	[be'tydandə]
similar (adj)	lik	['lik]
simple (easy)	enkel	['ɛŋkəlʲ]
skinny	benig, mager	['benig], ['magər]

small (in size)	liten, små	['litən], ['smo:]
smooth (surface)	glatt	['glʲat]
soft (~ toys)	mjuk	['mjʉ:k]
solid (~ wall)	solid, hållbar	[sɔ'lid], ['ho:lʲ,bar]

sour (flavor, taste)	syr	['syr]
spacious (house, etc.)	rymlig	['rʏmlig]
special (adj)	speciell	[spesi'ɛlʲ]
straight (line, road)	rak, rakt	['rak], ['rakt]
strong (person)	stark	['stark]

stupid (foolish)	dum	['dum]
suitable (e.g., ~ for drinking)	lämplig	['lʲɛmplig]
sunny (day)	solig	['sʊlig]
superb, perfect (adj)	utmärkt	['ʉt,mæ:rkt]
swarthy (adj)	mörkhyad	['mœ:rk,hyad]

sweet (sugary)	söt	['sø:t]
tan (adj)	solbränd	['sʊlʲ,brɛnd]
tasty (delicious)	läcker	['lʲɛkər]
tender (affectionate)	öm	['ø:m]
the highest (adj)	högst	['hœgst]

the most important	**viktigaste**	['viktigastə]
the nearest	**närmast**	['næ:rmast]
the same, equal (adj)	**samma, lika**	['sama], ['lika]
thick (e.g., ~ fog)	**tjock**	['ɕøk]
thick (wall, slice)	**tjock**	['ɕøk]

thin (person)	**mager**	['magər]
tight (~ shoes)	**snäv, trång**	['snɛv], ['trɔŋ]
tired (exhausted)	**trött**	['trœt]
tiring (adj)	**tröttande**	['trœtandə]

transparent (adj)	**genomskinlig**	['jenɔmˌhinlig]
unclear (adj)	**oklar**	[ʊ:'klʲar]
unique (exceptional)	**unik**	[u'nik]
various (adj)	**olika**	[ʊ:'lika]

warm (moderately hot)	**varm**	['varm]
wet (e.g., ~ clothes)	**våt**	['vo:t]
whole (entire, complete)	**hel**	['helʲ]
wide (e.g., ~ road)	**bred**	['bred]
young (adj)	**ung**	['uŋ]

MAIN 500 VERBS

252. Verbs A-C

to accompany (vt)	att följa	[at 'følja]
to accuse (vt)	att anklaga	[at 'aŋ,klʲaga]
to acknowledge (admit)	att erkänna	[at ɛ:'ɕɛna]
to act (take action)	att handla	[at 'handlʲa]
to add (supplement)	att tillfoga	[at 'tilʲ,foga]
to address (speak to)	att tilltala	[at 'tilʲ,talʲa]
to admire (vi)	att beundra	[at be'undra]
to advertise (vt)	att reklamera	[at rɛklʲa'mera]
to advise (vt)	att råda	[at 'ro:da]
to affirm (assert)	att påstå	[at 'pɔ,stɔ:]
to agree (say yes)	att samtycka	[at 'sam,tʏka]
to aim (to point a weapon)	att sikta på ...	[at 'sikta pɔ ...]
to allow (sb to do sth)	att tillåta	[at 'tilʲo:ta]
to amputate (vt)	att amputera	[at ampʉ'tera]
to answer (vi, vt)	att svara	[at 'svara]
to apologize (vi)	att ursäkta sig	[at 'ʉ:,sɛkta sɛj]
to appear (come into view)	att dyka upp	[at 'dyka up]
to applaud (vi, vt)	att applådera	[at aplʲo:'dera]
to appoint (assign)	att utnämna	[at 'ʉt,nɛmna]
to approach (come closer)	att närma sig	[at 'næ:rma sɛj]
to arrive (ab. train)	att ankomma	[at 'aŋ,kɔma]
to ask (~ sb to do sth)	att be	[at 'be:]
to aspire to ...	att aspirera	[at aspi'rera]
to assist (help)	att assistera	[at asi'stera]
to attack (mil.)	att angripa	[at 'an,gripa]
to attain (objectives)	att uppnå	[at 'upno:]
to avenge (get revenge)	att hämnas	[at 'hɛmnas]
to avoid (danger, task)	att undgå	[at 'und,go:]
to award (give medal to)	att belöna	[at be'lʲø:na]
to battle (vi)	att kämpa	[at 'ɕɛmpa]
to be (vi)	att vara	[at 'vara]
to be a cause of ...	att vara orsak	[at 'vara 'ʊ:ʂak]
to be afraid	att frukta	[at 'frukta]
to be angry (with ...)	att vara vred på ...	[at 'vara vred pɔ ...]

to be at war	att vara i krig	[at 'vara i ˌkrig]
to be based (on …)	att vara baserat på …	[at 'vara ba'serat pɔ …]
to be bored	att ha tråkigt	[at ha 'troːkit]
to be convinced	att vara övertygad	[at 'vara 'øːvəˌtygad]
to be enough	att vara nog	[at 'vara ˌnoːg]
to be envious	att avundas	[at 'avundas]
to be indignant	att bli indignerad	[at bli indi'nⁱerad]
to be interested in …	att intressera sig	[at intrɛ'sera sɛj]
to be lost in thought	att grubbla	[at 'grublⁱa]

to be lying (~ on the table)	att ligga	[at 'liga]
to be needed	att vara behövd	[at 'vara be'høːvd]
to be perplexed (puzzled)	att vara förvirrad	[at 'vara før'virad]
to be preserved	att bevaras	[at be'varas]

to be required	att vara nödvändig	[at 'vara 'nøːdˌvɛndig]
to be surprised	att bli förvånad	[at bli før'voːnad]
to be worried	att bekymra sig	[at be'çymra sɛj]
to beat (to hit)	att slå	[at 'slⁱoː]

to become (e.g., ~ old)	att bli	[at 'bli]
to behave (vi)	att uppföra sig	[at 'upˌføra sɛj]
to believe (think)	att tro	[at 'trʊ]
to belong to …	att tillhöra …	[at 'tilⁱˌhøːra …]

to berth (moor)	att förtöja	[at fœ:'ʈœːja]
to blind (other drivers)	att blända	[at 'blⁱɛnda]
to blow (wind)	att blåsa	[at 'blⁱoːsa]
to blush (vi)	att rodna	[at 'rɔdna]

to boast (vi)	att skryta	[at 'skryta]
to borrow (money)	att låna	[at 'lⁱoːna]
to break (branch, toy, etc.)	att bryta	[at 'bryta]
to breathe (vi)	att andas	[at 'andas]

to bring (sth)	att föra med sig	[at 'føra me sɛj]
to burn (paper, logs)	att bränna	[at 'brɛna]
to buy (purchase)	att köpa	[at 'çøːpa]
to call (~ for help)	att tillkalla	[at 'tilⁱˌkalⁱa]

to call (yell for sb)	att kalla	[at 'kalⁱa]
to calm down (vt)	att lugna	[at 'lʉgna]
can (v aux)	att kunna	[at 'kuna]
to cancel (call off)	att inställa, att annullera	[at in'stɛlⁱa], [at anʉ'lⁱera]
to cast off (of a boat or ship)	att kasta loss	[at 'kasta 'lⁱɔs]
to catch (e.g., ~ a ball)	att fånga	[at 'fɔŋa]
to change (~ one's opinion)	att ändra	[at 'ɛndra]
to change (exchange)	att växla	[at 'vɛkslⁱa]
to charm (vt)	att charmera	[at 'ʃarˌmera]
to choose (select)	att välja	[at 'vɛlja]

to chop off (with an ax)	att hugga av	[at 'huga av]
to clean (e.g., kettle from scale)	att rengöra	[at rɛn'jøːra]
to clean (shoes, etc.)	att rensa	[at 'rɛnsa]

to clean up (tidy)	att städa	[at 'stɛda]
to close (vt)	att stänga	[at 'stɛŋa]
to comb one's hair	att kamma	[at 'kama]
to come down (the stairs)	att gå ned	[at 'goː ˌned]

to come out (book)	att komma ut	[at 'kɔma ʉt]
to compare (vt)	att jämföra	[at 'jɛmˌføra]
to compensate (vt)	att kompensera	[at kɔmpen'sera]
to compete (vi)	att konkurrera	[at kɔŋku'rera]

to compile (~ a list)	att sammanställa	[at 'samanˌstɛlʲa]
to complain (vi, vt)	att klaga	[at 'klʲaga]
to complicate (vt)	att komplicera	[at komplʲi'sera]
to compose (music, etc.)	att komponera	[at kɔmpʉ'nera]

to compromise (reputation)	att kompromettera	[at kɔmprʉme'tera]
to concentrate (vi)	att koncentrera sig	[at kɔnsən'trera sɛj]
to confess (criminal)	att erkänna	[at ɛː'ɕɛna]
to confuse (mix up)	att förväxla	[at før'vɛkslʲa]

to congratulate (vt)	att gratulera	[at gratʉ'lʲera]
to consult (doctor, expert)	att konsultera	[at konsulʲ'tera]
to continue (~ to do sth)	att fortsätta	[at 'fʉtˌsæta]
to control (vt)	att kontrollera	[at kontrɔ'lʲera]

to convince (vt)	att överbevisa	[at 'øːvəˌbe'visa]
to cooperate (vi)	att samarbeta	[at 'samarˌbeta]
to coordinate (vt)	att koordinera	[at kʉɔɖi'nera]
to correct (an error)	att rätta	[at 'ræta]

to cost (vt)	att kosta	[at 'kosta]
to count (money, etc.)	att räkna	[at 'rɛkna]
to count on ...	att räkna med ...	[at 'rɛkna me ...]
to crack (ceiling, wall)	att spricka	[at 'sprika]

to create (vt)	att skapa	[at 'skapa]
to crush, to squash (~ a bug)	att krossa	[at 'krɔsa]
to cry (weep)	att gråta	[at 'groːta]
to cut off (with a knife)	att skära av	[at 'ʃæːra av]

253. Verbs D-G

| to dare (~ to do sth) | att våga | [at 'voːga] |
| to date from ... | att datera sig | [at da'tera sɛj] |

to deceive (vi, vt)	**att fuska**	[at 'fʉska]
to decide (~ to do sth)	**att besluta**	[at be'slʉ:ta]
to decorate (tree, street)	**att pryda**	[at 'pryda]
to dedicate (book, etc.)	**att tillägna**	[at 'tilˈɛgna]
to defend (a country, etc.)	**att försvara**	[at fœ:'ʂvara]
to defend oneself	**att försvara sig**	[at fœ:'ʂvara sɛj]
to demand (request firmly)	**att kräva**	[at 'krɛ:va]
to denounce (vt)	**att ange**	[at 'aŋnə]
to deny (vt)	**att förneka**	[at fœ:'ŋeka]
to depend on ...	**att bero på ...**	[at be'rʊ pɔ ...]
to deprive (vt)	**att beröva**	[at be'rø:va]
to deserve (vt)	**att förtjäna**	[at fœ:'ɕɛ:na]
to design (machine, etc.)	**att projektera**	[at prʊɧɛk'tera]
to desire (want, wish)	**att önska**	[at 'ønska]
to despise (vt)	**att förakta**	[at fø'rakta]
to destroy (documents, etc.)	**att förstöra**	[at 'fœ:ˌʂtø:ra]
to differ (from sth)	**att skilja sig från ...**	[at 'ɧilja sɛj frɔn ...]
to dig (tunnel, etc.)	**att gräva**	[at 'grɛ:va]
to direct (point the way)	**att visa vägen**	[at 'visa 'vɛ:gən]
to disappear (vi)	**att försvinna**	[at fœ:'ʂvina]
to discover (new land, etc.)	**att upptäcka**	[at 'upˌtɛka]
to discuss (vt)	**att diskutera**	[at diskʉ'tera]
to distribute (leaflets, etc.)	**att dela ut**	[at 'delˈa ʉt]
to disturb (vt)	**att störa**	[at 'stø:ra]
to dive (vi)	**att dyka**	[at 'dyka]
to divide (math)	**att dividera**	[at divi'dera]
to do (vt)	**att göra**	[at 'jø:ra]
to do the laundry	**att tvätta**	[at 'tvæta]
to double (increase)	**att fördubbla**	[at fœ:'dublˈa]
to doubt (have doubts)	**att tvivla**	[at 'tvivlˈa]
to draw a conclusion	**att dra en slutsats**	[at 'dra en 'slʉ:tsats]
to dream (daydream)	**att drömma**	[at 'drœma]
to dream (in sleep)	**att drömma**	[at 'drœma]
to drink (vi, vt)	**att dricka**	[at 'drika]
to drive a car	**att köra bil**	[at 'ɕø:ra ˌbilˈ]
to drive away (scare away)	**att jaga bort**	[at 'jaga bo:t]
to drop (let fall)	**att tappa**	[at 'tapa]
to drown (ab. person)	**att drunkna**	[at 'drʉŋkna]
to dry (clothes, hair)	**att torka**	[at 'tɔrka]
to eat (vi, vt)	**att äta**	[at 'ɛ:ta]
to eavesdrop (vi)	**att tjuvlyssna**	[at 'ɕʉ:vˌlˈysna]

to emit (diffuse - odor, etc.)	**att sprida**	[at 'sprida]
to enjoy oneself	**att ha roligt**	[at ha 'rʊlit]
to enter (on the list)	**att skriva in**	[at 'skriva in]
to enter (room, house, etc.)	**att komma in**	[at 'kɔma 'in]
to entertain (amuse)	**att underhålla**	[at 'undəˌhoːlʲa]
to equip (fit out)	**att utrusta**	[at 'ʉtˌrusta]
to examine (proposal)	**att undersöka**	[at 'undəˌsøːka]
to exchange (sth)	**att utväxla**	[at 'ʉtˌvɛksla]
to excuse (forgive)	**att ursäkta**	[at 'ʉːˌsɛkta]
to exist (vi)	**att existera**	[at ɛksi'stera]
to expect (anticipate)	**att förvänta**	[at før'vɛnta]
to expect (foresee)	**att förutse**	[at 'førʉtˌsə]
to expel (from school, etc.)	**att utesluta**	[at 'ʉtəˌslʉːta]
to explain (vt)	**att förklara**	[at før'klʲara]
to express (vt)	**att uttrycka**	[at 'ʉtˌtryka]
to extinguish (a fire)	**att släcka**	[at 'slʲɛka]
to fall in love (with ...)	**att förälska sig**	[at fø'rɛlʲska sɛj]
to feed (provide food)	**att mata**	[at 'mata]
to fight (against the enemy)	**att kämpa**	[at 'ɕɛmpa]
to fight (vi)	**att slåss**	[at 'slʲɔs]
to fill (glass, bottle)	**att fylla**	[at 'fylʲa]
to find (~ lost items)	**att finna**	[at 'fina]
to finish (vt)	**att sluta**	[at 'slʉːta]
to fish (angle)	**att fiska**	[at 'fiska]
to fit (ab. dress, etc.)	**att passa**	[at 'pasa]
to flatter (vt)	**att smickra**	[at 'smikra]
to fly (bird, plane)	**att flyga**	[at 'flʲyga]
to follow ... (come after)	**att följa efter ...**	[at 'følja 'ɛftər ...]
to forbid (vt)	**att förbjuda**	[at før'bjʉːda]
to force (compel)	**att tvinga**	[at 'tviŋa]
to forget (vi, vt)	**att glömma**	[at 'glʲœma]
to forgive (pardon)	**att förlåta**	[at 'fœːˌlʲoːta]
to form (constitute)	**att bilda, att forma**	[at 'bilʲda], [at 'forma]
to get dirty (vi)	**att smutsa ned sig**	[at 'smutsa ned sɛj]
to get infected (with ...)	**att bli smittad**	[at bli 'smitad]
to get irritated	**att bli irriterad**	[at bli iri'terad]
to get married	**att gifta sig**	[at 'jifta sɛj]
to get rid of ...	**att bli kvitt ...**	[at bli 'kvit ...]
to get tired	**att bli trött**	[at bli 'trœt]
to get up (arise from bed)	**att gå upp**	[at 'goː 'up]

| to give (vt) | att ge | [at je:] |
| to give a bath (to bath) | att bada | [at 'bada] |

to give a hug, to hug (vt)	att omfamna	[at 'ɔm‚famna]
to give in (yield to)	att ge efter	[at je: 'ɛftər]
to glimpse (vt)	att märka	[at 'mæ:rka]
to go (by car, etc.)	att åka	[at 'o:ka]

to go (on foot)	att gå	[at 'go:]
to go for a swim	att bada	[at 'bada]
to go out (for dinner, etc.)	att gå ut	[at 'go: ʉt]
to go to bed (go to sleep)	att gå till sängs	[at 'go: tilʲ 'sɛŋs]

to greet (vt)	att hälsa	[at 'hɛlʲsa]
to grow (plants)	att odla	[at 'ʊdlʲa]
to guarantee (vt)	att garantera	[at garan'tera]
to guess (the answer)	att gissa	[at 'jisa]

254. Verbs H-M

to hand out (distribute)	att dela ut	[at 'delʲa ʉt]
to hang (curtains, etc.)	att hänga	[at 'hɛŋa]
to have (vt)	att ha	[at 'ha]
to have a try	att försöka	[at fœ:'ʂø:ka]
to have breakfast	att äta frukost	[at 'ɛ:ta 'frʉ:kɔst]

to have dinner	att äta kvällsmat	[at 'ɛ:ta 'kvɛlʲs‚mat]
to have lunch	att äta lunch	[at 'ɛ:ta ‚lʉnɕ]
to head (group, etc.)	att leda	[at 'lʲeda]
to hear (vt)	att höra	[at 'hø:ra]
to heat (vt)	att värma	[at 'væ:rma]

to help (vt)	att hjälpa	[at 'jɛlʲpa]
to hide (vt)	att gömma	[at 'jœma]
to hire (e.g., ~ a boat)	att hyra	[at 'hyra]
to hire (staff)	att anställa	[at 'an‚stɛlʲa]
to hope (vi, vt)	att hoppas	[at 'hɔpas]

to hunt (for food, sport)	att jaga	[at 'jaga]
to hurry (vi)	att skynda sig	[at 'ɦynda sɛj]
to imagine (to picture)	att föreställa sig	[at 'førə‚stɛlʲa sɛj]
to imitate (vt)	att imitera	[at imi'tera]
to implore (vt)	att bönfalla	[at 'bøn‚falʲa]
to import (vt)	att importera	[at impɔ:'tera]
to increase (vi)	att öka	[at 'ø:ka]
to increase (vt)	att öka	[at 'ø:ka]
to infect (vt)	att smitta	[at 'smita]
to influence (vt)	att påverka	[at 'pɔ‚vɛrka]
to inform (e.g., ~ the police about)	att meddela	[at 'me‚delʲa]

to inform (vt)	**att informera**	[at infɔr'mera]
to inherit (vt)	**att ärva**	[at 'æ:rva]
to inquire (about …)	**att få veta**	[at fo: 'veta]
to insert (put in)	**att sätta in**	[at 'sæta in]
to insinuate (imply)	**att insinuera**	[at insinʉ'era]
to insist (vi, vt)	**att insistera**	[at insi'stera]
to inspire (vt)	**att inspirera**	[at inspi'rera]
to instruct (teach)	**att instruera**	[at instrʉ'era]
to insult (offend)	**att förolämpa**	[at 'førʊˌlʲɛmpa]
to interest (vt)	**att intressera**	[at intrɛ'sera]
to intervene (vi)	**att intervenera**	[at intərve'nera]
to introduce (sb to sb)	**att presentera**	[at presən'tera]
to invent (machine, etc.)	**att uppfinna**	[at 'upˌfina]
to invite (vt)	**att inbjuda, att invitera**	[at in'bjʉ:da], [at invi'tera]
to iron (clothes)	**att stryka**	[at 'stryka]
to irritate (annoy)	**att irritera**	[at iri'tera]
to isolate (vt)	**att isolera**	[at isʊ'lʲera]
to join (political party, etc.)	**att ansluta sig till …**	[at 'anˌslʉːta sɛj tilʲ …]
to joke (be kidding)	**att skämta, att skoja**	[at 'ʃɛmta], [at 'skɔja]
to keep (old letters, etc.)	**att behålla**	[at be'hoːlʲa]
to keep silent	**att tiga**	[at 'tiga]
to kill (vt)	**att döda, att mörda**	[at 'dø:da], [at 'mø:ɖa]
to knock (at the door)	**att knacka**	[at 'knaka]
to know (sb)	**att känna**	[at 'ɕɛna]
to know (sth)	**att veta**	[at 'veta]
to laugh (vi)	**att skratta**	[at 'skrata]
to launch (start up)	**att starta**	[at staːʈa]
to leave (~ for Mexico)	**att avresa**	[at 'avˌresa]
to leave (forget sth)	**att lämna**	[at 'lʲɛmna]
to leave (spouse)	**att efterlämna**	[at 'ɛftəˌlʲɛmna]
to liberate (city, etc.)	**att befria**	[at be'fria]
to lie (~ on the floor)	**att ligga**	[at 'liga]
to lie (tell untruth)	**att ljuga**	[at 'jʉːga]
to light (campfire, etc.)	**att tända**	[at 'tɛnda]
to light up (illuminate)	**att belysa**	[at be'lʲysa]
to like (I like …)	**att gilla**	[at 'jilʲa]
to limit (vt)	**att begränsa**	[at be'grɛnsa]
to listen (vi)	**att lyssna**	[at 'lʲysna]
to live (~ in France)	**att bo**	[at 'bʊ:]
to live (exist)	**att leva**	[at 'lʲeva]
to load (gun)	**att ladda**	[at 'lʲada]
to load (vehicle, etc.)	**att lasta**	[at 'lʲasta]
to look (I'm just ~ing)	**att se**	[at 'se:]
to look for … (search)	**att söka …**	[at 'sø:ka …]

to look like (resemble)	att likna	[at 'likna]
to lose (umbrella, etc.)	att mista	[at 'mista]
to love (e.g., ~ dancing)	att tycka om	[at 'tyka ɔm]

to love (sb)	att älska	[at 'ɛlˠska]
to lower (blind, head)	att sänka	[at 'sɛŋka]
to make (~ dinner)	att laga	[at 'lˠaga]
to make a mistake	att göra fel	[at 'jøːra ˌfelˠ]
to make angry	att göra arg	[at 'jøːra arj]

to make easier	att lätta	[at 'lˠæta]
to make multiple copies	att kopiera	[at kɔ'pjera]
to make the acquaintance	att göra bekantskap med	[at 'jøːra be'kantˌskap me]
to make use (of …)	att använda	[at 'anˌvɛnda]
to manage, to run	att styra, att leda	[at 'styra], [at 'lˠeda]

to mark (make a mark)	att markera	[at mar'kera]
to mean (signify)	att betyda	[at be'tyda]
to memorize (vt)	att memorera	[at memɔ'rera]
to mention (talk about)	att omnämna	[at 'ɔmˌnɛmna]
to miss (school, etc.)	att missa	[at 'misa]

to mix (combine, blend)	att blanda	[at 'blˠanda]
to mock (make fun of)	att håna	[at 'hoːna]
to move (to shift)	att flytta	[at 'flˠyta]
to multiply (math)	att multiplicera	[at mulˠtipli'sera]
must (v aux)	att måste	[at 'moːstə]

255. Verbs N-R

to name, to call (vt)	att kalla	[at 'kalˠa]
to negotiate (vi)	att förhandla	[at før'handlˠa]
to note (write down)	att notera	[at nʊ'tera]
to notice (see)	att märka	[at 'mæːrka]

to obey (vi, vt)	att underordna sig	[at 'undərˌɔːdna sɛj]
to object (vi, vt)	att invända	[at 'inˌvɛnda]
to observe (see)	att observera	[at ɔbsɛr'vera]
to offend (vt)	att förnärma	[at fœː'ɲæːrma]
to omit (word, phrase)	att utelämna	[at 'ʉteˌlˠɛmna]

to open (vt)	att öppna	[at 'øpna]
to order (in restaurant)	att beställa	[at be'stɛlˠa]
to order (mil.)	att beordra	[at be'oːdra]
to organize (concert, party)	att arrangera	[at aran'ʃera]
to overestimate (vt)	att övervärdera	[at 'øːvəvæˌdera]
to own (possess)	att besitta, att äga	[at be'sita], [at 'ɛːga]
to participate (vi)	att delta	[at 'dɛlˠta]
to pass through (by car, etc.)	att passera	[at pa'sera]

to pay (vi, vt)	**att betala**	[at be'talʲa]
to peep, spy on	**att kika, att titta**	[at 'ɕika], [at 'tita]
to penetrate (vt)	**att tränga in**	[at 'trɛŋa in]
to permit (vt)	**att tillåta**	[at 'tilʲoːta]
to pick (flowers)	**att plocka**	[at 'plʲɔka]

to place (put, set)	**att placera**	[at plʲa'sera]
to plan (~ to do sth)	**att planera**	[at plʲa'nera]
to play (actor)	**att spela**	[at 'spelʲa]
to play (children)	**att leka**	[at 'lʲeka]
to point (~ the way)	**att peka**	[at 'peka]

to pour (liquid)	**att hälla upp**	[at 'hɛlʲa up]
to pray (vi, vt)	**att be**	[at 'beː]
to prefer (vt)	**att föredra**	[at 'førədra]
to prepare (~ a plan)	**att förbereda**	[at 'førbəˌreda]
to present (sb to sb)	**att presentera**	[at presən'tera]

to preserve (peace, life)	**att bevara**	[at be'vara]
to prevail (vt)	**att dominera**	[at dɔmi'nera]
to progress (move forward)	**att gå framåt**	[at 'goː 'framoːt]
to promise (vt)	**att lova**	[at 'lʲɔva]

to pronounce (vt)	**att uttala**	[at 'ʉtˌtalʲa]
to propose (vt)	**att föreslå**	[at 'førəˌslʲoː]
to protect (e.g., ~ nature)	**att skydda**	[at 'ɧʏda]
to protest (vi)	**att protestera**	[at prʊtə'stera]

to prove (vt)	**att bevisa**	[at be'visa]
to provoke (vt)	**att provocera**	[at prʊvʊ'sera]
to pull (~ the rope)	**att dra**	[at 'dra]
to punish (vt)	**att straffa**	[at 'strafa]

to push (~ the door)	**att knuffa, att skjuta**	[at 'knufa], [at 'ɧʉːta]
to put away (vt)	**att lägga undan**	[at 'lʲɛga 'undan]
to put in order	**att bringa ordning**	[at 'briŋa 'ɔːdɳiŋ]
to put, to place	**att lägga**	[at 'lʲɛga]

to quote (cite)	**att citera**	[at si'tera]
to reach (arrive at)	**att nå**	[at 'noː]
to read (vi, vt)	**att läsa**	[at 'lʲɛːsa]
to realize (a dream)	**att realisera**	[at reali'sera]
to recognize (identify sb)	**att känna igen**	[at 'ɕɛna 'ijɛn]

to recommend (vt)	**att rekommendera**	[at rekɔmən'dera]
to recover (~ from flu)	**att återhämta sig**	[at 'oːterˌhɛmta sɛj]
to redo (do again)	**att göra om**	[at 'jøːra ɔm]
to reduce (speed, etc.)	**att minska**	[at 'minska]

to refuse (~ sb)	**att avslå**	[at 'avˌslʲoː]
to regret (be sorry)	**att beklaga**	[at be'klʲaga]

to reinforce (vt)	**att stärka**	[at 'stærka]
to remember (Do you ~ me?)	**att minnas**	[at 'minas]

to remember (I can't ~ her name)	**att minnas**	[at 'minas]
to remind of …	**att påminna**	[at po͵mina]
to remove (~ a stain)	**att ta bort**	[at ta 'bɔːt]
to remove (~ an obstacle)	**att undanröja**	[at 'undan͵røːja]

to rent (sth from sb)	**att hyra**	[at 'hyra]
to repair (mend)	**at reparere**	[at repa'rera]
to repeat (say again)	**att upprepa**	[at 'uprepa]
to report (make a report)	**att rapportera**	[at rapɔ'tera]

to reproach (vt)	**att förebrå**	[at 'førəbroː]
to reserve, to book	**att reservera**	[at resɛr'vera]
to restrain (hold back)	**att avhålla**	[at 'av͵hoːlʲa]
to return (come back)	**att komma tillbaka**	[at 'kɔma tilʲ'baka]

to risk, to take a risk	**att riskera**	[at ris'kera]
to rub out (erase)	**att radera ut**	[at ra'dera ʉt]
to run (move fast)	**att löpa, att springa**	[at 'lʲøːpa], [at 'spriŋa]
to rush (hurry sb)	**att skynda**	[at 'ʃʏnda]

256. Verbs S-W

to satisfy (please)	**att tillfredsställa**	[at 'tilʲfred͵stɛlʲa]
to save (rescue)	**att rädda**	[at 'rɛda]
to say (~ thank you)	**att säga**	[at 'sɛːja]
to scold (vt)	**att skälla**	[at 'ʃɛlʲa]

to scratch (with claws)	**att klösa**	[at 'klʲøːsa]
to select (to pick)	**att välja ut**	[at 'vɛlja ʉt]
to sell (goods)	**att sälja**	[at 'sɛlja]
to send (a letter)	**att skicka**	[at 'ʃika]

to send back (vt)	**att skicka tillbaka**	[at 'ʃika tilʲ'baka]
to sense (~ danger)	**att känna**	[at 'ɕɛna]
to sentence (vt)	**att döma**	[at 'døːma]
to serve (in restaurant)	**att betjäna**	[at be'ɕɛːna]

to settle (a conflict)	**att lösa**	[at 'lʲøːsa]
to shake (vt)	**att rista**	[at 'rista]
to shave (vi)	**att raka sig**	[at 'raka sɛj]
to shine (gleam)	**att skina**	[at 'ʃina]

to shiver (with cold)	**att skälva**	[at 'ʃɛlʲva]
to shoot (vi)	**att skjuta**	[at 'ʃʉːta]
to shout (vi)	**att skrika**	[at 'skrika]

to show (to display)	**att visa**	[at 'visa]
to shudder (vi)	**att rysa**	[at 'rysa]
to sigh (vi)	**att sucka**	[at 'suka]
to sign (document)	**att underteckna**	[at 'undəˌtɛkna]
to signify (mean)	**att betyda**	[at be'tyda]
to simplify (vt)	**att förenkla**	[at fø'rɛŋklʲa]
to sin (vi)	**att synda**	[at 'sʏnda]
to sit (be sitting)	**att sitta**	[at 'sita]
to sit down (vi)	**att sätta sig**	[at 'sæta sɛj]
to smell (emit an odor)	**att lukta**	[at 'lʉkta]
to smell (inhale the odor)	**att lukta**	[at 'lʉkta]
to smile (vi)	**att småle**	[at 'smoːlʲe]
to snap (vi, ab. rope)	**att gå sönder**	[at 'goː 'sœndər]
to solve (problem)	**att lösa**	[at 'lʲøːsa]
to sow (seed, crop)	**att så**	[at soː]
to spill (liquid)	**att spilla**	[at 'spilʲa]
to spill out, scatter (flour, etc.)	**att spillas ut**	[at 'spilʲas ʉt]
to spit (vi)	**att spotta**	[at 'spɔta]
to stand (toothache, cold)	**att tåla**	[at 'toːlʲa]
to start (begin)	**att börja**	[at 'bœrja]
to steal (money, etc.)	**att stjäla**	[at 'ɧɛːlʲa]
to stop (for pause, etc.)	**att stanna**	[at 'stana]
to stop (please ~ calling me)	**att sluta**	[at 'slʉːta]
to stop talking	**att tystna**	[at 'tʏsna]
to stroke (caress)	**att stryka**	[at 'stryka]
to study (vt)	**att studera**	[at stu'dera]
to suffer (feel pain)	**att lida**	[at 'lida]
to support (cause, idea)	**att stödja**	[at 'stœdja]
to suppose (assume)	**att anta, att förmoda**	[at 'anta], [at før'mʊda]
to surface (ab. submarine)	**att dyka upp**	[at 'dyka up]
to surprise (amaze)	**att förvåna**	[at før'voːna]
to suspect (vt)	**att misstänka**	[at 'misˌtɛŋka]
to swim (vi)	**att simma**	[at 'sima]
to take (get hold of)	**att ta**	[at ta]
to take a bath	**att tvätta sig**	[at 'tvæta sɛj]
to take a rest	**att vila**	[at 'vilʲa]
to take away (e.g., about waiter)	**att ta bort**	[at ta 'bɔːt]
to take off (airplane)	**att lyfta**	[at 'lʲyfta]
to take off (painting, curtains, etc.)	**att ta ned**	[at ta ned]

to take pictures	att fotografera	[at fʊtʊgra'fera]
to talk to …	att tala med …	[at 'talʲa me …]
to teach (give lessons)	att undervisa	[at 'undə‚visa]

to tear off, to rip off (vt)	att riva av	[at 'riva av]
to tell (story, joke)	att berätta	[at be'ræta]
to thank (vt)	att tacka	[at 'taka]
to think (believe)	att tro	[at 'trʊ]

to think (vi, vt)	att tänka	[at 'tɛŋka]
to threaten (vt)	att hota	[at 'hʊta]
to throw (stone, etc.)	att kasta	[at 'kasta]
to tie to …	att binda fast	[at 'binda fast]

to tie up (prisoner)	att binda	[at 'binda]
to tire (make tired)	att trötta	[at 'trœta]
to touch (one's arm, etc.)	att röra	[at 'rø:ra]
to tower (over …)	att höja sig	[at 'hø:ja sɛj]

to train (animals)	att dressera	[at drɛ'sera]
to train (sb)	att träna	[at 'trɛ:na]
to train (vi)	att träna	[at 'trɛ:na]
to transform (vt)	att transformera	[at trasfɔr'mera]

to translate (vt)	att översätta	[at 'ø:və‚sæta]
to treat (illness)	att behandla	[at be'handlʲa]
to trust (vt)	att lita på	[at 'lita pɔ]
to try (attempt)	att pröva	[at 'prø:va]

to turn (e.g., ~ left)	att svänga	[at 'svɛŋa]
to turn away (vi)	att vända sig bort	[at 'vɛnda sɛj 'bɔ:t]
to turn off (the light)	att släcka	[at 'slʲɛka]
to turn on (computer, etc.)	att slå på	[at 'slʲo: pɔ]
to turn over (stone, etc.)	att vända	[at 'vɛnda]

to underestimate (vt)	att underskatta	[at 'undə‚skata]
to underline (vt)	att understryka	[at 'undə‚stryka]
to understand (vt)	att förstå	[at fœ:'ʂto:]
to undertake (vt)	att företa	[at 'føre‚ta]

to unite (vt)	att förena	[at 'førena]
to untie (vt)	att lösa upp	[at 'lʲø:sa up]
to use (phrase, word)	att använda	[at 'an‚vɛnda]
to vaccinate (vt)	att vaksinera	[at vaksi'nera]

to vote (vi)	att rösta	[at 'rœsta]
to wait (vt)	att vänta	[at 'vɛnta]
to wake (sb)	att väcka	[at 'vɛka]
to want (wish, desire)	att vilja	[at 'vilja]

| to warn (of the danger) | att varna | [at 'va:ŋa] |
| to wash (clean) | att tvätta | [at 'tvæta] |

to water (plants)	**att vattna**	[at 'vatna]
to wave (the hand)	**att vinka**	[at 'viŋka]
to weigh (have weight)	**att väga**	[at 'vɛ:ga]
to work (vi)	**att arbeta**	[at 'arˌbeta]
to worry (make anxious)	**att bekymra, att oroa**	[at be'ɕymra], [at 'ʊ:rʊa]
to worry (vi)	**att vara orolig**	[at 'vara ʊ:'rʊlig]
to wrap (parcel, etc.)	**att packa in**	[at 'paka in]
to wrestle (sport)	**att brottas**	[at 'brɔtas]
to write (vt)	**att skriva**	[at 'skriva]
to write down	**att skriva ner**	[at 'skriva ner]